MODES

OF

CONSTITUTIONAL INTERPRETATION

By

CRAIG R. DUCAT

Associate Professor of Political Science
Northern Illinois University

ST. PAUL, MINN.
WEST PUBLISHING CO.
1978

Library of Congress Cataloging in Publication Data

Ducat, Craig R.
   Modes of constitutional interpretation.

   Includes index.
   1. United States—Constitutional law—Interpretation and construction—
Cases. I. Title.
KF4549.D8   342'.73'029   78–8496

ISBN 0–8299–2009–9

Ducat Const.Interpre. MTB

To

Mulford Q. Sibley,
an inspiring teacher,
an insightful scholar,
and an intrepid democrat.

*

PREFACE

The study of the construction of constitutional provisions by the judiciary is a multidimensional enterprise. At the lowest level of abstraction, it is the study of constitutional law. This approach proceeds case by case with a focus on what definition the court gave to a particular constitutional provision in a specific set of circumstances. For the skilled law student, this entails the serial examination of cases, comparing and contrasting their fact patterns and varied holdings with an eye toward discerning what rules and principles govern particular disputes of the kind clients may present him with sometime in the future. In much less sophisticated terms, a preoccupation with cases tends also to be the focus of the bewildered undergraduate. Mesmerized by the seemingly endless number and details of cases he feels obliged to memorize, he cannot see how the materials relate to one another much less how the opinions illustrate observations about law, judges, courts, or the political system. In many instances, the problem is intensified by what is known as "briefing the cases," the dissection of judicial decisions into their many parts, presumably for the purpose of understanding better what is going on. Not infrequently, the result is intellectual anarchy. For the undergraduate, the study of constitutional law is often a disorienting and pointless experience.

The centrifugal forces at work on the cases are frequently overcome and redirected in the study of constitutional politics. This approach is marked by the study of cases grouped according to policy area. The aggregation of cases by subject matter emphasizes the role of judges as policy-makers. Having gathered together all of the commerce cases, or all of the search and seizure cases, or all of the free speech cases, patterns can readily be seen in the decisions, and these patterns, in turn, serve as illustrations of certain broad explanations of how the judicial process operates. The study of constitutional politics often pro-

v

duces observations, for example, about the primacy of political attitudes in the making of judicial decisions, the limitations of courts as political institutions, and so forth.

A third perspective, and one that this volume adopts, is the study of constitutional interpretation. The hallmark of this approach is the emphasis given the principal frameworks employed by judges in justifying their decisions. Focusing attention on the major systematic justifications which are repeatedly offered over the entire range of constitutional decisions, without regard to policy area, goes a long way toward providing an integrative structure. The principal modes of constitutional interpretation are the means by which the debates that loom large in jurisprudence generally are injected into the judicial construction of constitutional provisions. The study of constitutional interpretation thus becomes the study of those questions which are of enduring importance to a legal order.

This volume was preceded by several essays which poked at some of the things that are much more fully developed here: "The Warren Court and the Second Constitutional Revolution," in Chase and Ducat, *Corwin's The Constitution and What It Means Today*, 13th ed. (Princeton: Princeton University Press, 1973), pp. 238–268; "Does the Supreme Court Have a Unique Function?" in Chase and Ducat, *Constitutional Interpretation* (St. Paul, Minn.: West Publishing Co., 1974), pp. 59–66; "Privacy and Constitutional Government," in Dionisopoulos and Ducat, *The Right to Privacy* (St. Paul, Minn.: West Publishing Co., 1976), pp. 1–14; and Flango and Ducat, "Toward an Integration of Public Law and Judicial Behavior," 39 *Journal of Politics* 41–72 (1977). The chapters which comprise this book much more fully treat the background against which these schools of thought evolved, articulate the basics of each model of interpretation, illustrate the application of each framework in the light of judicial opinions, and assess critically the strengths and weaknesses of each of the modes of constitutional interpretation. Insofar as possible, the illustrations, of which there are many, have been drawn from cases that are standard fare in most casebooks on the Constitution.

PREFACE

A project this long on the drawing board could not have reached completion without the help and support of others. Prominent among these, of course, have been my three collaborators on the publications listed above: Hal Chase, Allan Dionisopoulos, and Gene Flango. I am especially indebted to Gene for the continual probing and testing of ideas, for his boundless enthusiasm, and for helping me overcome what Sam Krislov once observed was "the schizoid quality of the field." I am also grateful to Davalene Cooper for her invaluable research assistance; to countless undergraduate and graduate students in my courses on the Constitution and on jurisprudence for some insightful observations and criticisms; and to Northern Illinois University for a sabbatical during the Fall, 1977 semester so that I could finish up the manuscript. Finally, I want to offer a special note of thanks to Chris Fosnaugh not only for daily encouragement, but for help in all those physical labors that make it possible to get a book to press. Needless to say, the short-comings in all the pages that follow are mine alone.

CRAIG R. DUCAT

DeKalb, Illinois
June, 1978

*

TABLE OF CONTENTS

TABLE OF CONTENTS

Chapter 4. The Preferred Freedoms Approach—Cont'd

*

XI

TABLE OF CASES

Cases refer to text or footnotes. References are to Pages.

TABLE OF CASES

TABLE OF CASES

TABLE OF CASES

TABLE OF CASES

TABLE OF CASES

†

MODES OF CONSTITUTIONAL INTERPRETATION

Chapter 1

The Justification of Judicial Review: *Marbury v. Madison* Revisited

There is scarcely a casebook on constitutional law that does not begin with *Marbury* v. *Madison*.[1] And small wonder. There is, after all, an almost inescapable logic about starting with the case in which the Supreme Court took for the judiciary ultimate authority in the disposition of constitutional questions.[2] It is

[1] 5 U.S. (1 Cr.) 137, 2 L.Ed. 60 (1803). Of four principal but traditional casebooks in constitutional law published by political scientists since 1960, only one (Cushman and Cushman, Cases in Constitutional Law [3d ed., 1968]) did not begin with *Marbury* v. *Madison*. (The other casebooks surveyed were: Chase and Ducat, Constitutional Interpretation [1974]; Mason and Beaney, American Constitutional Law [5th ed., 1972]; and Shapiro and Tresolini, American Constitutional Law [4th ed., 1975]). All four leading law school casebooks in constitutional law that were surveyed (Barrett, Bruton, and Honnold [4th ed., 1973]; Freund, Sutherland, Howe, and Brown, Constitutional Law [3d ed., 1967]; Gunther, Cases and Materials on Constitutional Law [9th ed., 1975];

and Lockhart, Kamisar, and Choper, Constitutional Law [4th ed., 1975]) began with *Marbury*. Interestingly enough, however, of five undergraduate casebooks produced by political scientists since 1960 that were of a judicial process or judicial behavior orientation, only one (Rosenblum and Castberg, Cases on Constitutional Law [1973]) began with *Marbury*. (The other four casebooks surveyed were: Grossman and Wells, Constitutional Law and Judicial Policy Making [1972]; Schmidhauser, Constitutional Law in the Political Process [1963]; Schubert, Constitutional Politics [1960]; and Shapiro and Hobbs, The Politics of Constitutional Law [1974]).

[2] While perhaps theoretically correct in some legal sense, this over-

states the finality of Supreme Court determinations much on the order of the oft-quoted passage from Justice Frankfurter's dissent in West Virginia State Board of Education v. Barnette, 319 U.S. 624, 651–652, 63 S.Ct. 1178, 1191 (1943): "A court can only strike down. It can only say 'This or that law is void.' It cannot modify or qualify, it cannot make exceptions to a general requirement. And it strikes down not merely for a day. At least the finding of unconstitutionality ought not to have ephemeral significance unless the Constitution is to be reduced to the fugitive importance of mere legislation."

First, this statement does not reflect the latitude of discretion in statutory construction which the Court is *obliged* to observe as a matter of honoring one of the cardinal principles of constitutional adjudication, *viz.*, that whenever a statute is drawn into question *vis-à-vis* a provision of the Constitution, the Court should make every effort to save the statute insofar as possible by construing it compatably with the Constitution (or, more accurately, since the Constitution does not construe itself, with the Court's interpretation of a given constitutional provision). Ashwander v. Tennessee Valley Authority, 297 U.S. 288, 348, 56 S.Ct. 466, 483–484 (1936) (concurring opinion of Brandeis, J.). Hence, to the extent that the Court abides by this principle, it will, in fact, "modify," "qualify," and "make exceptions to" statutes enacted by legislative bodies.

Second, attribution of finality to the Court's constitutional determina-

tions is at odds with the reality of pluralism in the American system. The idea of finality is really an adjunct of that simplistic and long-discredited notion of the American system—what Martin Shapiro has so astutely characterized as "the All Gaul" conception of American government (*i. e.*, that American government, like Gaul, in the classic description given by the opening sentence of Caesar's *Commentaries*, is divided into three parts: Congress, which makes the laws; the Presidency, which executes the laws; and the Courts, which interpret the laws). Law and Politics in the Supreme Court 32 (1964). In fact, of course, governmental functions are not so neatly bounded as the Gallic provinces—an observation readily confirmed by reading the text of the Constitution itself as it gives effect to the idea of checks and balances. With genuine insight, Richard Neustadt wrote over a decade and a half ago: "The constitutional convention of 1787 is supposed to have created a government of 'separated powers.' It did nothing of the sort. Rather, it created a government of separated institutions *sharing* powers." (Emphasis in original). Presidential Power 33 (1960).

The upshot of this is that there is no such thing as finality *anywhere* in the American system, but, instead, continuing adjustment, modification, and redefinition of policy by political interests as participants in the political system interact. Finality is simply not possible because interaction never ends. Judicial rulings, like any other form of policy—statutes, executive orders,

this long-recognized contribution of *Marbury* v. *Madison* that, as a matter of law, necessitates starting here.   If succeeding cases explore the Court's use of judicial review on particular substantive issues, common sense also dictates that it is best to begin at the point where the Court acquired the power in the first place. *Marbury,* therefore, receives its customary star billing because that's where it all began.

A book which sets for itself the task of examining the principal frameworks of constitutional interpretation should also logically begin with a discussion of *Marbury* v. *Madison* for quite a different reason.   Once the possibility or, more accurately, the reality of judicial review surfaces, so does an intractable dilemma.   For a century and three-quarters, now, it has been generally understood to stand as the central dilemma of constitutional interpretation in the American system: squaring the power of constitutional interpretation in the hands of appointed, life-tenured judges, on the one side, with democratic values, on the other.   In short, how is it that an essentially undemocratic institution, like the courts, can legitimately pass upon the decisions of popularly-elected officials in a democratic society?   The Court's

and administrative rulings—are being constantly reshaped in the system.   See Note, *Congressional Reversal of Supreme Court Decisions: 1945–1957*, 71 Harv.L.Rev. 1324 (1958).   And, in numerous instances, modification of the Court's policies takes place within the judicial institution itself as the result of external political pressure. See Murphy, Congress and the Court (1962); Nagel, *Court-Curbing Periods in American History*, 18 Vanderbilt L.Rev. 925 (1965), reprinted as *Curbing the Court: The Politics of Congressional Reaction,* in Nagel, The Legal Process from a Behavioral Perspective, ch. 21 (1969).   For discussions of the Court as it functions in the politi- cal context, see Latham, *The Supreme Court as a Political Institution*, 31 Minn.L.Rev. 205 (1947); Truman, The Governmental Process, ch. 15 (1951); Peltason, Federal Courts in the Political Process (1955); Rosenblum, Law as a Political Instrument (1955); Dahl, *Decision-Making in a Democracy: The Supreme Court as a National Policy-Maker*, 6 J.Pub.L. 275 (1957); Auerbach, Garrison, Hurst, and Mermin, The Legal Process (1961); Krislov, The Supreme Court in the Political Process (1965); Shapiro, Law and Politics in the Supreme Court (1964), and The Supreme Court and Administrative Agencies (1968).

opinion in *Marbury* must be assessed, then, not merely from the perspective of legal precedent, but from the standpoint of just how well the Court justified its acquisition of the power of judicial review.   In this respect, the opinion in *Marbury* suffers from serious if not fatal flaws, and, because of the inadequacy of that response, future jurists have each been obliged to confront the dilemma anew.   That continuing inquiry has, in turn, spawned the major schools of constitutional interpretation which are the focus of this book.   In this light, then, Chief Justice Marshall's opinion for the Court in *Marbury* v. *Madison* may well appear to be less important for what it did than for what it failed to do.

A Synopsis of the Controversy

Given the importance attached to *Marbury* v. *Madison* and the extent to which Chief Justice Marshall's opinion in that case will be examined, it might be useful to begin with a brief recapitulation of the facts:

Following their rout in the election of 1800, in which President John Adams was defeated for reelection and in which control of both houses of Congress fell to the Jeffersonians, the Federalists, who would never again gain a popular national mandate, sought to retain what political power they could by entrenching themselves in the national judiciary.

After the election, but before March 4th of the following year, the date prescribed by the Constitution on which President-Elect Thomas Jefferson would be sworn in, Oliver Ellsworth, then Chief Justice, resigned, ostensibly for reasons of ill health, permitting President Adams to name a new Chief Justice.   His choice for the post was his Secretary of State, John Marshall, Jefferson's cousin and arch political enemy.   Marshall also retained his cabinet post until the Adams administration went out of office.

The "lame duck" Congress attempted to shore up the declining political fortunes of the Federalists by passing legislation which created some 58 additional judgeships to be filled by the party faithful. First, it passed a law [3] on February 3, 1801, creating new federal circuit courts designed to free Supreme Court Justices from the burden of riding circuit in their dual capacities as appellate judges. These 16 vacancies were promptly filled by President Adams and their commissions delivered, though at a late hour, giving rise to their characterization as "the midnight judges." Second, Congress, two weeks after enactment of the circuit court legislation, passed a statute [4] providing 42 justices of the peace for the District of Columbia. It was this second piece of legislation which gave rise to the controversy in this case.

President Adams forwarded his nominations for this second wave of judicial appointments to the Federalist-controlled Senate and they were confirmed on March 3, 1801. The commissions for these posts were signed by President Adams and the Great Seal of the United States affixed by Secretary of State Marshall the same day, but Adams' term expired before all the commissions could be delivered by Marshall's brother, James, who returned four such commissions to the Secretary of State's office. Upon entering office, James Madison, the new Secretary of State, on explicit orders from President Jefferson, refused to deliver the remaining commissions, whereupon William Marbury, one of the four designated but uncertified judges, brought suit to recover his commission. Marbury lodged his suit directly with the Supreme Court, asking that it vindicate his right to the commission and, under § 13 of the Judiciary Act of 1789,[5] issue a writ of *mandamus* (*i. e.,* a court order commanding that a given officeholder fulfill some specific act within the purview of his office) directing Secretary of State Madison to deliver the commission.

---

3. 6th Cong., 2d Sess., ch. 4, 2 Stat. 89.

4. Act of Feb. 27, 1801, 6th Cong., 2d Sess., ch. 15, § 11, 2 Stat. 103, 107.

5. Act of Sept. 24, 1789, 1st Cong., 1st Sess., ch. 20, 1 Stat. 73.

Following the submission of Marbury's complaint to the Supreme Court, the Court set a date on which Madison was to be afforded an opportunity to appear and show cause why the Court should not issue the writ. Before such a hearing could be held, however, the new Congress, enraged over the Federalist maneuverings, acted not only to repeal the circuit courts legislation,[6] but also to cancel the Supreme Court's 1802 Term.[7] Consequently, argument in the case was postponed and the Court's decision delayed until 1803. Four of the six Justices on the Court,[8] a bare quorum,[9] participated in the decision.

An Analysis of Chief Justice Marshall's Opinion

The decision in *Marbury* v. *Madison* ranks perhaps as the classic example of a Chief Justice's sensitivity to the elements of judicial strategy.[10] Its worldly appreciation of political conse-

---

6. Act of Mar. 8, 1802, 7th Cong., 1st Sess., ch. 8, 2 Stat. 132. Soon thereafter, Congress passed legislation returning to much the same system which prevailed before the circuit courts act was passed, *i. e.*, Justices of the Supreme Court once again were required to ride circuit as circuit court judges, Act of Apr. 29, 1802, 7th Cong., 1st Sess., ch. 31, 2 Stat. 156.

7. Act of Apr. 29, 1802, 7th Cong., 1st Sess., ch. 31, § 1, 2 Stat. 156. The Judiciary Act of 1789 authorized two Terms per year for the Court. The legislation referred to here repealed authorization for a Term to begin on the first Monday of August; it empowered the Court to hold only a Term to start on the first Monday in February. Congress directed that proceedings before the Court be held over for its February (1803) Term, ch. 31, § 3, 2 Stat. 156, 157.

8. The four Justices who participated were: John Marshall (1801–1835), William Paterson (1793–1806), Samuel Chase (1796–1811), and Bushrod Washington (1798–1829). Justices William Cushing (1789–1810) and Alfred Moore (1799–1803) were absent. All, of course, were Federalists.

9. Act of Sept. 24, 1789, 1st Cong., 1st Sess., ch. 20, § 1, 1 Stat. 73.

10. The phrase is used here in recognition of Walter Murphy's fine study, Elements of Judicial Strategy (1964), examining the leadership possibilities open to the Chief Justice and detailing options in the mobilization of political power inside and outside the Court. For discussion of strategy open to the Chief Justice within the Court see, Danelski, *The Influence of the Chief Justice in the Decisional Process*, in Murphy and Pritchett, eds., Courts, Judges, and Politics

quences marks the decision as a masterstroke.[11] In the jargon of political calculation, Chief Justice Marshall mobilized the Court to take a short-term loss for a long-term gain. Faced with an implacable President, who would never permit his Secretary of State to honor a judicial command to turn over the commission, Marshall opted to make Marbury the victim of a sacrifice play. The Court's decision, dismissing the suit and precluding the possibility of relief in any other forum,[12] averted a collision with the executive branch that was fraught with almost certain disaster for an institution which has no way of forcing compliance with its decisions.[13] By virtue of the manner in which Marshall pulled off this strategic retreat, he managed to acquire for the Court the power of judicial review.[14]

525–534 (2d ed. 1974). Justice Frankfurter contends that Marshall's reputation for an ability to mesmerize his brethren and single-handedly control the Court is blown out of proportion and neglects the reality of the Court as a collegial institution. *John Marshall and the Judicial Function*, 69 Harv.L.Rev. 217, 220–221 (1955).

11. The decision has been widely characterized as a *tour de force*. Professor Corwin concluded that the decision "bears many of the earmarks of a deliberate partisan coup." The Doctrine of Judicial Review 10 (1914). In the same vein, Professor McLaughlin wrote that Marshall "really manufactured an opportunity to declare an act void." Marbury *v.* Madison *Again*, 13 A.B.A.J. 156, 157 (1928). In Professor Crosskey's view, Marshall's motivation was entirely "political." 2 Politics and the Constitution in the History of the United States 1040 (1953). Professor Haines regards the political aspects of *Marbury* as "obvious."

The American Doctrine of Judicial Supremacy 199 (1932). See also, Swisher, The Growth of Constitutional Power in the United States 55–56 (1946).

12. That another form existed, *viz.*, the circuit court for the District of Columbia, is apparent from the same legislation pursuant to which Marbury was appointed, Act of Feb. 27, 1801, 6th Cong., 2d Sess., ch. 15, § 3, 2 Stat. 103; Marbury was appointed under § 11 of the Act. That court was subsequently held to possess the authority to *mandamus* an executive officer acting in a ministerial capacity in Kendall v. United States ex rel. Stokes, 37 U.S. (12 Pet.) 524, 9 L. Ed. 1181 (1838).

13. See the text, *infra*, at pp. 35–36, and accompanying notes.

14. Many years ago, it was hotly contested whether the Supreme Court had "usurped" the power of judicial review. The pro and con positions were briefly noted by

Professor Corwin in his seminal work, The Doctrine of Judicial Review 1–2 (1914), the first chapter of which was originally published as Marbury v. Madison *and the Doctrine of Judicial Review*, 12 Mich.L.Rev. 538 (1914). Arrayed against those who, in Corwin's words, held "that the power owes its existence to an act of sheer usurpation by the Supreme Court itself, in the decision of *Marbury* v. *Madison*" (*e. g.*, Boudin, *Government by Judiciary*, 26 Pol.Sci.Q. 238 [1911] and Government by Judiciary [2 vols., 1932]; McDonough, *Usurpation of Power by Federal Courts*, 46 Am.L.Rev. 45 [1912]; Trickett, *The Great Usurpation*, 40 Am.L.Rev. 356 [1906]; Pennoyer, *The Case of* Marbury v. Madison, 30 Am.L.Rev. 188 [1896]), were other scholars who argued: (1) that specific provisions of the Constitution, notably the Supremacy Clause (Art. VI, § 2), conferred the power (*e. g.*, Coxe, Judicial Power and Unconstitutional Legislation [1893]; Dougherty, Power of the Federal Judiciary over Legislation [1912]); (2) that the Framers of the Constitution intended that the Court have the power (*e. g.*, Beard, The Supreme Court and the Constitution [1912], published originally as *The Supreme Court—Usurper or Grantee?* 27 Pol.Sci.Q. 1 [1912]; Meigs, *The Relation of the Judiciary to the Constitution*, 19 Am.L.Rev. 175 [1885]; Melvin, *The Judicial Bulwark of the Constitution*, 8 Am.Pol.Sci.Rev. 167 [1914]; Burr, *Unconstitutional Law and the Federal Judicial Power*, 60 U. Pa.L.Rev. 624 [1912]; Elliott, *The Legislatures and the Courts*, 5 Pol. Sci.Q. 224 [1890]; Mullan, *Allegiance to the Constitution*, 52 Am.

L.Rev. 51 [1918]; but *cf.* Davis, *Annulment of Legislation by the Supreme Court*, 7 Am.Pol.Sci.Rev. 541 [1913]); or (3) that the power was "the natural outgrowth of ideas that were common property in the period when the Constitution was established" (*e. g.*, Corwin, *ibid.*, and *The Rise and Establishment of Judicial Review*, 9 Mich.L.Rev. 102, 284 [1910–1911]; McLaughlin, The Courts, the Constitution, and Parties [1912]; Haines, The American Doctrine of Judicial Supremacy [1914]; Meigs, *ibid.*, and *The American Doctrine of Judicial Power and Its Early Origin*, 47 Am.L.Rev. 683 [1913]; Warren, Congress, the Constitution, and the Supreme Court [1935]; but *cf.* Crosskey, 2 Politics and the Constitution in the History of the United States, Chs. 27–29 [1953]). Though the debate no longer continues with the same intensity or volume, three relatively recent contributions are worth noting: Wechsler, *Toward Neutral Principles of Constitutional Law*, 73 Harv.L.Rev. 1 (1959), reprinted in Principles, Politics, and Fundamental Law 3–48 (1961); and Black, The People and the Court (1960), are additions to (1) above; and Berger, Congress v. The Supreme Court (1969), fits with the materials in (2).

Given the fact that it has become part and parcel of our constitutional fabric, two contemporary scholars have a point when they conclude, "Whether or not the Supreme Court 'usurped' the practice of judicial review is now purely an academic question." Binkley and Moos, A Grammar of American Politics 519 (3d ed. 1958). Though

The Court's decision—that it could not issue a writ of *mandamus* for delivery of the commission because Congress was without the constitutional power to grant the Court jurisdiction in such cases—simultaneously extracted the Court from a nasty and futile confrontation and yet gave it the means to return again and fight another day. By its demonstration that § 13 of the Judiciary Act contradicted the Constitution, the Court disengaged itself from immediate peril and, at the same time, secured the power of constitutional interpretation. Moreover, Chief Justice Marshall was afforded the opportunity of announcing the doctrine of judicial review from a sheltered position where it could not readily be challenged by the President.[15] And unchal-

this may dispose of the historical question, it is unlikely to prove adequate in response to a demand for a *justification* of judicial review. The reason is that durable and forceful justifications of the power are likely to be built around the advancement of certain highly-regarded values, not the ambiguities of historical inference (at least not without giving us some reason why we should feel obliged to honor the intent of individuals long since dead). The question of justifying the power, unlike the question of explaining how, exactly, in retrospect, the Court got the power, is not limited by considerations of timeliness.

15. As Justice Jackson keenly observed:

The strategy of giving the Jeffersonians a victory by invoking a doctrine of which they were the bitter opponents was masterly. Marshall knew his politics as well as his law. The Jeffersonians could not well arouse the people against the doctrine by which they had won their case. Marshall had

fixed in the law the doctrine of judicial supremacy, and he had fixed it in a most sheltered position. Had he declared the doctrine in a case where the decision went against Mr. Jefferson, there is little doubt that the President would have defied the Court and at that time the people would probably have sustained him. But Jefferson could not defy a decision in his favor; he could make no issue over a legal theory. Judicial supremacy in constitutional interpretation was so snugly anchored in a Jeffersonian victory that it could not well be attacked.

The Struggle for Judicial Supremacy 27 (1941).

Moreover, it would appear that at that time the focus of popular attention on the case was not on the issue of judicial review, a matter that seems clear to us in retrospect, but on the issue of executive accountability in the courts, *i. e.*, on "the alleged trespass of the Judges on the Presidential field of power * * *." 1 Warren, The

lenged exercises of power are the stuff of which precedents are made.

Beginning with *Marbury*, the Supreme Court, heretofore afflicted with such weakness, began to take on new possibilities. If Marshall's decree—that "[i]t is emphatically, the province and duty of the judicial department, to say what the law is" [16] —did not transform the Court into the brightest star in the political constellation,[17] it did single-handedly save that branch of government from obscurity. Though Marshall's words would pose no particular threat to Jefferson, reliance upon them would seal the fate of another President 171 years later.[18] The decision in *Marbury* v. *Madison* stands, then, as a monument to Marshall's genius at statecraft.

What it may or may not stand for is an adequate justification of the practice of judicial review. That Marshall's opinion demonstrates a skilled use of power, subordinating the disposition of legal considerations to paramount political objectives, is undeniable. That it can stand the test of reason in fashioning a way out of the central dilemma of constitutional interpretation is a

Supreme Court in United States History 245 (1926).

16. 5 U.S. (1 Cr.) at 175, 2 L.Ed. at 73.

17. Our preoccupation with only those cases in which the Supreme Court exercises the power of judicial review, writes Professor Shapiro, distorts the role of the Court. Such a focus makes both too much and too little of the Court. It makes too much of the Court because it magnifies out of all proportion the importance of the Court as a policy-making institution and gives an illusion of finality to what is really an on-going political process. Law and Politics in the Supreme Court 1–6 (1964).

See note 2, *supra*. A precursor to Shapiro's view was Meigs, *The Relation of the Judiciary to the Constitution*, 19 Am.L.Rev. 175 (1885). The focus on the Supreme Court as Constitutional Court also makes too little of the institution because it obscures or eliminates from our view entirely the Court's dominant business of statutory interpretation. Once this sphere of the Court's functioning is restored to view, the Court can be seen as a dynamic institution, *i. e.*, one in interaction with other branches and agencies of government in a continuing process of modifying policies.

18. United States v. Nixon, 418 U.S. 683, 705, 94 S.Ct. 3090, 3106 (1974).

very different matter, for the acquisition of judicial review should not be confused with its justification. When it comes to opinions, the test is one of reason, not power. The question to be asked, then, is: How well has the Court justified the conclusion it has chosen to reach? To answer this question, the Court's opinion must be examined in detail.[19] To the extent that the arguments offered in Marshall's opinion constitute the means by which the accepted justification of judicial review has been supported, the merit of the Court's claim will be no stronger than the weakest link in the proverbial chain.

1. Some Preliminary Considerations

To begin with, there would appear to be a serious conflict of interest on the part of Chief Justice Marshall. His participation in the Court's consideration of the case, not to mention his authorship of the Court's opinion, violates the expectation we have that judges not sit in cases in which they have either experi-

---

19. The discussion which follows makes no attempt to comprehensively evaluate all of the manifold legal problems presented by Chief Justice Marshall's opinion, but instead seeks to highlight some of the more critical difficulties. For those seeking a more detailed, comprehensive, and definitive critical analysis, two relatively recent, superbly-executed dissections are: Van Alstyne, *A Critical Guide to* Marbury *v.* Madison, 1969 Duke L. J. 1, and Rhodes, Marbury *v.* Madison *Revisited*, 33 U.Cin.L.Rev. 23 (1964). The classic study is Corwin, The Doctrine of Judicial Review (1914), the first chapter of which was originally published as Marbury *v.* Madison *and the Doctrine of Judicial Review*, 12 Mich. L.Rev. 538 (1914). Another traditional critique is Haines, The American Doctrine of Judicial Supremacy 193–203 (1959), and also

his The Role of the Supreme Court in American Government and Politics 1789–1835 245–258 (1944). See also McLaughlin, The Courts, the Constitution, and Parties (1912), and his Marbury *v.* Madison *Again*, 14 A.B.A.J. 155 (1928), as well as Grant, Marbury *v.* Madison *Today*, 23 Am.Pol.Sci.Rev. 673 (1929). For additional background and discussion of the case, see 3 Beveridge, The Life of John Marshall, Chs. 2, 3 (1919), 1 Warren, The Supreme Court in United States History, Ch. 5 (1926), and Burton, *The Cornerstone of Constitutional Law: The Extraordinary Case of* Marbury *v.* Madison, 36 A.B.A.J. 805, 881 (1950). See also the sources listed in note 14, *supra*. While the observations that follow were not specifically drawn from these sources, some overlap will necessarily be found.

enced personal involvement or in which they have close personal or professional relationships with the affected parties or their counsel.[20] His disregard for this principle concerning the avoid-

20. For over 60 years, the United States Code has contained a provision requiring disqualification of judges in cases under certain circumstances which may render their participation suspect. The current version of the statute, 28 U.S.C.A. § 455, revised in 1974, reads in part as follows:

(a) Any justice, judge, magistrate, or referee in bankruptcy of the United States shall disqualify himself in any proceeding in which his impartiality might reasonably be questioned.

(b) He shall also disqualify himself in the following circumstances:

(1) Where he has a personal bias or prejudice concerning a party, or personal knowledge of disputed evidentiary facts concerning the proceeding;

(2) Where in private practice he served as lawyer in the matter in controversy, or a lawyer with whom he previously practiced law served during such association as a lawyer concerning the matter, or the judge or such lawyer has been a material witness concerning it;

(3) Where he has served in governmental employment and in such capacity participated as counsel, adviser, or material witness concerning the proceeding or expressed an opinion concerning the merits of the particular case in controversy;

(4) He knows that he, individually or as a fiduciary, or his spouse or minor child residing in his household, has a financial interest in the subject matter in controversy or in a party to the proceeding, or any other interest that could be substantially affected by the outcome of the proceeding;

*   *   *

For a discussion of the background of the law, see the House Report on the measure, 1974 U.S. Code Cong. & Admin.News 6351. The report also discusses Canon 3C of the American Bar Association's Code of Judicial Conduct upon which the above provisions of the law were based. For a discussion of the parameters of judicial disqualification, see particularly the expert commentaries by John P. Frank: *Disqualification of Judges*, 47 Yale L.J. 605 (1947); *Disqualification of Judges: In Support of the Bayh Bill*, 35 L. & Contemp.Probs. 43 (1970); *Commentary on Disqualification of Judges—Canon 3C*, 1972 Utah L.Rev. 377. See also the symposium on the Code of Judicial Conduct generally, 1972 Utah L. Rev. 333–464, and Note, *Disqualification of Judges and Justices in the Federal Courts*, 86 Harv.L.Rev. 736 (1973). The principle that a man not be the judge in his own case was recognized at least as far back as Dr. Bonham's Case, 8 Co. Rep. 1136, 77 Eng.Rep. 646 (K.B. 1609), also reported as College of Physicians' Case, 2 Br.&Gold. 256,

ance of impropriety or even the appearance of impropriety is alleviated neither by the fact that a quorum of four justices was required for the case to be heard and Justices Cushing and

123 Eng.Rep. 928; see Note, *Disqualification of Judges for Bias in the Federal Courts*, 79 Harv.L.Rev. 1435 (1966).

Marshall, however, did disqualify himself in several land title cases, notably Martin v. Hunter's Lessee, 14 U.S. (1 Wheat.) 304, 4 L.Ed. 97 (1816), where he and his brother were personally involved in the purchase of several large tracts of Virginia real estate. In more recent times, disqualification of Justices Reed, Murphy, and Jackson, who variously had been involved in prosecutions as Attorney General or Solicitor General of the United States during Franklin Roosevelt's first two administrations, came close to impairing the operation of the Stone Court. Later, a heated wrangle over Justice Black's participation in Jewell Ridge Coal Corp. v. Local No. 6167, United Mine Workers of America, 325 U.S. 161, 65 S.Ct. 1063 (1945), a case in which counsel for the union happened to be Black's old law partner, developed when Justice Jackson objected (see his concurring opinion in the Court's denial of a petition for rehearing, 325 U.S. 897, 65 S.Ct. 1550). That disagreement festered in private until Jackson, committing what is alleged by some to be perhaps the greatest breach of judicial ethics in the history of the Court, exposed the feud to public view in a rash cable to the House and Senate Judiciary Committees in an at-

tempt to blunt what he thought was a movement to name Black as Stone's successor to the Chief Justiceship. See Schubert, Dispassionate Justice: A Synthesis of the Judicial Opinions of Robert H. Jackson 16–17, 165–168, 292 (1969); see also Gerhart, America's Advocate: Robert H. Jackson 235–277 (1958). And as recently as 1972, controversy flared when Justice Rehnquist refused to disqualify himself in Laird v. Tatum, 408 U.S. 1, 92 S. Ct. 2318 (1972). In that case, which involved military surveillance of political activities by civilians, the appellees alleged bias since Rehnquist, as an Assistant U. S. Attorney General prior to his appointment to the Court, had testified before a subcommittee of the Senate Judiciary Committee and had spoken publicly on other occasions in favor of government data collection activities. Rehnquist defended his participation in the *Laird* case in a separate memorandum opinion, 409 U.S. 824, 93 S.Ct. 7 (1972). See Note, *Justice Rehnquist's Decision to Participate in* Laird v. Tatum, 73 Colum.L.Rev. 106 (1973). *Laird* v. *Tatum*, like the *Jewell Ridge* case, was decided by a 5–4 vote. For an example of a controversy in which a federal judge displayed such aggressiveness and bias that he functioned, in the words of a federal appeals court, as a veritable "advocate," see Reserve Mining Co. v. Lord, 529 F.2d 181 (8th Cir. 1976).

Moore were not present for some or all of the proceedings,[21] or by the outcome which seems at variance with any partisan interests Marshall might be thought to have had in this controversy.[22]

Another unusual aspect of the Court's disposition of *Marbury* is the order in which it takes up the three questions posed by the case. In Marshall's words:

> In the order in which the court has viewed this subject, the following questions have been considered and decided: 1st. Has the applicant a right to the commission he demands? 2d. If he has a right, and that right has been violated, do the laws of this country afford him a remedy? 3d. If they do afford him a remedy, is it a *mandamus* issuing from this court? [23]

Consistent with the conventional practice that courts do not rule on matters not pertaining to the immediate disposition of the case,[24] one would expect Marshall to have placed the jurisdic-

---

21. Cushing was not present at any trial sessions or for the decision; Moore was present when the decision was announced, but not for trial. Burton, *The Cornerstone of Constitutional Law: The Extraordinary Case of* Marbury v. Madison, 36 A.B.A.J. 805, 807 (1950).

22. The customary practice in such circumstances is to postpone hearing the dispute until a fuller complement of judges is available. In view of the absence of any extenuating circumstances in this case, it is difficult to understand why there was any necessity to choose between overlooking Marshall's involvement and not attaining a quorum. It is also difficult to see how the outcome justifies Marshall's participation for, if that were to be so, it would imply that a participant in his position prejudge the case.

23. 5 U.S. (1 Cr.) at 154, 2 L.Ed. at 66.

24. Compare the treatment of jurisdiction *vis-à-vis* the merits of the controversy here with the Court's consideration of a petition for *habeas corpus* as it was affected by an Act of Congress withdrawing the Court's appellate jurisdiction in such cases in Ex parte McCardle, 74 U.S. (7 Wall.) 506, 512, 514, 19 L.Ed. 264, 265 (1869):

> The first question necessarily is that of jurisdiction; for, if the Act * * * takes away * * * jurisdiction * * * it is useless, if not improper, to enter into any discussion of other questions.
>
> * * *
>
> * * * Without jurisdiction the court cannot proceed at all in any cause. Jurisdiction is the power to declare the law, and

tional question first since, if the Court possessed no authority to render a binding decision, a ruling on the merits of the controversy would seem completely unnecessary.

One explanation of why the questions are positioned as they are, proceeding from right to remedy to jurisdiction, is that the result Marshall is aiming at is really not credible unless the merits of the dispute are resolved first. Had the Court failed to jell the facts into a concrete case and controversy at the outset, its treatment of the important constitutional issues would likely be seen as wholly speculative and gratuitous, if, in fact, discussion of them could be sustained at all. The answer to the first question establishes the integrity of the Court's inquiry, that this is not a hypothetical case. If the positioning of the questions does not reflect the norm in conventional judicial practice, it nonetheless has a logic of its own. As they are sequenced by Marshall, the questions are so interlocked that their thrust seems not only commonsensical but compelling.

Another explanation is that the disposition of the questions in the order Marshall has arrayed them affords some moral consolation to disgruntled Federalists. True, the consolation it offers is something like that in the story of the pedestrian who, crossing the street on the crosswalk, fails to look before he steps out from the curb and is struck and killed by a car—he's right, but dead—nevertheless, to extreme partisans and ideologues moral rightness is not an irrelevant consideration. And, inasmuch as

when it ceases to exist, the only function remaining to the court is that of announcing the fact and dismissing the cause. And this is not less clear upon authority than upon principle.

Moreover, given the conventional practice of not reaching constitutional issues (and there are two of them in this case: directing a *mandamus* at an executive officer of the government and passing upon the legitimacy of an Act of Congress) if a disposition of the case can be made on other grounds (Ashwander v. Tennessee Valley Authority, 297 U.S. 288, 345–348, 56 S.Ct. 466, 482–484 (1936) [concurring opinion of Brandeis, J.]), straightforward dismissal of the case on jurisdictional grounds if possible would appear to be the most appropriate tack. For an extended discussion, see Van Alstyne, *A Critical Guide to* Marbury *v.* Madison, 1969 Duke L.J. 1, 6–8.

Marshall has to discuss the merits anyway, it doesn't cost anything to give them some feeling of satisfaction. It also offers the chance to tweak Jefferson's nose, an opportunity not to be missed.

2. Marbury's Right to the Commission

Marshall appears to have little difficulty disposing of the question whether Marbury has a right to the commission. The Court's affirmative answer reflects a conclusion that all of the constitutional and statutory procedures required for appointing and commissioning an officer of the government have been carried out.

Because the Constitution provides for them under different sections of Article II,[25] the processes of appointing and commissioning are separable.[26] The former has been completed when the President signs the commission, thus accepting the Senate's confirmation of his nominee. Says Marshall:

> Some point of time must be taken when the power of the executive over an officer, not removable at his will, must cease. That point of time must be when the constitutional power of appointment has been exercised. And this power has been exercised when the last act, required from the person possessing the power, has been performed. This last act is the signature of the commission. * * *

25. The President's power to "nominate, and, by and with the advice and consent of the Senate, * * * appoint" is granted by Art. II, Sec. II, ¶ 2. His power to "commission all officers of the United States" is granted by Art. II, Sec. III.

26. In cases of appointment by the President, though, they run together at the point where the President signs the commission. The President's signature ends the process of appointment and constitutes half of the commissioning process; the other half being the affixing of the Great Seal by the Secretary of State. Conceivably, the processes of appointing and commissioning can be completely separate when the President commissions officers appointed by others, since "the Congress may by law vest the appointment of such inferior officers, as they think proper, * * * in the courts of law, or in the heads of departments." Art. II, Sec. II, ¶ 2.

The signature is a warrant for affixing the great seal to the commission; and the great seal is only to be affixed to an instrument which is complete. It attests, by an act supposed to be of public notoriety, the verity of the presidential signature.

It is never to be affixed till the commission is signed, because the signature, which gives force and effect to the commission, is conclusive evidence that the appointment is made.

The commission being signed, the subsequent duty of the secretary of state is prescribed by law, and not to be guided by the will of the president. He is to affix the seal of the United States to the commission, and is to record it.[27]

Delivery of the commission cannot be regarded as a stage in the appointment process both because the process is concluded well before that event can take place and because "transmission of the commission is a practice directed by convenience, but not by law." [28] Indeed, argues Marshall, were possession of the commission to be equated with appointment, then loss or destruction of the certificate would displace the officeholder from his post, which it surely does not. Under the law, a certified copy of the commission obtainable from the Secretary of State is a valid substitute. Jefferson, however, refused to accept Marshall's characterization of the appointment and commissioning processes as distinctly different. In his view, delivery of the commission constituted the final act of appointment.[29]

27. 5 U.S. (1 Cr.) at 157–158, 2 L.Ed. at 67.

28. 5 U.S. (1 Cr.) at 160, 2 L.Ed. at 68.

29. Characterizing Marshall's ruling on this point as a "perversion of law," Jefferson writes:

For if there is any principle of law never yet contradicted it is that delivery is one of the essentials to the validity of the deed. Although signed and sealed, yet as long as it remains in the hands of the party himself, it is in *fieri* only, it is not a deed, and can be made so only by its delivery. In the hands of a third person it may be made an escrow. But whatever is in the executive offices is certainly deemed to be in the hands of the President; and in this case, was actually in my hands, because, when I countermanded them, there was as yet no Secretary of State.

Letter to William Johnson, June 12, 1823, in Basic Writings of Thomas Jefferson 780, at 781–782 (Foner, ed. 1950).

In sum, with respect to the first question, the Court holds:

> Mr. Marbury, then, since his commission was signed by the President, and sealed by the Secretary of State, was appointed; and as the law creating the office, gave the officer a right to hold for five years, independent of the executive, the appointment was not revocable, but vested in the officer legal rights, which are protected by the laws of this country.

> To withhold his commission, therefore, is an act deemed by this court not warranted by law, but violative of a vested legal right.[30]

3. The Limits of the Remedy

Unless the system is a sham, and hence unworthy of even being called a legal system, an individual who possesses a vested legal right must have some remedy with which to vindicate that right when it is encroached upon by others.   Yet, where, as here, such a remedy would call into question the actions of an executive officer of the government, a countervailing concern surfaces, namely, that executive officers not be intruded upon or

---

30. 5 U.S. (1 Cr.) at 160, 2 L.Ed. at 68.   Speaking for the Court in Myers v. United States, 272 U.S. 52, 47 S.Ct. 21 (1926), a case upholding the President's authority to remove first, second, and third class postmasters without Senate approval, Chief Justice Taft, after quoting Marshall above, observed that "the expression of opinion that the officer was not removable by the President was unnecessary, even to the conclusion that a writ in a proper case could issue. However this may be, the whole statement was certainly obiter dictum with reference to the judgment actually reached." 272 U.S. at 141, 47 S.Ct. at 33.   Moreover, continued Taft, even if the conclusion in *Marbury*, quoted above, were not taken as dictum, subsequent decisions of the Court have plainly overruled it as a statement of law. See the discussion, 272 U.S. at 142–164, 47 S.Ct. at 34–41. See also McLaughlin, Marbury *v*. Madison *Again*, 14 A.B.A.J. 155 (1928).

We should also note that, since Marbury was clearly appointed as an Article I and not an Article III judge (his term of office being for only five years instead of life), the usual concern for protecting the independence of the judiciary is significantly reduced. For a discussion of Article I and Article III courts, see Ex parte Bakelite Corp., 279 U.S. 438, 49 S.Ct. 411 (1929), but *cf.* Glidden Co. v. Zdanok, 370 U.S. 530, 82 S.Ct. 1459 (1962).

impeded in their legitimate operation of the government. The exact parameters of a remedy hinge upon the following inquiry:

> It follows, then, that the question, whether the legality of an act of the head of a department be examinable in a court of justice or not must always depend on the nature of that act.
>
> If some acts be examinable, and others not, there must be some rule of law to guide the court in the exercise of its jurisdiction.[31]

The principle which circumscribes the proper scope of the remedy, Marshall explains, is one separating "discretionary" from "ministerial" acts. In the parlance of political science, the distinction is one between "politics" and "administration."[32] Discretionary acts (such as those of the President in the appointing process) entail political choices, and the leeway of government officials in making those kinds of choices is protected by the Constitution.[33] If there is disagreement over the wisdom

31. 5 U.S. (1 Cr.) at 165, 2 L.Ed. at 70.

32. See Wilson, *The Study of Administration*, 2 Pol.Sci.Q. 197, 209–210 (1887); for a discussion of the paradigm in the study of political science, see Ostrom, The Intellectual Crisis in American Public Administration, Ch. 2 (Rev. ed. 1974).

Conceding the substantial inaccuracy of characterizing administrators as people who "don't make policy" but who "just work here," nevertheless the distinction between making policy choices and executing the law is essential in constitutional law because of critical considerations related to the separation of powers concept. Obviously, all government officials exercise some discretion, so that the distinction is necessarily a matter of degree. Such a formal distinction must be made, however, if the equities in a given controversy are to have a chance of being fairly resolved. Without the ability to draw such a formal distinction, and thus be afforded an opportunity to balance the contending interests, we would be compelled to accept one of two extreme alternatives: either vested rights will go completely unprotected, or government officials will have their legitimate discretion supplanted by that of judges deciding questions of policy clearly committed by the Constitution to other branches of government.

33. Just as no court could order the President to appoint a particular individual to public office, no court could order the Chief Executive to veto a bill, or enjoin him from executing a law passed by Congress. See Mississippi v. Johnson, 71 U.S. (4 Wall.) 475, 18 L.Ed. 437 (1867).

of those policy choices, it must be resolved at the ballot box. The delivery of a commission, however, does not share this quality of a discretionary act; rather, it is one of simple administration. The actions of the Secretary of State in the commissioning process are specifically and unequivocally directed by law and he is afforded no policy choice. Hence, "where a specific duty is assigned by law, and individual rights depend upon the performance of that duty, it seems equally clear that the individual who considers himself injured, has a right to resort to the laws of his country for a remedy." [34]

4. Jurisdiction to Grant the Remedy

Having answered the first two questions affirmatively, Marshall at last reaches the third question, the answer to which constitutes by far the most crucial and, as it turns out, certainly the most controversial part of the Court's opinion. Whether Marbury is entitled to the remedy is a question the Court separates into two subordinate inquiries: first, as to the nature of the available writ, and second, as to the Court's jurisdiction to grant it.

Without much extended discussion, the Court finds a writ of *mandamus*, directed to the Secretary of State within the limits sketched out in answer to the second question, to be the proper remedy. Such an order, in keeping with the traditional use of the writ, would direct him to fulfill a function associated with his office, namely, delivery of the commission.[35]

One federal district court, determined to implement a constitutional right to treatment for individuals involuntarily committed to state mental institutions, has come pretty close, however, to trenching upon a legislature's appropriation power. See Wyatt v. Stickney, 344 F.Supp. 373 (M.D.Ala.1972).

35. Even in cases where the President has removed inferior officers, the remedy granted by the courts has never been reinstatement, but rather an award of salary. See Myers v. United States, 272 U.S. 52, 47 S.Ct. 21 (1926), and Humphrey's Executor v. United States, 295 U.S. 602, 55 S.Ct. 869 (1935).

34. 5 U.S. (1 Cr.) at 166, 2 L.Ed. at 70.

Whether or not the remedy of *mandamus* is one that may issue from the Supreme Court is a matter of jurisdiction. The long and short of it, Marshall says, is that, though Marbury may have a right to the commission, and though *mandamus* is a proper remedy with which to vindicate that right, nevertheless it is not a remedy which can issue from the Supreme Court. This is so despite § 13 of the Judiciary Act which gives the Court the power to issue the writ in some circumstances, because, as Marshall reads the statute, it runs contrary to provisions regarding the Court's original and appellate jurisdiction set down in Article III of the Constitution. The essence of the conflict, as Marshall sees it, is that § 13 of the Judiciary Act has unconstitutionally expanded the Court's original jurisdiction by permitting writs of *mandamus* to be granted. And, following along the same lines as Hamilton in *Federalist No. 78*, Marshall argues: Both the Constitution and elementary logic dictate that, given a conflict between a statute and a provision of the Constitution, it is the Constitution which must prevail. Insofar as courts are agencies of government called upon to apply the law, then they are forced to make such a choice when laws conflict. The exercise of judicial review, therefore, is an inescapable aspect of the adjudicative function.

Most of the answer to the third question is, in fact, reducible to a simple syllogism:

Major Premise: The Constitution and all laws passed pursuant to it are the law of the land.

Minor Premise: Section 13 of the Judiciary Act contradicts the Constitution.

Conclusion: Section 13 of the Judiciary Act cannot be law.

Marshall's discussion of this argument, and his embellishment of it, constitute the bulk of the most critical section of the opinion.

His answer to Question 3 is controversial and unsettling, and, because of its importance, merits extensive consideration. Analysis of it will focus initially on the validity of the minor premise [36] and ultimately on the argument presented in the syllogism as an argument justifying the power of judicial review.

Since an argument, after all, is no stronger than the premises upon which it is based, it is important to understand the reasoning behind the minor premise. Because the minor premise in the syllogism is but a conclusion drawn with respect to § 13 of the Judiciary Act, it remains for us to probe Marshall's opinion further to see why § 13 of the Judiciary Act is incompatible with the provisions of Article III of the Constitution concerning the Court's original and appellate jurisdiction.

The relevant portion of Marshall's opinion consumes less than three pages of the original Court reports.[37]   His discussion is straightforward, even somewhat belabored, on the difference between the two kinds of jurisdiction.   The drift of what Marshall has to say is, in effect, that original jurisdiction is original jurisdiction, appellate jurisdiction is appellate jurisdiction, and, if the Constitutional Convention had intended no significance in the distinction between the two, it would not have so explicitly distinguished them and provided respectively for their immutability and alteration in Article III.   Thus, were Congress to expand the Court's original jurisdiction by permitting it to issue writs of *mandamus*, Congress would be acting clearly contrary to the Constitution.   Only aspects of the Court's appellate jurisdiction can be modified by legislative enactment.   As even a cursory examination of the text of § 13 will show, however, Congress intended no such adjustment in the Court's original jurisdiction.[38]

---

36. The validity of the major premise is established by the Supremacy Clause of the Constitution, Art. VI, ¶ 2.

37. 5 U.S. (1 Cr.) at 173–176, 2 L.Ed. at 72–73.

38. The relevant portion of the statute, Act of Sept. 24, 1789, 1st

Cong., 1st Sess., ch. 20, 1 Stat. 73, 80–81, reads as follows:

SEC. 13.   *And be it further enacted,* That the Supreme Court shall have exclusive jurisdiction of all controversies of a civil nature, where a state is a party, except between a state and its citizens; and except also between a state and

The statute indicates with undeniable clarity that only in respect to its appellate jurisdiction is the Court permitted to issue writs of prohibition and *mandamus.*

It would, perhaps, be difficult to understand why Marshall does not dismiss the case at this point and suggest to Marbury that he pursue the matter in the proper lower federal court,[39] allowing the controversy in time to reach the Supreme Court by the appellate route. Instead, Marshall goes on to foreclose the option of appellate review by taking up the question of whether the Court may issue a writ of *mandamus* in the exercise of its appellate jurisdiction. In this regard, he writes:

> It is the essential criterion of appellate jurisdiction, that it revises and corrects the proceedings in a cause already instituted, and does not create that cause. Although, therefore, a mandamus may be directed to courts, yet to issue such a writ to an officer for the delivery of a paper, is in effect the same as to sustain an original action for that paper, and, therefore, seems not to belong to appellate but to original jurisdiction. Neither is it necessary in such a case as this, to enable the court to exercise its appellate jurisdiction.[40]

citizens of other states, or aliens, in which latter case it shall have original but not exclusive jurisdiction. And shall have exclusively all such jurisdiction of suits or proceedings against ambassadors, or other public ministers, or their domestics, or domestic servants, as a court of law can have or exercise consistently with the law of nations; and original, but not exclusive jurisdiction of all suits brought by ambassadors, or other public ministers, or in which a consul, or vice consul, shall be a party. And the trial of issues in fact in the Supreme Court, in all actions at law against citizens of the United States, shall be by jury. The Supreme Court shall also have appellate jurisdiction from the circuit courts and courts of the several states, in the cases herein after specially provided for; and shall have power to issue writs of prohibition to the district courts, when proceeding as courts of admiralty and maritime jurisdiction, and writs of *mandamus,* in cases warranted by the principles and usages of law, to any courts appointed, or persons holding office, under the authority of the United States.

39. The Circuit Court for the District of Columbia was available, it having been created by the same legislation that created Marbury's job, Act of Feb. 27, 1801, 6th Cong., 2d Sess., ch. 15, § 3, 2 Stat. 103, 105.

40. 5 U.S. (1 Cr.) at 175, 2 L.Ed. at 73.

To those who have just sat through several paragraphs of Marshall's making the point that original jurisdiction is original jurisdiction and appellate jurisdiction is appellate jurisdiction, this seems downright contradictory. It is all the more curious since he appears to make jurisdiction turn upon parties to suits rather than upon the forums in which suits begin. If *mandamus* has a different effect in terms of the Court's jurisdiction when it is directed to "persons" instead of "courts," we need to know more than the brief statement above tells us. Given the importance of what is said here, it seems strange that he has opted for such economical expression. Compared with his laborious treatment of original and appellate jurisdiction earlier and the fulsome rhetoric yet to come as to why a superior law should prevail over an inferior law, it is surprising to find Marshall so nonchalant, almost cryptic, at this critical juncture.

What Marshall is driving at may be explained in a statement by two leading commentators on practice before the Supreme Court as they discuss the relation between the granting of the principal "extraordinary writs" (*mandamus*, prohibition, *habeas corpus*, and *certiorari*) and the Court's original jurisdiction:

> Since the jurisdiction of the Court to issue an extraordinary writ is invoked as a means of correcting error in a lower court, the writs are an exercise of the Supreme Court's appellate jurisdiction, not its original jurisdiction under Article III of the Constitution. But the application for the writ before the Supreme Court institutes a new case which has never been heard by a lower court even though its object is to correct error below. For that reason the case in the Supreme Court is, in a sense, an original action * * *. Indeed, until recent years, the extraordinary writ cases were placed on the Original Docket along with cases arising under the Court's original jurisdiction. Inasmuch as the constitutional and statutory bases for the two types of cases are entirely different, the writs are now placed on the Court's Miscellaneous Docket. * * *[41]

41. Stern and Gressman, Supreme Court Practice 411 (4th ed. 1969).

Another possible explanation lies in the fact that, at the time of *Marbury* v. *Madison,* lower federal courts [42] may have been without jurisdiction to issue writs of *mandamus* in such circumstances.   The authority of the circuit courts was governed in this respect by the Judiciary Act of 1789,[43] a provision of which, while empowering the lower federal courts "to issue writs of *scire facias, habeas corpus,* and all other writs not specially provided for by statute," [44] nevertheless confined them in the issuance of those orders to writs *"which may be necessary for the exercise of their respective jurisdictions,* and agreeable to the principles and usages of law." [45]   (The names of the specific writs are italicized in the original; otherwise emphasis is supplied.)   Thus, the refusal of a circuit court to issue a writ of *mandamus* for want of jurisdiction (given that the remedy sought by Marbury was a *mandamus* directed to the Secretary of State), and subsequent appeal to the Supreme Court, which alone had the power to issue a *mandamus* to "persons," might

---

42. Clearly the circuit courts were the more important of the two inferior federal tribunals. The district courts were confined largely to hearing nonserious federal criminal cases and small civil suits. Act of Sept. 24, 1789, 1st Cong., 1st Sess., ch. 20, § 9, 1 Stat. 73, 76–77. The circuit courts, in addition to having original jurisdiction in cases of serious federal offenses and civil suits over $500, had appellate jurisdiction in those cases that began in the district courts. *Ibid.,* § 11, 1 Stat. 73, 78–79.

43. Both before passage of the Midnight Judges Act, which significantly expanded the jurisdiction of the circuit courts, and after its repeal approximately a year later, the authority of the circuit courts was controlled by the Judiciary Act of 1789. See notes 4 and 6, *supra.* The legislation enacted following repeal of the Midnight Judges Act merely reinstated the jurisdictional provisions of the Judiciary Act of 1789. See Act of Apr. 29, 1802, 7th Cong., 1st Sess., ch. 31, § 5, 2 Stat. 156, 158.

44. Act of Sept. 24, 1789, 1st Cong., 1st Sess., ch. 20, § 14, 1 Stat. 73, 81–82.

45. *Ibid.,* 82. This limitation would appear to confine the issuance of a *mandamus* to courts. For example, a circuit court might rely upon the writ to direct a district court to take action in a particular instance or to force a recalcitrant district judge to act in conformity with a prior ruling of the circuit court.

make issuing the writ tantamount to an original action by the Court.

Since the paragraph of Marshall's in question only states a conclusion without providing a reason to justify it, it is impossible to tell from the opinion which of these two possible explanations he had in mind. The former would seem to stretch a formality on pleading to the point of annihilating the essence of appellate review acknowledged by Marshall in the first sentence of the paragraph. Subsequent Supreme Court decisions have accepted the latter.[46] Indeed, Court decisions following *Marbury* affirmed the power of the Circuit Court for the District of Columbia, as distinguished from that of the other circuit courts, to *mandamus* federal officers,[47] based in part on that court's common law jurisdiction acquired from the State of Maryland, and based in part on terms of the act creating a system of courts within the District of Columbia [48] which incorporated the sweeping jurisdiction given the circuit courts by the Midnight Judges Act, then in effect.

The classic objection which is offered to Marshall's syllogistic argument justifying judicial review is not merely that it belabors the answer to a question, but that it belabors an answer to the *wrong* question.[49] The question is not "Which should prevail when a statute conflicts with a provision of the Constitution?" but "Why should such a determination be a function of the Court?" It is, after all, not simply constitutional but *judicial* review we are talking about.

Marshall's effort at driving home what is obvious, but not to the point, is coupled with a prose style that frequently resorts to the rhetoric of certitude. Conclusions appear inevitable; the net effect is one of irrefutability. It becomes nearly impossible to see any other alternatives. We don't have to read much of

46. Hart and Wechsler, The Federal Courts and the Federal System 1180–1187 (1953).

47. The principal case in point is Kendall v. United States ex rel. Stokes, 37 U.S. (12 Pet.) 524, 9 L. Ed. 1181 (1838).

48. See note 39, *supra*

49. See note 19, *supra*

Marshall's opinion to know this is no place to be looking for any examination of the null hypothesis. What we have here is an advocate building a case.

That there is at least another conceivable position on the question of judicial review is pointed up by Justice Gibson in an opinion dissenting from the decision of the Pennsylvania Supreme Court in *Eakin* v. *Raub*.[50] In sum, Gibson argues that courts are agencies of distributive justice only—that they merely apply the written law in concrete cases. It is, of course, quite possible for courts to uniformly apply the law passed by a legislative body without getting into the business of deciding the separable issue of whether the legislature has the power to enact a given law.

To some extent, Marshall may have anticipated this kind of attack on judicial review in *Marbury* v. *Madison*. In substance, he seems to counter by taking the position that judges asked to apply the law may encounter a conflict among the laws to be applied—that between a statute and the Constitution, for example. Resolution of that conflict is an inescapable function of judicial power because, without it, there can be no uniform application of the laws. Failure to undertake resolution of this conflict, therefore, is an abdication of judicial responsibility, and judges, after all, take an oath to live up to the responsibilities of their office. They swear to uphold the Constitution.

Gibson's rejoinder is that, if judges take an oath of office to uphold the Constitution, legislators—and executives, for that matter—do too. Each branch of government must make its own determination.[51] While clever, this tilt does not unhorse Marshall. To impeach Marshall's argument, he has to be confronted on his own ground, that is in terms of his characterization of the adjudicative process.

50. 12 S.&R. 330 (1825).

51. As several of his letters indicate, this was Jefferson's view: Letter to Abigail Adams, June 11, 1804, 8 Writings of Thomas Jefferson 310 (Ford, ed. 1897); Letter to Judge Spencer Roane, Sept. 6, 1819, 10 Writings of Thomas Jefferson 140 (Ford, ed. 1899); Letter to William C. Jarvis, Sept. 12, 1820, *ibid.*, 160.

At the time, Gibson's everybody-takes-an-oath rebuttal may have been the best response that could have been mustered. But 175 years of judicial review by the United States Supreme Court raise a serious question about the truth of Marshall's argument. And it is the kind of plain empirical observation, not possible in 1803, which calls into question the accuracy of Marshall's portrayal of the adjudicative process. Much of the seeming irrefutability of Marshall's syllogism and the grip of his supporting judges-take-an-oath argument rests on the tacit premise that adjudication is a process of logic, not discretion—a premise that is squarely at odds even with Marshall's own doings in this very case. To flesh out Marshall's argument: It is the inexorable collision between some statutes and the Constitution that justifies the power of judicial review; it is a logical contradiction between the two that impels responsible judges, charged with applying the law, to confront the reality of inescapable choice.

Looking at those statutes, both federal and state, invalidated by the Court, the fact is that the overwhelming majority have been held unconstitutional not because of any inescapable logical contradiction with the plain wording of the Constitution, but rather because the Court, at certain moments in American history, deliberately chose to read certain fundamental rights— whether of an economic or civil libertarian character—into the Constitution.[52] Either by expanding the meanings of words ex-

52. A complete roster of cases decided by the Supreme Court to June, 1972, in which it declared unconstitutional laws passed by Congress, state acts, and municipal ordinances, can be found in the standard reference work prepared by the Congressional Research Service of the Library of Congress, The Constitution of the United States of America: Analysis and Interpretation, 1595–1785 (1973). The list of cases in which the Court has struck down acts of Congress has been updated to 1976 by P. Allan

Dionisopoulos in his article, *Judicial Review in the Textbooks*, recently featured in the Fall, 1976 issue of the DEA News, a publication of the American Political Science Association's Division of Educational Affairs. Based upon the Court's use of judicial review with respect to 59 laws in 44 cases between 1943 and 1976, Professor Dionisopoulos criticizes most contemporary introductory American government texts for the grossly misleading impressions they convey about the modern Court's use of

plicitly appearing in the document—an approach sometimes known as "the accordion theory" of constitutional interpretation —or by fashioning entirely new rights where none existed before, the Court has engineered the demise of legislation it thought incompatible with certain basic values. Likewise, an incalculable number of statutes have been rescued either due to the Court's willingness—oftentimes sheer ingenuity—in adopting a congenial construction of either statute or Constitution so as to avoid conflict, whether real or imagined, or due to periodic change in the composition of the Court.[53] These are not matters governed by some inexorable logic.

judicial review; to wit, "that (1) judicial review has rarely been used in national cases since 1937; (2) federal laws voided in the recent past are insignificant; (3) the Supreme Court's record of defending civil liberties is less than inspirational; and (4) the Nixon appointees have fulfilled his 1968 campaign promise 'to turn the Court around.' "

Reviewing those cases in which the Court held that statutes passed by Congress ran afoul of the Constitution, one scholar, on the eve of the Constitutional Revolution of 1937, observed:

Congress does not contravene the black-and-white clauses of the Constitution, like that which allots two Senators to each State. The conflicts between Congress and the Court have related to the indefinite clauses, like those which deal with interstate commerce, due process, and executive power. It is familiar that the relation of a law to these broad clauses is not a matter of fact but a matter of opinion. Congress in all the cases to be considered, and members of the Court in many, differed in opinion from the majority of the Court.

* * *

Edgerton, *The Incidence of Judicial Control Over Congress*, 22 Cornell L.Q. 299, 300 (1937). Judicial supremacy, Judge Edgerton concluded, had been far from "neutral in its incidence" but, instead, tended overwhelmingly to advance the interests of "the well-to-do minority" at the expense of "common men." More recent scholarly works have continued to underscore the connection between the political outlook of a majority of Justices sitting on the Court at a given time and particular trends in constitutional interpretation: see Twiss, Lawyers and the Constitution (1942); Bickel, The Supreme Court and the Idea of Progress (1970); Levy, Against the Law: The Nixon Court and Criminal Justice (1974); and Wasby, Continuity and Change: From the Warren Court to the Burger Court (1976).

53. The classic illustration remains the Court's celebrated about-face in its receptiveness to New Deal legislation in the late 1930s. Who

The exercise of judicial review, like the process of statutory construction, is conditioned by discretion, that is to say, in substantial measure, by the values of the individual judges. Marshall's characterization of the decisional process is palpably untrue as demonstrated by the unmistakable experience of the Court. In sum, then, an argument for the necessity of judicial review which stems from postulated logical contradictions that may arise between statute and written Constitution fails to accurately characterize that range of choice open to judges and which they do, in fact, exercise. Indeed, to repeat a point made earlier, Marshall's exercise of discretion in this very case belies the truth of his own overly modest characterization of the adjudicative process.

could deny that the Constitutional Revolution of 1937—a reorientation of political values, legal method, and the policy-making focus of the Court—was the product of accumulated political pressure, not legal logic, and that the guarantee of permanent triumph for the new constitutional order was the rapid change in the composition of the Court, beginning that June with the retirement of Justice Van Devanter? As against history's average of two appointments to the Court per presidential term, it is well worth noting that the ideological gulf separating the Court from the administration was sustained largely because FDR had no opportunities to make appointments to the Court during his first term (1933–1937), whereas, in his second term (1937–1941), he made eight (including the elevation of Stone to the Chief Justiceship). See Chase and Ducat, Corwin's The Constitution and What It Means Today 238–239 (13th ed. 1973); Schubert, Quantitative Analysis of Judicial Behavior 192–210 (1959); Jackson, The Struggle for Judicial Supremacy (1941); Leonard, The Search for a Judicial Philosophy: Mr. Justice Roberts and the Constitutional Revolution of 1937 (1971).

For works which focus on the Court's policy-making as it relates to dominant values and forces of the day, see Mendelson, *Judicial Review and Party Politics*, 12 Vanderbilt L.Rev. 447 (1959); Nagel, The Legal Process from a Behavioral Perspective, Chs. 20, 21 (1969); Funston, *The Supreme Court and Critical Elections*, 69 Am.Pol.Sci.Rev. 795 (1975); Dahl, *Decision-Making in a Democracy: The Supreme Court as a National Policy-Maker*, 6 J.Pub.L. 279 (1957); Dahl, Pluralist Democracy in the United States: Conflict and Consensus, Ch. 6 (1967); Casper, *The Supreme Court and National Policy Making*, 70 Am.Pol.Sci.Rev. 50 (1976); Schubert, Judicial Policy Making (Rev. ed. 1974); Mason, The Supreme Court from Taft to Warren (Rev. ed. 1968).

That this criticism is repeatedly articulated in the writings of modern jurisprudence [54] and the research of contemporary political science,[55] and vividly illustrated by decades of the Court's own experience—things neither Marshall nor anyone else could have been expected to know back in 1803—is neither unfair or irrelevant.   To be valid, the argument for judicial review must

54. For some observations in general, see Bodenheimer, Jurisprudence: The Philosophy and Method of Law, Chs. 8, 17, 18 (1962); Friedmann, Legal Theory, Chs. 25–28 (5th ed. 1967), Paton, Jurisprudence 22–28, 198–242 (4th ed. 1972); Stone, Social Dimensions of Law and Justice (1966). Specific examples would include: Arnold, The Symbols of Government (1935); Cairns, The Theory of Legal Science (1941); Cardozo, The Nature of the Judicial Process (1921); Cardozo, The Growth of the Law (1924); Cohen, Law and the Social Order (1933); Dewey, *Logical Method and the Law*, 10 Cornell L. Q. 17 (1924); Frank, Law and the Modern Mind (1930); Frank, Courts on Trial (1949); Garlan, Legal Realism and Justice (1941); Gray, The Nature and Sources of Law (1909); Holmes, *The Path of the Law*, 10 Harv.L.Rev. 457 (1897); Llewellyn, Bramble Bush (1930); Llewellyn, Jurisprudence: Realism in Theory and Practice (1962); Pound, *Mechanical Jurisprudence*, 8 Colum.L.Rev. 605 (1908); Pound, *The Scope and Purpose of Sociological Jurisprudence*, 25 Harv.L.Rev. 489 (1912); Pound, The Spirit of the Common Law (1921); Pound, An Introduction to the Philosophy of Law (1922); Pound, *The Call for a Realist Jurisprudence*, 44 Harv.L.Rev. 697 (1931); Pound, Law Finding

Through Experience and Reason (1960). See also, White, Social Thought in America: The Revolt Against Formalism, Chs. 2, 5, 7, 8 (1957).

55. Overviews of public law and judicial behavior research, centered mainly in political science, are provided in two superb review essays by Glendon Schubert, *Behavioral Research in Public Law*, 57 Am. Pol.Sci.Rev. 433 (1963), and *Judicial Process and Behavior 1963–1971*, in Robinson, ed., 3 Political Science Annual 73–280 (1972). Since Schubert's 1972 monograph, several other notable works have appeared: Murphy and Tanenhaus, The Study of Public Law (1972); Eisenstein, Politics and the Legal Process (1973); Sheldon, The American Judicial Process (1974); Schubert, The Judicial Mind Revisited (1974); Rohde and Spaeth, Supreme Court Decision Making (1976).

The link between modern legal theory and empirical political science research is developed in Becker, Political Behavioralism and Modern Jurisprudence, Chs. 1–3 (1964). A structure of the public law and judicial behavior field within political science, and its relationship to other disciplines, is provided by Schubert, *Academic Ideology and the Study of Adjudication*, 61 Am. Pol.Sci.Rev. 106 (1967).

be timeless. It must not be left to hang on historic limitations of thought or experience, or else the argument for judicial review reduces to something like: We have it because way back then the Court took it, and even though the argument is no longer any good, judicial review is here to stay. This makes the mistake of equating an explanation of why the Court has the power with a justification for that power. To explain the existence of something, however, is not the same as justifying it. We can explain many things that we can and do regard as completely unjustifiable.

However one may feel about either the persuasiveness of Gibson's answers to Marshall's arguments or the fact that, in time, he, too, came to accept the notion of judicial review,[56] nothing can detract from the fact that it was Gibson, not Marshall, who began, at least, by asking the right question. Gibson put his finger on it when he wrote:

> The constitution and the right of the legislature to pass the act, may be in collision; but is that a legitimate subject for judicial determination? If it be, the judiciary must be a *peculiar* organ, to revise the proceedings of the legislature, and to correct its mistakes *   *   *.[57] [Emphasis supplied.]

Recasting these sentiments in the form of a direct question, responses to which would be capable of furnishing a *justification* for judicial review, Justice Gibson's suggestion for our inquiry reduces to the query, "Does the Supreme Court have a unique function?"

Ultimately, the success of the argument for judicial review, and for those philosophies of constitutional interpretation that would use it freely, rests upon the assertion that the judiciary possesses some superior quality not possessed by other branches of government which can countervail the basically undemocratic character of judicial review. Such a value must be superior to that of democracy itself. There is, perhaps, only one such

56. Norris v. Clymer, 2 Pa. 277, 281 (1845).   57. Eakin v. Raub, 12 S.&R. 330, 348 (1825).

widely-respected value, and that is justice. Thus, to justify the exercise of the review power by an inherently undemocratic institution, those who make a case for it must show that the Court has the unique function of doing justice.

The Study of Politics and the Justification of Judicial Review

It is important to point out how this focus differs from much of the thrust of contemporary political science. Few themes in the modern study of politics and the judicial process have received greater emphasis, or been greeted with a larger sense of professional self-satisfaction among political scientists, than that courts are political institutions.[58] Though scholars often have been careful to show how particular features of judicial institutions constrain the impact of universal political variables, such as power and values, for example, few would dispute the proposition that the study of courts and how they make policy is squarely within David Easton's definition of the study of politics as inquiry into "the authoritative allocation of values for a society."[59], [60] Conceding the truth of the proposition,

---

58. See notes 2 and 55, *supra*.

59. The Political System 134 (1953). An oft-repeated criticism of Easton's definition of what political scientists study, as distinguished, say, from what sociologists or economists study, is that it is too narrow, too conservative, a definition. "If 'political' is confined to governmental decision-making and that which relates to it, the clearly nongovernmental institutions, irrespective of the power which they may wield and the impact of their decisions on society, are not political." This is of consequence because "this narrow concept supports the legitimacy of the elite decision-making process within the corporations and other large pri-

vate institutions" with the net effect that "by accepting a rigid and narrow concept of political, the elite theorist removes from consideration (within the context of democratic theory) the question of the feasibility of increasing participation in decision-making by enlarging the political scope to include more powerful private institutions." Bachrach, The Theory of Democratic Elitism: A Critique 97 (1967).

The rebuttal to this is, of course, not only that when the word "authoritative" is removed from Easton's definition, there will be nothing to separate the study of politics from

---

60. See note 60 on page 34.

that of the other social sciences, but also that such a modification may move us significantly from a constitutional democracy to a totalitarian state. Consider the following observation drawn by Stanley Benn, writing on the importance of privacy to a free society:

The totalitarian claims that everything a man is and does has significance for society at large. He sees the state as the selfconscious organization of society for the well-being of society; the social significance of our actions and relations overrides any other. Consequently, the public or political universe is all inclusive, *all* roles are public, and every function, whether political, economic, or artistic, can be interpreted as involving a public responsibility.

The liberal, on the other hand, claims not merely a private capacity—an area of action in which he is not responsible to the state for what he does so long as he respects certain minimal rights of others; he claims further that this is the residual category, that the onus is on anyone who claims he is accountable. * * *

This ideal of the private citizen provides no very precise criteria for distinguishing the private realm; it is rather that no citizen other than actual employees of the administration can be held culpable —even morally culpable—for any action as a failure in public duty unless special grounds can be shown why this is a matter in which he may not merely please himself. Of course, there will be duties associated with roles he has voluntarily assumed—as husband, employee, and so on—but such re-

sponsibilities are of his own choosing, not thrust upon him, like his public roles of juror, or taxpayer.

Benn, *Privacy, Freedom, and Respect for Persons*, in Pennock and Chapman, eds., Privacy 22–23 (1971). Reprinted by Permission of the Publishers, Lieber-Atherton, Inc. Copyright ⓒ 1971 All Rights Reserved.

60. The connection between law and politics—that, in a larger sense, the study of one is necessarily the study of the other—is underscored if one sees that each of the key words comprising Easton's definition highlights the emphasis given the definition of law by each of the three great schools of jurisprudence. "Authoritative" captures the contribution of the analytical positivists with their emphasis on law as "the command of the sovereign," stressing the importance of sanctions and finality in decisionmaking. See Wolin, *Hobbes: Political Society as a System of Rules*, in Politics and Vision 239–285 (1960); Kelsen, The Pure Theory of Law (1967); Bodenheimer, Jurisprudence: The Philosophy and Method of the Law, Ch. 7 (1962); Friedmann, Legal Theory, Chs. 22–24 (5th ed. 1967); Stone, Legal System and Lawyers' Reasonings (1964). "Allocation" highlights the emphasis of sociological jurisprudence, that judges make choices among competing interests in society in the formulation of social policy. See note 54, *supra*. And "values" symbolizes the concern of philosophical jurisprudence and natural law, that law is not value-free; indeed, that to be law, the policy of the state must have some minimum moral content. See d'Entrèves, Natural Law (1951);

then, that, in interaction with other officeholders, judges, too, resolve problems pressed on them as to "who gets what, when, how" [61] still, the observation that the judicial process is a political process and that judges, whether intentionally or unwittingly, are policy-makers is not the end of the discussion, but its beginning.

The possibilities of judicial power do not stem from any demonstration of how courts are like other governmental institutions, but from an accentuation of their differences.   The reason why this must be so is suggested in part by Hamilton's characterization of the Supreme Court in *Federalist No. 78*:

> Whoever attentively considers the different departments of power must perceive, that in a government in which they are separated from each other, the judiciary, from the nature of its functions, will always be the least dangerous to the political rights of the constitution; because it will be least in a capacity to annoy or injure them.   The executive not only dispenses the honors, but holds the sword of the community. The legislature not only commands the purse, but prescribes the rules by which the duties and rights of every citizen are to be regulated.   The judiciary on the contrary has no influence over either the sword or the purse, no direction either of the strength or of the wealth of the society, and can take no active resolution whatever. It may truly be said to have neither Force nor Will, but merely judgment; and must ultimately depend upon the aid of the executive arm even for the efficacy of its judgments.[62]

Accepting the accuracy of Hamilton's characterization of the Court as "the weakest of the three departments of power," [63] it

Fuller, The Morality of Law (1964); Bodenheimer, Jurisprudence: The Philosophy and Method of the Law, Chs. 1–4, 9 (1962); Friedmann, Legal Theory, Chs. 2, 7–15 (5th ed. 1967); Stone, Human Law and Human Justice (1965). The interrelationships, disclosed by Easton's conception, make clear at a glance why past debates among these schools of jurisprudence, as to which presented the "correct" definition of law, have been essentially fruitless.

61. Lasswell, Politics: Who Gets What, When, How (1958).

62. The Federalist 522–523 (Cooke, ed. 1961).

63. *Ibid.*, 523. Hamilton's statement is true only in a narrow sense,

can hardly serve the interests of judicial power to emphasize what the judiciary has in common with the other avowedly "political" branches if, unlike the Congress or the Executive, it has no attendant sanction.[64]

The weakness that comes with an inability of the judiciary to force its will on the other branches, coupled with its vulnerability to attack by Congress,[65] dictates a strategy for the Court that places it above the "political" battle. Ultimately, considerations of compliance with the Court's judgments and of its institutional safety hinge on moral respect for it as an institution. The "peculiar" quality of the judiciary that simultaneously links it to the doing of justice, extracts it from the morass of explicit politics, and offers the prospect of furnishing lasting moral respect has been identified by Herbert Wechsler:

> The courts have both the title and the duty when a case is properly before them to review the actions of the other branches in light of constitutional provisions, even though the action involves value choices, as invariably action does. In doing so, however, they are bound to function otherwise than as a naked power organ; they participate as courts of law. This calls for facing how determinations of this kind can be asserted to have any legal quality. The answer, I suggest, inheres primarily in that they are—or are obliged to be —entirely principled. A principled decision, in the sense I have in mind, is one that rests on reasons with respect to all the issues in the case, reasons that in their generality and

however, where strength is defined as the capacity of one branch of government to force its will on another. If one adopts a larger view —that power also inheres in the manipulation of symbols that legitimate exercises of power—the Court, operating as it does in an American culture that is highly legalistic, is far from being weak. See Arnold, The Symbols of Government (1935); Edelman, The Symbolic Uses of Politics (1964).

Also see the discussion in Chapter 5, *infra*, at pp. 280–285.

64. See especially the discussion by Shapiro, Law and Politics in the Supreme Court 24–32 (1964), particularly as it focuses on Miller and Howell, *The Myth of Neutrality in Constitutional Adjudication*, 27 U. Chi.L.Rev. 661 (1960).

65. See note 2, *supra*.

their neutrality transcend any immediate result that is involved.[66]

There is, of course, substantial disagreement as to the content and scope of such principles, disagreement especially over the degree to which the notion of a "rule of law" presents an attainable goal,[67] yet what is striking is the agreement about the core of truth in Martin Shapiro's observation that what is essentially distinctive about adjudication is its method of generalization in the resolution of controversies—that judges generalize to a solution when problems are presented to them.[68]

The next three chapters of this book explore and critically analyze three different modes of constitutional interpretation. Each philosophy of constitutional adjudication confronts the question which should have been asked in *Marbury* v. *Madison* and then develops an accompanying framework of constitutional interpretation. Each of these modes of constitutional interpretation reflects a judicial role which stands at the intersection of two important dimensions: the relation of the judge to written law, and the relation of the Court to other branches of government.

The dimension underlying judicial role that reflects the judge's attitude toward constraints imposed by written law has been collapsed to form two polar, "pure" types. The "rule-ori-

---

66. *Toward Neutral Principles of Constitutional Law*, 73 Harv.L.Rev. 1, 19 (1959), reprinted in Principles, Politics, and Fundamental Law 27 (1961). Adds Professor Wechsler, "No legislature or executive is obligated by the nature of its function to support its choice of values by the type of reasoned explanation that I have suggested is intrinsic to judicial action—however much we may admire such a reasoned exposition when we find it in those other realms." *Ibid.*, at 15–16, and 22, respectively.

67. *Cf.* Hart, *Foreword: The Time Chart of the Justices*, 73 Harv.L. Rev. 84 (1959), and Arnold, *Professor Hart's Theology*, 73 Harv.L. Rev. 1298 (1960).

68. Shapiro, The Supreme Court and Administrative Agencies, Ch. 2 (1968); *cf.* the slashing attack on such legalistic problem-solving in Menninger, The Crime of Punishment, Chs. 1, 2, 4 (1966).

ented" perspective embodies the following views: that legal rules are the principal if not the sole determinant in adjudication; that the resolution of controversies is discoverable and deducible from a given body of legal rules; that the ideal legal system is one accentuates the job of the judge as law-applier and minimizes the opportunities for the discretionary exercise of power; and that the successful resolution of a case furnishes a rule for the disposition of all future like cases. Conversely, the "policy-making" orientation stresses a quite different aggregation of beliefs: that a judge's values are the principal determinant in adjudication, modified to an uncertain degree by existing but vague and incomplete legal rules and precedents; that judicial opinions do not explain how a judge reaches his decisions, but present only reconstructed logic by which he justifies a decision reached in a much less orderly and more value-laden manner; that law is a tentative statement of the accumulated solutions to past legal problems; and that solutions to controversies reflect a mix of trends apparent in the resolution of past cases and a commonsense appreciation of the consequences that will follow from the selection of a particular solution in the instant case.[69]

---

69. Though there is less than complete agreement in the literature on judicial role as to exactly what labels to give these role types, there is no disagreement whatever that one of the dimensions of judicial role in an appellate context is that delineating the amount of discretion possessed by the decision-maker *vis-à-vis* written law. See Becker, Political Behavioralism and Modern Jurisprudence (1964); Becker, *A Survey of Hawaiian Judges: The Effect on Decisions of Judicial Role Variations*, 60 Am.Pol.Sci.Rev. 677 (1966); Flango and Schubert, *Two Surveys of Simulated Judicial Decision-Making: Hawaii and the Philippines*, in Schubert and Danelski, eds., Comparative Judicial Behavior 197–220 (1969); Glick, Supreme Courts in State Politics (1971); Glick and Vines, State Court Systems (1973); Ungs and Baas, *Judicial Role Perceptions: A Q-Technique Study of Ohio Judges*, 6 L.&Soc.Rev. 343 (1972); Vines, *The Judicial Role in the American States: An Exploration*, in Grossman and Tanenhaus, eds., Frontiers of Judicial Research 461–485 (1969). For a comparative discussion of these and other studies, see Flango, Wenner, and Wenner, *The Concept of Judicial Role: A Methodological Note*, 19 Am.J. Pol.Sci. 277 (1975).

The second independent dimension of judicial role is the judge's perception of the ideal relationship between the judiciary and the other branches of government, or, in the parlance of constitutional law, judicial activism and judicial self-restraint. This conception is not far different from Glendon Schubert's contention that "the Court is activist whenever its policies are in conflict with those of other major decision-makers." [70] Judicial activism is the willingness of judges to use their power to either expand present policy or to create new policy. Self-restraint, on the other hand, is a position which counsels the limited and infrequent use of judicial power. Clearly, one would expect these two schools of thought to differ significantly with respect to: the scope of the questions to be decided, the decision of a case on the merits versus decision on narrower, procedural grounds, the amount of deference to be accorded the legislature, the willingness of judges to formulate new policies before the "political" branches have had a chance to act, and finally, the degree of deference to be accorded a primary fact-finder (*e. g.*, a jury or administrative agency).[71]

Figure 1 depicts the correspondence of the three modes of constitutional interpretation—absolutism, the balancing of interests, and the preferred freedoms approach—in terms of these two dimensions of judicial role. The three subsequent chapters will argue for the goodness of fit. It bears emphasizing that these modes of constitutional interpretation are independent of any particular political philosophy, though at times they may be used to advance certain sets of political values. Absolutism, for example, should not necessarily be regarded either as conservative in itself or by comparison with the balancing of interests,

In his volume, Becker discusses at some length the commonality of this dimension of judicial role with the delegate-trustee categorization long-noted in the literature on legislative roles. Political Behavioralism and Modern Jurisprudence 71–77.

70. Judicial Policy Making 213 (Rev. ed. 1974).

71. Flango and Ducat, *Toward an Integration of Public Law and Judicial Behavior*, 39 J.Politics 41, 53 (1977).

though Chapter 5 will conclude that, on the whole, resolution of political problems by way of the courts is an option with usually conservative consequences.

FIGURE 1. MODES OF CONSTITUTIONAL INTERPRETATION: THE INTERSECTION OF JUDGE'S ATTITUDE TOWARD WRITTEN LAW AND THE SCOPE OF JUDICIAL INVOLVEMENT

| | | Relation between the Court and other branches of government | |
		Activism	Restraint
Relation between the judge and written law	Rule-Oriented	Absolutism	
	Problem-Solving	Preferred Freedoms	Balancing of Interests

In sum, what has been suggested is that any difference which inheres in the judiciary exists because of the justification which judges are expected to offer for the decisions they make. Roles structure political values. No political actor is valueless. All political actors are asked to resolve problems, the pressing of divergent claims upon them by contending interests in the political system. Like other government officials, judges must solve problems. In doing so, there is considerable latitude for discretion because there is no one and only true and correct solution for every problem. In the allocation of values among competing interests of society, reasonable men and women can and do disagree. The vast majority of people who go on to become judges spend years before that intimately involved with the political process and its pressures; [72] they do not leave their values and experiences behind them merely by donning a black robe. They must respond to problems, too; and, if de Tocqueville's classic observation can be regarded as correct—that "[t]here is hardly a political question in the United States which does not sooner or later turn into a judicial one" [73]—judges will be asked to respond to the same problems as legislators, executives, and administrators. In doing so, however, they will generally be expected to offer written justification. Their discretion will be constrained by a need for consistency and will be tempered by an expectation of fairness and even-handedness. In short, the reaction of judges to problems over the long-run cannot present a reflection of prejudice, expediency, party allegiance, constituency loyalty, or personal advancement.

Above all, it has been suggested that the solutions which individual judges bring to problems in constitutional law will display a pattern of resolution—a pattern colored strongly by their answer to the critical question which eluded the Court in *Marbury* v. *Madison*. Though they face constitutional questions that are diverse, individual judges respond to those problems through common frameworks—modes of constitutional interpretation— which derive from the function of the judiciary itself.

72. See Chase, Federal Judges: The Appointing Process (1972); Danelski, A Supreme Court Justice Is Appointed (1964); Eulau and Sprague, Lawyers in Politics (1964); Grossman, Lawyers and Judges: The ABA and the Politics of Judicial Selection (1965); Watson and Downing, The Politics of the Bench and the Bar (1969).

73. Democracy in America 270 (Mayer ed. 1969).

Chapter 2

Absolutism

The mode of constitutional interpretation closest in form and style to the argument offered by Chief Justice Marshall in *Marbury* v. *Madison* I shall designate as "absolutism." It seems logical to begin with a consideration of this legal framework not only because we have just concluded a discussion of *Marbury* but also because, historically speaking, absolutism [1] preceded rival modes of interpretation. Indeed, as we proceed through the three principal interpretive frameworks, it will become readily apparent that any given school of thought reacts in the first instance most strongly to the perceived flaws of that legal philosophy which directly preceded it.[2]

It might also be useful at this point to sketch out the general format of our survey and to offer a few caveats. This chapter, like the two which follow, will explore a principal mode of constitutional interpretation in turn by: positing a justification for the practice of judicial review or lack thereof; outlining the

1. Known in jurisprudence as "analytical positivism." For commentaries on legal theory which discuss it, see Chapter 1, note 60. I have adopted the term "absolutism" because it seems less ponderous, because it readily conveys the gist of the approach, and because of its common use already in the study of constitutional law due to the First Amendment views of Justice Black.

2. Thus the balancing of interests approach, discussed in Chapter 3, is largely the product of dissatisfaction with absolutism; and the preferred freedoms mode, covered

in Chapter 4, grew out of the perceived short-comings of interest balancing. Analytical positivism was itself prompted by discontent with the prevailing natural law coloration of law at the beginning of the nineteenth century in Britain. It was particularly associated with reform of the criminal law, and not entirely coincidentally did analytical positivism adopt the criminal law as its model for all law. See Bentham, The Limits of Jurisprudence Defined (1782); Austin, Lectures on Jurisprudence (1832), and The Province of Jurisprudence Determined (1832).

consequent structure of a framework for interpreting the Constitution; illustrating the operation of the interpretive framework with several judicial opinions; and assessing critically several problems which arise when reliance is placed on that mode of interpretation.

Given the size and survey nature of this volume, the sketch of each mode of interpretation is necessarily a rough approximation. We cannot hope to do justice here (though many of the footnotes try) to the infinite shadings of thought which have been collected together under one common rubric, except, of course, to acknowledge that many variations on a theme are possible and that the criticisms supplied will prove more or less telling on each of the subtle hues as the circumstances warrant. Secondly, as indicated in the preface, illustrations are drawn from among those commonly appearing in constitutional law casebooks. The examples chosen surely do not exhaust the realm of the possible. Hopefully, they are among the best of those which might have been chosen. At any rate, the pool of examples provided is a sample only and not the entire universe of possible illustrations. Moreover, attention to the opinions selected is restricted to the manner in which they capture the form and style of particular schools of legal thought. This is neither the time nor the place for the complete parsing of cases whatever their importance in other respects. Finally, it would fly in the face of all we know about the complexity of human beings to suppose that one legal worldview could account for the entire behavior of a whole judge, let alone that of entire courts. Our latitude in characterizing the outlook of specific Justices must, therefore, be restricted to the context of particular opinions illustrative of a given mode of interpretation. Even Justice Hugo Black, for example, renown for his literal reading of the First Amendment, took a much more discretionary view of other parts of the Constitution.[3]

---

3. The classic example is Black's acknowledgement of the latitude in judicial discretion permitted by the Fourth Amendment's ban on only "unreasonable" searches and seizures. Coolidge v. New Hampshire,

Bearing these thoughts in mind, I want to turn presently to a discussion of absolutism.

Law as a System of Rules

Long venerated as perhaps *the* shining ideal in Anglo-American jurisprudence, the concept of the Rule of Law lies at the heart of the absolutist tradition. It is customarily contrasted with the Rule of Men, generally with pejorative effect to the latter: While the Rule of Law mandates the decision of controversies objectively according to general, impartial, and fixed rules which do not acknowledge the individual identity of or personal consequences for particular litigants before a court, the Rule of Men implies that judgments in individual cases are otherwise politically motivated and tend to be made on the basis of "whose ox is being gored." The absolutist school subscribes not merely to the rhetoric of the Rule of Law as an ideal for which judges should strive; it is distinguished by its deep commitment to the distinctive view that the ideal *can* be made actual because law is a science.

Implicit in the Rule of Law concept is the vision of society as held together by a system of rules which set out in definitive terms the rights and obligations of its component members. The organization and governance of social relations by an authoritative system of rules, implemented by the coercive power of the state, allowed the peace and orderliness of civil society to replace the anarchy and chaos of self-help in the state of

403 U.S. 443, 493, 91 S.Ct. 2022, 2051 (1971) (concurring and dissenting opinion); Chimel v. California, 395 U.S. 752, 770, 89 S.Ct. 2034, 2044 (1969) (dissenting opinion of White, J., in which Black joined). Compare his attitude toward the standard of "reasonableness" in this context with his attitude toward the use of that standard generally in constitutional interpretation. Black, A Constitutional Faith 25–26 (1969); Reich, *Mr. Justice Black and the Living Constitution*, 76 Harv.L.Rev. 673, 686, 692 (1963); Ball, The Vision and the Dream of Justice Hugo L. Black 30–31, 115ff. (1975).

nature.[4] With the rise of the importance of the individual, it was possible for much of the focus of law to shift, but not entirely by any means, from an almost single-minded preoccupation with "insur[ing] domestic tranquility" to such other goals as "establish[ing] justice," "promot[ing] the general welfare," and "secur[ing] the blessings of liberty," and was generally accompanied by a movement to restructure rights and obligations on the basis of contract instead of status.[5]

Reflecting perhaps a substantial intellectual debt in form and style to sciences such as geometry, enthusiasm erupted during the nineteenth century for the model of the legal system as a highly-integrated, internally-consistent body of norms. The ordering of rules within this formal abstract system was the province of logic: inferior norms were deducible from superior ones and, of course, all were deducible from the Constitution. The argument offered in *Marbury* for judicial review fits this scheme rather well because once one concedes that courts are charged with applying the law in concrete cases, there is a certain logic to the inevitability of judicial determination as to which norm is valid when two laws conflict.

It bears emphasizing that a system of rules so ordered constitutes a totally closed system; that is, a system the norms of which are immune to external evaluation. Rules can only be valid or invalid—consistent or inconsistent with higher legal norms—not good or bad. Indeed, as between law and morals, there is at bottom an assertion that propositions of moral rightness are unprovable; they can be persuasive or unpersuasive,

---

4. The general tenets of the Rule of Law concept set out in this section have been drawn from numerous sources, among the best of which are: Wolin, *Hobbes: Political Society as a System of Rules*, in Politics and Vision, Ch. 8 (1960); Hayek, *Planning and the Rule of Law*, in The Road to Serfdom, Ch. 6 (1944); Kelsen, General Theory of Law and State (1945); Kelsen, The Pure Theory of Law (1967); Kelsen, What Is Justice? (1971); Hohfeld, Fundamental Legal Conceptions (1919); Wasserstrom, The Judicial Decision, Chs. 2–4 (1961) [hereafter referred to as Wasserstrom]. See also Chapter 1, note 60.

5. Maine, Ancient Law (1861).

but the moral rightness of anything cannot be logically proved. This is so, goes the argument, because questions of what should be are matters of emotion not reason. Questions of rightness, fairness, and morality are undeterminable in any authoritative way and, hence, ultimately reflect arbitrary judgments. To throw a system of legal rules open to such objections, where no fixed demonstrable standards exist, invites every member of society to judge for himself which laws are good and, therefore, which he will obey. Moreover, since moral objections to legal rules, like political criticisms of legal norms, may be heavily infected with self-interest, evaluation of a system of legal rules on the basis of any external criteria, whether moral or political, invites anarchy and returns us to a state of nature.

This is not to say, however, that the Rule of Law concept, and particularly current versions of it such as absolutism, are unconcerned with justice. Quite the contrary. Though it is true, strictly speaking, that questions of justice are irrelevant to the application of particular legal rules in concrete cases, clearly there is a systemic concern for justice. The whole notion of a system of interlocking rules ordered and applied by deductive logic is predicated on a definite conception of justice: justice defined as formal equality.[6] This is apparent, first of all, in the emphasis given objectivity as a cardinal virtue. Objectivity, as it pertains to the meaning of legal norms, does not signify that the rules are value-free. Indeed, how could they be? Rules, which attach sanctions to and thus penalize certain forms of conduct but encourage others, inescapably reflect a choice among competing values. Instead, objectivity refers to the fact that once a rule is set down or its meaning spelled out, the rule will have the same meaning for everyone. Regardless of its content, then, the rule will have an objective meaning as between

---

6. Honoré, *Social Justice*, in Summers, ed., Essays in Legal Philosophy 61–94 (1968); Shklar, Legalism (1964) [hereafter referred to as Shklar]; Hart, The Concept of Law, Ch. 8 (1961) [hereafter referred to as Hart]; Wasserstrom, 69–72. See also Del Vecchio, Justice (Campbell, ed. 1952).

individuals. Our concern for following precedent in judicial applications of a valid rule similarly reflects a commitment to justice defined as formal equality. Where A and B are individuals who have committed similar acts, we expect that, unless the pattern of facts in the second case is different such that B falls under another rule, the outcome in the two instances should be the same; that is, B should be treated like A. This is an expectation of treatment of cases by a standard of formal equality: like cases should be treated alike. Ultimately, then, the Rule of Law concept carries a commitment to a certain brand of justice, specifically, procedural or formal equality. Irrespective of the content of the legal norms, the touchstone of their proper application is, at minimum, respect for a sort of equal protection of the laws writ large.

Important as all of this is to an appreciation of the heritage from which absolutism took its distinctive posture as a framework for constitutional interpretation, still we have not yet considered how legal norms yield results in particular cases. Indeed, of all the aspects of the Rule of Law tradition, its characterization of the process of fitting the rules to concrete cases, or, more accurately, the fitting of cases to concrete rules, has come in for the harshest criticism from modern jurists and political scientists.[7]

The keystone in the representation of judicial decision-making, offered by the Rule of Law tradition, is the firm belief that judges merely apply law, they do not make it. In constitutional adjudication, this view was succinctly set forth by Justice Roberts in an oft-quoted excerpt from his opinion for the Court in *United States* v. *Butler*:

> There should be no misunderstanding as to the function of this court in such a case. It is sometimes said that the court assumes a power to overrule or control the action of the people's representatives. This is a misconception. The Constitution is the supreme law of the land ordained and established by the people. All legislation must conform to the

---

7.   Chapter 1, notes 54 and 55.

principles it lays down. When an act of Congress is appropriately challenged in the courts as not conforming to the constitutional mandate, the judicial branch of the government has only one duty; to lay the article of the Constitution which is invoked beside the statute which is challenged and to decide whether the latter squares with the former. All the court does, or can do, is to announce its considered judgment upon the question. The only power it has, if such it may be called, is the power of judgment. This court neither approves nor condemns any legislative policy. Its delicate and difficult office is to ascertain and declare whether the legislation is in accordance with, or in contravention of, the provisions of the Constitution; and, having done that, its duty ends.[8]

This conception of what it is that judges do has been variously dubbed "mechanical jurisprudence," "slot-machine jurisprudence," and "the phonograph theory"[9] of the decisional process. Needless to say, this view was hardly peculiar to Justice Roberts and has recurrently surfaced in American constitutional law.

An understanding of the decisional process, so the argument goes, begins and ends with the study of the written opinions of the judges. This is so because judicial opinions were thought to both justify and explain the decisional process. Consistent with our earlier observations about the structuring of legal norms, the style of the opinion was that of deductive logic and the format of the explanation/justification offered was a syllogism. In its simplest form, this cast a rule of law as the major premise, a pertinent finding of fact as the minor premise, and the conclusion of law as the conclusion offered by the syllogism. Indeed, the critical argument presented in answer to the third question put by Chief Justice Marshall in *Marbury* (see p. 21) is in just this form. Though this style of argument was touted as the paradigm for all judicial decisions, invariably in constitutional law cases, the rule of law constituting the

---

8. 297 U.S. 1, 62–63, 56 S.Ct. 312, 318 (1936).

9. That theory of the judge's function "according to which the judge merely repeats the words that the law has spoken into him * * *." Cohen, Law and the Social Order 113 (1933).

major premise was a command embodied in a constitutional provision and the minor premise was a finding of fact and law mixed since it was an observation about a particular piece of legislation. An opinion drawn along these lines not only justified the conclusion reached by the court in a given case, but for many years was believed to explain the process of decision simply because rules were perceived to be the only operative force in reaching a legal judgment.

The paradigm drawn from deductive logic bolstered proponents of the Rule of Law concept in their claim that judges, therefore, did not create law, but only discovered and applied it. It implied that if only one thought long enough and hard enough, an answer would appear. More than that. If only one knew enough black letter law (for constitutional cases, read: if only one read the Constitution and other relevant historical documents *carefully*, and got from them their *true* meaning), if only one were steeped long enough in legal, that is deductive, method, *the correct* answer would emerge. And it was the belief in the certain, successful replication of this exercise that infused the enterprise with the feeling that law was a science rather like geometry: Judicial opinions were proofs that had been worked in which a logical manipulation of factual "givens" and legal axioms had been made to yield up the inexorable legal judgment, Q.E.D.

It is this belief that law is "there" [10] and that the proper function of judges is simply to *apply* it that puts the ring of truth in Professor Fuller's appellation of Rule of Law advocates as believers in "first rules, then courts." [11] Indeed, it is the insistence on the existence of law prior to adjudication that makes fairness possible in a second sense, the sense of forewarning. If the legal judgment is not to be *ex post facto,* and thus entirely arbitrary, the principles of law must precede their application. Otherwise, the losing party in a suit is not being punished for his failure to

---

10. Shklar, 33.

11. Fuller, *Adjudication and the Rule of Law,* 54 Proc.Am.Soc.Int.L. 1, 6 (1960).

perform some existing legal duty but rather on account of judicial innovation and creativity. Conversely, only when it is possible for us to know what the law is can the aphorism which summarizes our traditional expectation of citizen responsibility —"Ignorance of the law excuses no one"—have any real meaning.

At the core of the Rule of Law concept lies a genuine suspicion about the exercise of governmental power. Historically, in terms of constitutional interpretation, this meant that Rule of Law advocates usually have been strict constructionists. To be sure this was not always the case. One could point to John Marshall himself who often assumed the pose of the Rule of Law advocate replete with the rhetoric of mechanical jurisprudence, and Marshall was surely no strict constructionist; but the link between the Rule of Law outlook and the philosophy of negative government—that government is best which governs least—held true generally. Even if one concedes that judges may not embrace strict construction in every facet of constitutional adjudication, it is significant that, for each of the celebrated illustrations of an absolutist approach discussed later in this chapter, adoption of that perspective has entailed acceptance in some area of constitutional law of a strict construction-negative government outlook. This is a logical association. Closely confining the power of government officials to channels delineated by fixed and well-defined rules of law likely will have the effect of limiting their range of policy-making and thus curbing the activities of government. Both the method of mechanical jurisprudence and the philosophy of limited government are bolstered when emphasis is placed on the fact that it is a *written* Constitution that is being expounded. Furthermore, the basic denial that judges exercise discretion in rendering legal judgments is itself evidence of the suspicion of judges as *political* decision-makers. Judges, presumably held in check by an elaborate system of rules, become instead instruments of revealed truth rather than conscious policy-makers. And, in fact, the claim to judicial review is strongly attached to this very denial of judicial discretion:

Judgments about the constitutionality of acts by the political branches of the government are the product not of political choice but nonpolitical, legal expertise, training in the science of law not in the art of politics. *Marbury* is an implicit statement of just such a position: Judicial review follows from the fact of inexorable choice thrust upon the Justices that must proceed if the rules comprising the legal system are to be consistently applied.

A Sketch of the Absolutist Framework

Twenty years ago, when Professor Wechsler sounded the call for a return to "neutral principles" in constitutional adjudication, it was widely assumed that this was also a call for a return to absolutist jurisprudence. Yet, as the following passage (which does little else than once again give us the gist of the excerpt quoted earlier [pp. 36–37]) shows, Wechsler exhorted more than he explained:

> [W]hether you are tolerant, perhaps more tolerant than I, of the *ad hoc* in politics, with principle reduced to a manipulative tool, are you not also ready to agree that something else is called for from the courts? I put it to you that the main constituent of the judicial process is precisely that it must be genuinely principled, resting with respect to every step that is involved in reaching judgment on analysis and reasons quite transcending the immediate result that is achieved. To be sure, the courts decide, or should decide, only the case they have before them. But must they not decide on grounds of adequate neutrality and generality, tested not only by the instant application but by others that the principles imply? Is it not the very essence of judicial method to insist upon attending to such other cases, preferably those involving an opposing interest, in evaluating any principle avowed? [12]

Nor did his subsequent writings systematically develop a scheme of such principles.[13] The call for a return to "general" or "neu-

---

12. *Toward Neutral Principles of Constitutional Law*, 73 Harv.L.Rev. 1, 15 (1959), reprinted in Principles, Politics, and Fundamental Law 21 (1961).

13. *The Nature of Legal Reasoning*, in Hook, ed., Law and Philosophy 290–300 (1964); *Courts and the Constitution*, 65 Colum.L.Rev. 1001 (1965). He has said, "No one can

tral" principles of constitutional law remained just that. Piling inference upon inference, friend [14] and foe [15] alike jousted with, what for all anyone knew, were straw men. And the "debate" took on the quality of two trains passing in the night. It is possible, as some of the discussion in Chapter 3 will show, that Wechsler was not advocating absolutism at all, but was instead seeking to strengthen its antithesis, the balancing of interests.

state a formula that will determine when such reasons are sufficient but surely there are things that can be said." *ibid.*, 1012, following which he indicated some of the relevant considerations to be taken into account. See the discussion in Chapter 3 at pp. 128–129. Perhaps the central problem of ambiguity is best described in Pollak, *Constitutional Adjudication: Relative or Absolute Neutrality*, 11 J.Pub.L. 46 (1962).

14. For example, see Hart, *Foreword: The Time Chart of the Justices*, 73 Harv.L.Rev. 84 (1959); Pollak, *Racial Discrimination and Judicial Integrity: A Reply to Professor Wechsler*, 108 U.Pa.L.Rev. 1 (1959); Black, *The Lawfulness of the Segregation Decisions*, 69 Yale L.J. 421 (1960); Griswold, *Of Time and Attitudes: Professor Hart and Judge Arnold*, 74 Harv.L.Rev. 81 (1960); Henkin, *Some Reflections on Current Constitutional Controversy*, 109 U.Pa.L.Rev. 637 (1961); Bickel, The Least Dangerous Branch (1962); Gunther, *The Subtle Vices of the "Passive Virtues" —A Comment on Principle and Expediency in Judicial Review*, 64 Colum.L.Rev. 1 (1964); Henkin, *"Neutral Principles" and Future Cases*, in Hook, ed., Law and Philosophy 301–309 (1964); Golding,

Principled Decision-Making and the Supreme Court, in Summers, ed., Essays in Legal Philosophy 208–236 (1968); Bickel, The Supreme Court and the Idea of Progress (1970); Bork, *Neutral Principles and Some First Amendment Problems*, 47 Ind.L.J. 1 (1971).

15. For example, see Miller and Howell, *The Myth of Neutrality in Constitutional Adjudication*, 27 U.Chi.L.Rev. 661 (1960); Arnold, *Professor Hart's Theology*, 73 Harv.L.Rev. 1298 (1960); Wright, *The Supreme Court Cannot Be Neutral*, 40 Tex.L.Rev. 599 (1961); Rostow, *American Legal Realism and the Sense of the Profession*, 34 Rocky Mt.L.Rev. 123 (1962); Shapiro, *The Supreme Court and Constitutional Adjudication: Of Politics and Neutral Principles*, 31 Geo.Wash.L.Rev. 587 (1963) [hereafter referred to as Shapiro, *Neutral Principles*]; Shapiro, The Supreme Court in Law and Politics 17–32 (1964); Deutsch, *Neutrality, Legitimacy, and the Supreme Court: Some Intersections Between Law and Political Science*, 20 Stan.L.Rev. 169 (1968) [hereafter referred to as Deutsch]; Wright, *Professor Bickel, the Scholarly Tradition, and the Supreme Court*, 84 Harv.L.Rev. 769 (1971).

Putting aside the vagaries of the "neutral principles" debate, then, the task ahead will be to sketch out in some detail the absolutist framework of constitutional interpretation; for only against such a background can vague phrases such as "adequate generality" have any meaning.

It might be helpful to begin with an explanation of the placement of absolutism on the chart designated as Figure 1 (p. 40). As the discussion in Chapter 1 pointed out, the modes of constitutional interpretation are composed of two principal dimensions: an attitude about the relation of the judge to written law, and an attitude about the Court's relation to coordinate branches of government. A judge with an absolutist outlook is one who stresses the importance of formulating and applying rules in the resolution of legal controversies without any particular regard for whether those resolutions tend to run with or against the grain of policy pursued by other branches of government.

Absolutism reflects a commitment to solving problems by generalizing toward a solution, it is true, but with distinct overtones of finality; that is, reaching a conclusion in the instant case by formulating or applying a broad rule of law that can effectively dictate the resolution of all future like cases. The values that underlie such a commitment were discussed when we took up the Rule of Law concept. By constructing well-delineated pigeonholes of legal categories, each covered by its own rule, the process, after a time, can be seen as strictly controlled by *stare decisis* (adherence to precedent) such that continued replication of the process becomes automatic. The deductive possibilities of such a procedure, of course, depend upon the fact that the categories in law are mutually exclusive; that is, that they are separated by precepts that articulate how the fact situations in one category are different in kind from those in another. Further, the rules which divide and govern categories in law tend to remain unqualified since the introduction of qualifications multiplies the opportunity for the exercise of discretion.

The allure of certainty and finality that comes with the operation of such interlocking systems of rules was so considerable that, despite the ferocity with which such an approach was denounced in some quarters,[16] even such redoubtable advocates of interest balancing as Roscoe Pound conceded its validity in certain areas of law. Dean Pound wrote:

> Philosophically the apportionment of the field between rule and discretion which is suggested by the use of rules and of standards respectively in modern law has its basis in the respective fields of intelligence and intuition. Bergson tells us that the former is more adapted to the inorganic, the latter more to life. Likewise rules, where we proceed mechanically, are more adapted to property and to business transactions; and standards, where we proceed upon intuitions, are more adapted to human conduct and to the conduct of enterprises. * * * [17]

Others imagined a concept embodied in legal rules as a sphere-like figure which had a core meaning that paled as one moved toward the perimeter, or which had a penumbra comprised of a range of shaded meanings.[18] Easy cases were those where the core meaning was evident and so automatically evoked application of the rule; hard cases lay on the periphery of the concept, at a point where perhaps one concept overlapped another, such that resolution of the problem could only be achieved through reasoning by analogy. Likewise, a distinction was often drawn between the open texture of the law at some point, and matters, on the other hand, which were well-settled, where the legal fabric was tightly woven.[19] Older versions of the Law School Aptitude Test, for example, tended to give credence to the use of the

16. See Chapter 1, note 54.

17. Pound, An Introduction to the Philosophy of Law 70 (1922). For a devastating critique of this distinction as largely an artifact of how the facts in a given case are stated, see Wasserstrom, 98–105. But see also Horwitz, *The Rise of Legal Formalism*, 19 Am.J. Legal Hist. 251 (1975).

18. Hart, Ch. 7. See also Hart, *Positivism and the Separation of Law and Morals*, 71 Harv.L.Rev. 593 (1958); *cf.* Fuller, *Positivism and Fidelity to Law—A Reply to Professor Hart*, 71 Harv.L.Rev. 630 (1958).

19. Llewellyn, The Common Law Tradition (1960). See also Morris, How Lawyers Think (1937); Morris, The Justification of the Law, Ch. 4 (1971).

deductive approach by presenting candidates with problems in one section of the exam in which they were asked to apply a rule or definition of law to a given factual situation and select the *correct* conclusion from among a set of five alternatives identified as a, b, c, d, or e.

The absolutist approach is one that focuses on the form and structure of legal rules rather than their content. Adherence to the form of the principled decision simultaneously meets the expectation of fairness and constrains the power of the judge. It also provides a certain amount of institutional, that is to say, political, support.[20] Individuals whose interest has suffered an adverse judgment are more likely to tolerate the decision, comply with it, and respect the judges who made it, if the decision is justified in the form of a principle which states a rule broad enough so that if today's losers are someday put in the position of the other party they can be expected to be treated accordingly.

20. The generation of popular support for the Court because of the form in which its decisions are justified has been characterized as perhaps the trump card of those who argue for the necessity of "principled" decisions as against those who have called upon the Court to take into account the political effects of its decisions or to candidly acknowledge the value choices behind them. Shapiro, *Neutral Principles*, 598–601; Shapiro, Law and Politics in the Supreme Court 24–29; Deutsch, 196–197, 216–217, 237–238, 240. But, as the literature on public opinion and the Court suggests, this link could hardly be an immediate one. Support for the Court, it appears, is compounded generally of public ignorance of what it does and acceptance of something like the Rule of Law concept as a given. Kessell, *Public Perceptions of the Supreme Court*, 10 Mw.J.Pol.Sci. 171 (1966); Dolbeare, *The Public Views the Supreme Court*, in Jacob, ed., Law, Politics, and the Federal Courts 194–212 (1967); Murphy and Tanenhaus, *Public Opinion and the United States Supreme Court: A Preliminary Mapping of Some Prerequisites for Court Legitimation of Regime Changes*, in Grossman and Tanenhaus, eds., Frontiers of Judicial Research 273–303 (1969); Murphy, Tanenhaus, and Kastner, *Public Evaluations of Constitutional Courts: Alternative Explanations*, Sage Professional Paper in Comparative Politics, 4, 01–045 (1973); Casey, *The Supreme Court and Myth: An Empirical Investigation*, 8 L. & Soc.Rev. 385 (1974).

It still remains for us to point up the minimum demands that such a systematic mode of interpretation imposes. Because absolutism is an approach that talks in terms of the form an acceptable opinion must take, it is essential that we highlight the structural requirements of such a framework. Though it may become apparent from the illustrations which follow in the next section that there are more details which could be fleshed out, still, it seems to me, the absolutist approach makes essentially three principal structural assumptions:

1. There are a finite number of constitutional precepts.

2. These precepts are capable of being stated in rather precise terms.

3. No two constitutional precepts must ever collide.[21]

The first proposition is important because, without it, the absolutist faces the twin problems of arbitrariness and lack of warning; if the pot of legal principles continues to be enlarged without end, the hazards of innovation cannot be held in check. The second proposition is critical to assuring consistency in the application of rules and to affording the citizen reasonable understanding of his rights and obligations; if constitutional rules are not stated exactly, contradictory applications will follow. And the third proposition is imperative because if two constitutional precepts are allowed to collide, the judge could not deductively apply either principle; he would be forced to balance the contending interests and therefore make a policy decision. Needless to say, more will be said of this later.

21. The third of these structural requisites is discussed in Mueller and Schwartz, *The Principle of* *Neutral Principles*, 7 U.C.L.A. L. Rev. 571, 586 (1960); Deutsch, 232.

Illustrations

Several examples, drawn from quite different areas of constitutional adjudication, illustrate the essentials of the absolutist approach to constitutional interpretation:

1. *Dual Federalism*

Few chapters in American constitutional history better illustrate the absolutist approach to constitutional interpretation than the era between 1895 and 1936 when a majority of Justices on the Supreme Court succeeded in cutting back the scope of Congress' regulatory power under the interstate commerce and taxing and spending clauses by developing and applying the doctrine of dual federalism. The doctrine rested upon the assertions that, as a matter of law, the national government and the states were dual sovereigns and that, as a matter of practical politics, the accretion of power in the political system would be checked most effectively if intergovernmental relations sustained a constant tension; hence the view of national and state powers as mutually exclusive, conflicting, and antagonistic.

The status of dual federalism as constitutional theory was nurtured by accepting the proposition that the Constitution was a compact among the states which ceded certain specified powers to the national government and retained all others. An important corollary in the implementation of this constitutional theory was the belief that regulatory functions could be neatly parcelled out between the two levels of government. Applying the doctrine of dual federalism, the Court looked to two constitutional instruments: First and foremost was a literal interpretation given the enumerated powers of the national government and an extraordinarily limited reliance upon any amplification of these powers added by the necessary and proper clause. In sum, the dual federalists came to read Article I, section 8 much as one would read a statute. Unless the national government were granted a power specifically, the assumption was against the exercise of power. Secondly, the dual federalists saw the Tenth Amendment as a viable base of support from which actions of the national government could be ruled unconstitutional. Congress, in their view, may not invade the reserved powers of the states. In their heyday, advocates of dual federalism took the position that if, in the exercise of its enumerated powers, the national government happened to touch upon the functions reserved to the states, then the action of the national government was unconstitutional.

Morton Grodzins likened this view of the federal system to a layer cake, each level of government clearly distinct from the other.[22] Given the fact that this was the Age of Industry, however, and the devastating impact which dual federalism had as a constitutional doctrine used by the Court to waylay congressional efforts at regulating business enterprise, perhaps the more appropriate vision of the federal system was James Bryce's: "The system is like a great factory wherein two sets of machinery are at work, their revolving wheels apparently intermixed, their bands crossing one another, yet each set doing its own work without touching or hampering the other." [23] Indeed, there seems a quaint correspondence here: a mechanical view of the federal system applied, as it turned out, by a mechanical judicial process.

The telltale signs of absolutism were everywhere in the Court's decisions applying the precepts of dual federalism to limit Congress' power to regulate commerce. What the Court did was to rigidly dichotomize economic functions and then parcel out jurisdiction over them to the national government and the states. As Figure 2 shows, the two immutable categories of economic activity which the Court recognized were distribution and production. "Commerce" was taken to mean distribution; production was something which preceded commerce and, therefore, was not a part of it. Included within production were "local" economic activities such as manufacturing, mining, and agriculture, while distribution was thought to encompass such things as

22. Grodzins, *The Federal System*, in American Assembly, Goals for Americans 265–282 (1960).

23. 1 Bryce, The American Commonwealth 325 (3d ed. 1896).

navigation, interstate transportation of goods, and regulation of interstate carriers. As the Court pointed out in a decision placing a manufacturing conglomerate controlling 98% of the sugar refining capacity of the country beyond the reach of the Sherman Antitrust Act, national and state powers over business regulation were mutually exclusive: "That which belongs to commerce is within the jurisdiction of the United States, but that which does not belong to commerce is within the jurisdiction of the police power of the state." [24]

FIGURE 2. DUAL FEDERALISM AND THE REGULATION OF COMMERCE: DICHOTOMIZING ECONOMIC FUNCTIONS

Commerce	Not Commerce
DISTRIBUTION	PRODUCTION
• navigation	• manufacturing
• interstate transportation of goods	• mining
• interstate carriers	• agriculture
Producing "direct" effects on interstate commerce which may be regulated by Congress	Producing "indirect" effects on interstate commerce which may not be regulated by Congress; exclusively within the jurisdiction of the states

Often the Court chose to discuss jurisdiction over economic functions in terms of the "direct" or "indirect" effects which the economic activity in question exerted on interstate commerce.

24. United States v. E. C. Knight Co., 156 U.S. 1, 12, 15 S.Ct. 249, 252 (1895).

Yet the conclusion about whether the national government might constitutionally regulate a particular business enterprise was not formed from any empirical assessment of economic effects; it was dictated by the absolute rules that surrounded the categories of production and distribution. Economic activity was not treated as a continuous process made up of many steps which imperceptibly flowed into the next such that matters of regulation became questions of degree. Rather, the two categories which the Court had created were seen as *different in kind*. Jurisdictionally speaking, said the Court in its 1935 decision invalidating the NRA: "The precise line can be drawn only as individual cases arise, but the distinction is clear in principle." [25] Exactly how principled the distinction was between "direct" and "indirect" effects became crystal clear the following year as the Court struck down the Guffey Coal Act, saying:

> The distinction between a direct and an indirect effect turns, not upon the magnitude of either the cause or the effect, but entirely upon the manner in which the effect has been brought about. If the production by one man of a single ton of coal intended for interstate sale and shipment, and actually so sold and shipped, affects interstate commerce indirectly, the effect does not become direct by multiplying the tonnage, or increasing the number of men employed, or adding to the expense or complexities of the business, or by all combined. It is quite true that rules of law are sometimes qualified by considerations of degree, as the government argues. But the matter of degree has no bearing upon the question here, since that question is not—What is the extent of the local activity or condition, or the extent of the effect produced upon interstate commerce? but—What is the relation between the activity or condition and the effect? [26]

In sum, then, the distinction between "direct" and "indirect" effects precisely overlay the difference in kind that distinguished distribution from production. The dichotomies were one and the same. Any exercise of discretion in which the Court en-

25. Schechter Poultry Corp. v. United States, 295 U.S. 495, 546, 55 S. Ct. 837, 850 (1935).

26. Carter v. Carter Coal Co., 298 U.S. 238, 307–308, 56 S.Ct. 855, 871 (1936).

gaged where constitutional adjudication of the commerce power was concerned ended really with the finding as to whether the economic activity in question was a variant of distribution or production. All else was foreclosed by the deductive operation of the existing constitutional rules once the economic activity in question had been correctly pigeonholed.[27]

27. Compare the approach of Chief Justice Hughes, speaking for the Court, in National Labor Relations Board v. Jones & Laughlin Steel Corp., 301 U.S. 1, 57 S.Ct. 615, one of the two decisions which effected the Constitutional Revolution of 1937. Holding that labor-management legislation, enacted by Congress under the commerce power, applied to Jones & Laughlin, the nation's fourth largest steel producer and a sprawling "completely integrated enterprise" which controlled mining, transportation, manufacturing, and distribution, he observed:

It is the effect upon commerce, not the source of the injury, which is the criterion. * * * Whether or not particular action does affect commerce in such a close and intimate fashion as to be subject to federal control, and hence to lie within the authority conferred upon the Board, is left by the statute to be determined as individual cases arise. We are thus to inquire whether in the instant case the constitutional boundary has been passed.

* * *

Although activities may be intrastate in character when separately considered, if they have such a close and substantial relation to interstate commerce that their control is essential or appropriate to protect that commerce from burdens and obstructions, Congress cannot be denied the power to exercise that control. * * * The question is necessarily one of degree. * * *

* * *

The close and intimate effect which brings the subject within the reach of federal power may be due to activities in relation to productive industry although the industry when separately viewed is local. * * *

* * *

It is thus apparent that the fact that the employees here concerned were engaged in production is not determinative. The question remains as to the effect upon interstate commerce of the labor practice involved. * * *

* * * [T]he fact remains that the stoppage of those operations by industrial strife would have a most serious effect upon interstate commerce. In view of respondent's far-flung activities, it is idle to say that the effect would be indirect or remote. It is obvious that it would be immediate and might be catastrophic. We are asked to shut our eyes to the plainest facts of our national life and to deal with the question of direct and indirect effects in an intellectual vacuum. * * * When

When Congress sought to regulate production through the exercise of the taxing and spending power, the Court proved equal to the task: first, by distinguishing between a tax, on the one hand, and a penalty or special purpose levy, on the other; and second, by assessing the constitutionality of the only-incidentally revenue-raising measure in light of the basic dichotomy between production and distribution. For example, when Congress attempted to resurrect child labor legislation, following its demise at the hands of the Court as an interference with state jurisdiction over manufacturing,[28] by placing a prohibitive levy on the interstate transportation of products manufactured by youngsters, the Court concluded that the child labor tax was, in fact, a penalty imposed for the violation of manufacturing regulations. The so-called tax was not a tax at all, reasoned the Court, but a penalty because: (1) "[i]t provides a heavy exaction for a departure from a detailed and specified course of conduct in business"; (2) if the employer "does not know the child is within the named age limit, he is not to pay; that is to say, it is only where he knowingly departs from the prescribed course that payment is to be executed"; and (3) "[t]he employer's factory is to be subject to inspection at any time not only by the taxing officer of the Treasury * * * but also by the Secretary of Labor and his subordinates, whose normal function is the advancement and protection of the welfare of the workers."[29] The statute's "prohibitory and regulatory effect and purpose are palpable" said the Court, and its revenue-raising purpose and effect only incidental, instead of vice versa. Stripped of its pre-

---

industries organize themselves on a national scale, making their relation to interstate commerce the dominant factor in their activities, how can it be maintained that their industrial labor relations constitute a forbidden field into which Congress may not enter when it is necessary to protect interstate commerce from the paralyzing consequences of industrial war? * * *

301 U.S. at 32, 37–38, 40–41, 57 S.Ct. at 622, 624–626.

28. Hammer v. Dagenhart, 247 U.S. 251, 38 S.Ct. 529 (1918).

29. Bailey v. Drexel Furniture Co., 259 U.S. 20, 36–37, 42 S.Ct. 449, 450 (1922).

tentions as a tax, the Court held, relying on its commerce clause precedents, the levy was a penalty imposed by Congress on manufacturing and, therefore, violated the Tenth Amendment.

A similar fate befell the First Agricultural Adjustment Act. That statute levied a tax on food processors the proceeds of which were earmarked as subsidy payments to farmers in return for their agreement to reduce crop production. In addition to the requirement that a tax have the primary purpose of raising revenue and that it regulate only incidentally, the Court began by pointing out that the fiscal prerogatives of Congress were confined by Article I, section 8 to taxing and spending for the "general welfare": "A tax, in the general understanding of the term, and as used in the Constitution, signifies an exaction for the support of the government. The word has never been thought to connote the expropriation of money from one group for the benefit of another." [30]   In the context of the AAA, the levy was not really a tax since: "The tax is to cease when rental or benefit payments cease. The rate is fixed with the purpose of bringing about crop reduction and price raising. * * * The whole revenue from the levy is appropriated in aid of crop control; none of it is made available for general governmental use." [31]   Thus the Court concluded that "the act is one regulating agricultural production; that the tax is a mere incident of such regulation * * * ." [32]   The so-called tax, being in reality a special-purpose levy, whose "stated purpose is the control of

---

30. United States v. Butler, 297 U.S. 1, 61, 56 S.Ct. 312, 317 (1936). To a student, like me, who was raised on the writings of Burns and Peltason, David Truman, and V. O. Key, Jr., Roberts' characterization has always seemed the quintessence of old-time, formalistic political science. All that remains to be done is capitalize the "g" on "government." Even giving the critics of pluralism their due, what does government do if it does not distribute or redistribute resources among contending groups? Lowi, *American Business, Public Policy, Case Studies, and Political Theory,* 17 World Politics 677 (1964).

31. 297 U.S. at 59, 56 S.Ct. at 316.

32. 297 U.S. at 61, 56 S.Ct. at 317.

agricultural productivity, a purely local activity," [33] violated the Tenth Amendment because:

> The act invades the reserved rights of the states. It is a statutory plan to regulate and control agricultural production, a matter beyond the powers delegated to the federal government. The tax, the appropriation of the funds raised, and the direction for their disbursement, are but parts of the plan. They are but means to an unconstitutional end.[34]

Whatever the approach taken by Congress, whether it was the overt regulation of production or regulation concealed in a taxing scheme, the Court's assessment of constitutionality was ultimately and inexorably determined by the application of a system of absolute rules embedded in the distinction between production and distribution.

2. Justice Black and the First Amendment

Undoubtedly, the best known modern exponent of absolutism was Justice Hugo Black. While the opinions he penned during his first decade on the Court tend to discount an early commitment to this mode of constitutional interpretation, the opinions Black wrote during the remainder of his tenure, dating from the post-war years, vividly demonstrate the grip on his thought which absolutism came to have.[35] While this approach permeates his construction of constitutional provisions generally,[36] it was especially evident in his treatment of First Amendment questions.

33. 297 U.S. at 63–64, 56 S.Ct. at 318.

34. 297 U.S. at 68, 56 S.Ct. at 320.

35. Ulmer, *The Longitudinal Behavior of Hugo Lafayette Black: Parabolic Support for Civil Liberties, 1937–1967*, paper delivered at the annual meeting of the American Political Science Ass'n, Sept. 1970.

36. In addition to the sources indicated in note 3, *supra*, see Black, *The Bill of Rights*, 35 N.Y.U.L.Rev. 865 (1960); Cahn, *Justice Black and First Amendment "Absolutes": A Public Interview*, 37 N.Y.U.L. Rev. 549 (1962) [hereafter referred to as Public Interview]; *Text of Historic TV Interview with Justice Black*, 1969 Cong. Quart. Wkly. Rep. 6.

The bonds between Justice Black's absolutism and tenets of the Rule of Law concept are quite strong.[37] Black frequently emphasized the paramount importance of a *written* Constitution in the prevention of oppression and in the protection of minorities from the tyranny of the majority.[38] Congress, while distin-

37. Yarbrough, *Mr. Justice Black and Legal Positivism*, 57 Va.L.Rev. 375 (1971). This outstanding research effort not only persuasively demonstrates that Black's opinions and other statements jibe well with the tenets of analytical positivism, but also discloses, as often only an analysis of written opinions can, the *role* which dominated Black's voting behavior during most of his years on the Court. Reliance solely upon votes cast in Supreme Court decisions can lead one to label Black a doctrinaire liberal. See Schubert, The Judicial Mind, Chs. 5–8 (1965), and The Judicial Mind Revisited, Chs. 5–7 (1974). That Black voted frequently with Justice Douglas—who was, I venture to say, a real "doctrinaire liberal"—does not mean Black was too. As important as the number of times Black did *not* vote with Douglas were his *reasons* for not doing so. One theory explaining their increasing divergence during their later years on the Court is that Black became much more conservative. See Schubert, The Constitutional Polity 118–129 (1970). More plausible, in light of Yarbrough's analysis, I think, is the explanation that Black's position, defined by the absolutist role, remained constant and the majority dominating the Warren Court gradually moved up to and past him, particularly in the latitude it gave

the First Amendment and the speed of its selective incorporation process. See also Yarbrough, *Justices Black and Douglas: The Judicial Function and the Scope of Constitutional Liberties*, 1973 Duke L.J. 441; Howard, *Mr. Justice Black: The Negro Protest Movement and the Rule of Law*, 53 Va. L.Rev. 1030 (1967). And, wrote Justice Harlan, "Those who have purported to discern in some of Mr. Justice Black's recent opinions a shift from 'liberalism' to 'conservatism' have, it seems to me, missed the true essence of his judicial philosophy." *Mr. Justice Black—Remarks of a Colleague*, 81 Harv.L.Rev. 1, 2 (1967).

38. Black, A Constitutional Faith 3, 7, 35, 41–42; Barenblatt v. United States, 360 U.S. 109, 150–151, 79 S. Ct. 1081, 1105–1106 (1959) (dissenting opinion). Though support for these observations on the ideas of Justice Black could be drawn from many sources and from numerous opinions of his as well, I have restricted such citations mainly to the collection of lectures published under the above title to avoid unnecessary clutter, because these lectures present his ideas most coherently (instead of in snatches as is the case with opinions), and to reduce the likelihood of quoting out of context.

guishable from other agencies of government by virtue of the fact that it was the legitimate law-making body in a democratic society, was not supreme however. The American system, after all, was a constitutional not a parliamentary system of government.[39] The people through the Constitution, Black argued, were sovereign and, thus, the Court, as the ineluctable guarantor of the Rule of Law was obligated to enforce constitutional restraints on legislators. It was, therefore, incumbent on the Supreme Court, as Constitutional Court, to discover the true meaning of the words comprising constitutional provisions so that the original balance of interests struck in the Constitution might be maintained.[40] To repeat: Congress was constitutionally constrained by this balance originally struck, and, of course, by subsequent amendments, understood in terms of their original intentions. This, said Black, did not smack of judicial supremacy or imply that the Court was to have the last word on matters of policy. The reason why not is provided by allegiance to the Rule of Law: Questions of constitutional interpretation were not to be decided by judges promulgating their personal value preferences, but by divining the original intent and true meaning of existing constitutional rules.[41] The proper role of judges, then, was as rule-appliers, not rule-makers.

It followed, then, that considerations of judicial activism or self-restraint *per se* were irrelevant. "Activist" judges were those who deviated from the proper judicial function by reading into the Constitution their personal policy preferences and thereby usurped legislative power. But equally reprehensible was the

---

39. Black, *The Bill of Rights*, 870.

40. Baldwin v. New York, 399 U.S. 66, 74, 90 S.Ct. 1886, 1891 (1970) (concurring opinion); see also Barenblatt v. United States, 360 U.S. 109, 134, 79 S.Ct. 1081, 1097 (1959) (dissenting opinion); Konigsberg v. State Bar of California, 366 U.S. 36, 56, 81 S.Ct. 997, 1010 (1961) (dissenting opinion).

41. Black, A Constitutional Faith 8, 10, 14. Reinforcing this distinction between judges as rule-appliers and rule-makers, Black pointedly distinguished between constitutional and common law adjudication. Linkletter v. Walker, 381 U.S. 618, 641–644, 85 S.Ct. 1731, 1744–1745 (1965) (dissenting opinion).

posture of judicial "self-restraint" since, when it meant deference to the legislative will in the face of transgressing a provision of the Constitution, "restraint" equalled the evasion of judicial responsibility.[42]

Above all, law, in Black's view, was to be spelled out in advance of the imposition of sanctions and in terms people could
understand. Judges, consequently, bore an obligation to encourage this climate of settled expectations by resolving cases in
clear and straight-forward terms and by relying on precise language. Perhaps Justice Black's general orientation toward the
task of constitutional interpretation is best summarized in a passage from his dissenting opinion in a narcotics case decided by
the Court approximately a year and a half before his death. He
wrote:

> The Framers of our Constitution and Bill of Rights were too
> wise, too pragmatic, and too familiar with tyranny to attempt
> to safeguard personal liberty with broad, flexible words and
> phrases like "fair trial," "fundamental decency," and "reason-
> ableness." Such stretchy, rubberlike terms would have left
> judges constitutionally free to try people charged with crime
> under will-o'-the-wisp standards improvised by different
> judges for different defendants. Neither the Due Process
> Clause nor any other constitutional language vests any judge
> with such power. Our Constitution was not written in the
> sands to be washed away by each wave of new judges blown
> in by each successive political wind which brings new politi-
> cal administrations into temporary power. Rather, our Con-
> stitution was fashioned to perpetuate liberty and justice by
> marking clear, explicit, and lasting constitutional boundaries
> for trials. One need look no further than the language of
> that sacred document itself to be assured that defendants
> charged with crime are to be accorded due process of law—
> that is, they are to be tried as the Constitution and the laws
> passed pursuant to it prescribe and not under arbitrary pro-
> cedures that a particular majority of sitting judges may see
> fit to label as "fair" and "decent." I wholly, completely, and
> permanently reject the so-called "activist" philosophy of some
> judges which leads them to construe our Constitution as

42. *Ibid.*, 14–21.

meaning what they now think it should mean in the interest of "fairness and decency" as they see it.[43]

Though the excerpt above is set in the context of due process issues, the essentials of Black's approach were no different in First Amendment cases. Indeed, the shift in focus heightens the absolutist tenor of his analysis because of the explicit wording of the Amendment. In Black's words:

> My view is, without deviation, without exception, without any ifs, buts, or whereases, that freedom of speech means that government shall not do anything to people * * * either for the views they have or the views they express or the words they speak or write. Some people would have you believe that this is a very radical position, and maybe it is. But all I am doing is following what to me is the clear wording of the First Amendment that "Congress shall make no law * * * abridging the freedom of speech or of the press." These words follow Madison's admonition that there are some powers the people did not mean the federal government to have at all. As I have said innumerable times before I simply believe that "Congress shall make no law" means Congress shall make no law. * * * Thus we have the absolute command of the First Amendment that no law shall be passed by Congress abridging freedom of speech or the press. * * * [44]

As distinguished from others who applied a test as to the content of the speech in order to distinguish protected from unprotected speech, Black was quick to point out that "[t]here is nothing in the language of the First Amendment to indicate that it protects only *political* speech, although to provide such protection was no doubt a strong reason for the Amendment's passage." [45] Consequently, "[s]ince the language of the Amend-

---

43. Turner v. United States, 396 U. S. 398, 426, 90 S.Ct. 642, 657 (1970) (dissenting opinion).

44. Black, A Constitutional Faith 45–46. Copyright 1969. Reprinted by permission of the publisher, Alfred A. Knopf, Inc. See also Black,

The Bill of Rights, 867; Public Interview, 552–554.

45. Black, A Constitutional Faith 46; Public Interview, 559. *Cf.* Meiklejohn, Free Speech and Its Relation to Self-Government (1948).

ment contains no exceptions," [46] Black voted repeatedly to invalidate all obscenity and libel laws.[47]

The parallel between Justice Black's approach to constitutional interpretation and that adopted by the Old Court in its formulation of dual federalism is heightened further by the fact that the absolute guarantee of constitutional protection was qualified by a dichotomous classification of the individual's activity. As Black explained, "In giving absolute protection to free speech, however, I have always been careful to draw a line between speech and conduct."[48] Absolute protection extended only to "pure speech"; that meant government could not impose "punishment of a person because he says [or writes] something, believes something or associates with others who believe the same thing * * *."[49] But such protection did not extend to "speech

46. *Ibid.*

47. *Ibid.*, 48. Obscenity: Roth v. United States, 354 U.S. 476, 508, 77 S.Ct. 1304, 1321 (1957) (dissenting opinion of Douglas, J., in which Black joined); Kingsley International Pictures Corp. v. Regents, 360 U.S. 684, 697, 79 S.Ct. 1362, 1370 (1959) (concurring opinion of Douglas, J., in which Black joined); Smith v. California, 361 U.S. 147, 155, 80 S.Ct. 215, 220 (1959) (concurring opinion); Jacobellis v. Ohio, 378 U.S. 184, 196, 84 S.Ct. 1676, 1682 (1964) (statement of Justice Black); Ginzburg v. United States, 383 U.S. 463, 476, 86 S.Ct. 942, 950 (1966) (dissenting opinion); Mishkin v. New York, 383 U.S. 502, 515, 86 S.Ct. 958, 968 (1966) (dissenting opinion); Ginsberg v. New York, 390 U.S. 629, 650, 88 S.Ct. 1274, 1286 (1968) (dissenting opinion of Douglas, J., in which Black joined); United

States v. 37 Photographs, 402 U.S. 363, 379, 91 S.Ct. 1400, 1416 (1971) (dissenting opinion). Libel: Beauharnais v. Illinois, 343 U.S. 250, 267, 72 S.Ct. 725, 736 (1952) (dissenting opinion); New York Times Co. v. Sullivan, 376 U.S. 254, 293, 84 S.Ct. 710, 733 (1964) (concurring opinion); Rosenblatt v. Baer, 383 U.S. 75, 94, 86 S.Ct. 669, 680 (1966) (concurring and dissenting opinion); Time, Inc. v. Hill, 385 U.S. 374, 398, 87 S.Ct. 534, 547 (1967) (concurring opinion); Curtis Publishing Co. v. Butts and Associated Press v. Walker, 388 U.S. 130, 170, 87 S.Ct. 1975, 1999 (1967) (concurring and dissenting opinion); Rosenbloom v. Metromedia, Inc., 403 U.S. 29, 57, 91 S.Ct. 1811, 1826 (1971) (opinion concurring in the judgment).

48. *Ibid.*, 53.

49. *Ibid.*, 50–51.

plus"; that is, activity which couples speech and action. As elaborated by Justice Black:

> Picketing, demonstrating, and similar activity usually consists in walking or marching around a building or place carrying signs or placards protesting against something that has been or is being done by the person picketed. Thus a person engaged in such activities is not only communicating ideas—that is, exercising freedom of speech or press—but is pursuing a course of conduct in addition to constitutionally protected speech and press. * * * This is not a new idea either with me or the Supreme Court since it has long been accepted constitutional doctrine that the First Amendment presents no bar to the passage of laws regulating, controlling, or entirely suppressing such a course of marching conduct even though speaking and writing accompany it. As picketing is made up of speech and press plus other conduct, so are what are popularly called demonstrations and street marches. And the conduct of demonstrators and street marchers, like that of pickets, can be regulated by government without violating the First Amendment.[50]

The reason why such regulation is necessary is simply because "this conduct by its very nature tends to infringe the rights of others." [51] In sum, then, "the peace and tranquillity of society absolutely compel the foregoing distinction between constitutionally protected freedom of religion, speech and press, and nonconstitutionally protected conduct like picketing and street marching. It marks the difference between arguing for changes in the governing rules of society and in engaging in conduct designed to break and defy valid regulatory laws." [52] It is not surprising, therefore, that, in addition to joining in certain decisions hospitable toward the basic regulatory power of government over picketing and demonstrations,[53] Justice Black came down hard on flag and draft-card burning.[54]

50. *Ibid.*, 54–55. Reprinted from Black, A Constitutional Faith, by permission of the publisher, Alfred A. Knopf, Inc., copyright 1969.

51. *Ibid.*, 57.

52. *Ibid.*, 55.

53. See Walker v. Birmingham, 388 U.S. 307, 87 S.Ct. 1824 (1967);

54. See note 54 on page 71.

In Black's view, it was also important to bear in mind that the First Amendment guaranteed protection to speak, write, believe, and associate. It did not obligate the government to furnish places to speak, write, or associate.[55] While the First Amendment did guarantee the right to petition, Black observed, "it should be noted that the petition is to be made to 'government,' not to the public in general. Propagandizing on the streets can hardly be the same as presenting a petition to 'government' to redress grievances."[56] In sum, this meant that constitutional rights to oral and written expression and to association were bounded by time and place limitations. Said Black, the First Amendment "does not guarantee that people can, wholly regardless of the rights of others, go where they please and when they please to argue for their views."[57] The upshot of this position was a number of votes cast by Justice Black against the First Amendment claims of individuals in a series of what were once called the "public forum" cases.[58] And Justice Black became

Shuttlesworth v. Birmingham, 394 U.S. 147, 89 S.Ct. 935 (1969); Carroll v. President and Com'rs of Princess Anne, 393 U.S. 175, 89 S. Ct. 347 (1968); Gregory v. Chicago, 394 U.S. 111, 113, 89 S.Ct. 946, 947 (1969) (concurring opinion). While these decisions upheld First Amendment claims against the *application* of existing ordinances, it is significant that Black voted to join the majority opinion affirming a contempt citation in the first case, concurred in the result only without opinion in the second and third, and wrote a concurring opinion in the fourth. Black's concurring opinion in *Gregory* clearly recognizes the authority of government to regulate demonstrations and picketing, but insists on a "narrowly drawn" law. 394 U.S. at 118, 89 S.Ct. at 950.

54. United States v. O'Brien, 391 U. S. 367, 88 S.Ct. 1673 (1968); Street v. New York, 394 U.S. 576, 609, 89 S.Ct. 1354, 1374 (1969) (dissenting opinion). Black also voted against First Amendment claims in other "symbolic speech" cases, Tinker v. Des Moines Indep. Community School Dist., 393 U.S. 503, 515, 89 S.Ct. 733, 741 (1969) (dissenting opinion); Cohen v. California, 403 U.S. 15, 27, 91 S.Ct. 1780, 1789 (1971) (dissenting opinion of Blackmun, J., in which Black joined).

55. Black, A Constitutional Faith 58.

56. *Ibid.*

57. *Ibid.*, 61.

58. Cox v. Louisiana (*Cox II*), 379 U.S. 559, 575, 85 S.Ct. 476, 466

particularly exercised about the notion, temporarily accepted by the Court, that the owners of private property had some constitutional obligation to furnish a place for picketers.[59]

Two correlative limitations on legislation regulating conduct or "speech plus" were also recognized by Justice Black. First, "regulatory laws in this area [must] be applied to all groups alike, and these laws must never be used as a guise to suppress particular views which the government dislikes," otherwise it "amounts to precisely the kind of governmental censorship the First Amendment was written to proscribe." [60] Second, "the First Amendment prohibits * * * [government] from regulating conduct in such a way as to affect speech indirectly where other means are available to accomplish the desired result without burdening speech or where the need to control the conduct in question is insufficient even to justify an indirect effect on speech." [61] These features of Black's approach to related First Amendment questions are extrinsic to the focus on absolutism, but they are worth noting for the way in which they underscore the respective values of equal protection and a commitment to limited government inherent in the Rule of Law concept.

One further observation is worth making both to forestall confusion and to illuminate the absoluteness of Black's First Amendment conceptions. The distinction between "speech" and

(1965) (opinion dissenting); Brown v. Louisiana, 383 U.S. 131, 151, 86 S.Ct. 719, 729 (1966) (dissenting opinion); Adderley v. Florida, 385 U.S. 39, 87 S.Ct. 242 (1966). Compare these cases with those in which Black joined the majority to uphold the First Amendment claim, Garner v. Louisiana, 368 U.S. 157, 82 S.Ct. 248 (1961); Taylor v. Louisiana, 370 U.S. 154, 82 S.Ct. 1188 (1962); Edwards v. South Carolina, 372 U.S. 229, 83 S.Ct. 680 (1963); Cox v. Louisiana (*Cox I*), 379 U.S. 536, 575, 85 S.Ct. 453, 466 (1965) (opinion concurring).

59. Amalgamated Food Employees Union v. Logan Valley Plaza, 391 U.S. 308, 88 S.Ct. 1601 (1968); modified by Lloyd Corp. v. Tanner, 407 U.S. 551, 92 S.Ct. 2219 (1972); finally overruled by Hudgens v. National Labor Relations Board, 424 U.S. 507, 96 S.Ct. 1029 (1976). Black's views are aired in his *Logan Valley Plaza* dissent, 391 U.S. at 327, 88 S.Ct. at 1613.

60. Black, A Constitutional Faith 59.

61. *Ibid.*, 60.

"action" or "conduct" has become a commonplace in constitutional law. We tend to associate it most readily with Justice Holmes who made the distinction such an integral part of his "clear and present danger" analysis of free speech cases. Precisely because of its traditional association with Holmes, it is important to explain how Black's conception of the two terms differs.

A useful place to begin would appear to be with Black's reason for rejecting Holmes' "clear and present danger" test for the analysis of free speech disputes. In Black's words, "The problem with this test is that it can be used to justify the punishment of advocacy." [62] This position is elaborated in the following excerpt from his dissenting opinion in *Yates* v. *United States*:

> The Court says that persons can be punished for advocating action to overthrow the Government by force and violence, where those to whom the advocacy is addressed are urged "to *do* something, now or in the future, rather than merely to *believe* in something." Under the Court's approach, defendants could still be convicted simply for agreeing to talk as distinguished from agreeing to act. I believe that the First Amendment forbids Congress to punish people for talking about public affairs, whether or not such discussion incites to action, legal or illegal. *   *   * [63]

That the test could be used to reach advocacy is a conclusion which does not have to rest on Justice John Harlan, Jr.'s [64] qua-

62. *Ibid.*, 52.

63. 354 U.S. 298, 340, 77 S.Ct. 1064, 1088 (1957).

64. One of the apparently insurmountable problems of constitutional law texts lies in distinguishing between the two Harlans. Technically, of course, it is wrong to differentiate between them by calling one "Sr." and the other "Jr." since John M. Harlan (1833– 1911) was the grandfather and not the father of John M. Harlan (1899–1971). Other alternatives, however, seem to risk duplicating the error (calling them Harlan I and Harlan II), or appear unnecessarily clumsy (using the full name for one and only the first name for the other, or using their dates), or accentuate the trivial (referring to the different states [Ky. and N. Y., respectively] in which they resided).

si-"clear and present danger" analysis in the *Yates* opinion. It is evident from Holmes' original formulation in *Schenck* and its restatement and embellishment in subsequent cases by both Holmes and Brandeis. Recall that *Schenck* involved a prosecution for conspiracy to print and circulate to men who had been called and accepted for military service copies of a pamphlet aimed at encouraging resistance to military service. In affirming the defendant's conviction under the Espionage Act, Justice Holmes, speaking for the Court, wrote:

> We admit that in many places and in ordinary times the defendants in saying all that was said in the circular would have been within their constitutional rights. But the character of every act depends upon the circumstances in which it is done. * * * The most stringent protection of free speech would not protect a man in falsely shouting fire in a theatre and causing a panic. It does not even protect a man from an injunction against uttering words that may have all the effect of force. * * * The question in every case is whether the words used are used in such circumstances and are of such a nature as to create a clear and present danger that they will bring about the substantive evils that Congress has a right to prevent. It is a question of proximity and degree. When a nation is at war many things that might be said in time of peace are such a hindrance to its effort that their utterance will not be endured so long as men fight and that no Court could regard them as protected by any constitutional right. * * * [65]

In his dissent with Justice Brandeis in *Abrams* later that year, Holmes emphasized that, in addition to elements such as the gravity of the evil and the immediacy of the danger, it was also incumbent upon the government to demonstrate that the defendant had a specific intent to achieve a criminal goal.[66] Also, in the same dissent, and in Brandeis' dissenting opinion in *Whitney* eight years later in which Holmes joined too, the duo sought to shore up the test against abusive application to remote develop-

---

65. Schenck v. United States, 249 U.S. 47, 52, 39 S.Ct. 247, 249 (1919).

66. Abrams v. United States, 250 U. S. 616, 626–627, 40 S.Ct. 17, 21 (1919).

ments by substituting the phrase "clear and imminent" in place of "clear and present." [67] Still, whatever may be said of these modifications in other respects, it is undeniable from what happened in *Schenck* and from the following words of Brandeis in the *Whitney* dissent that the "clear and imminent danger" test could, in the right set of circumstances, reach advocacy:

> Fear of serious injury cannot alone justify suppression of free speech and assembly. Men feared witches and burnt women. It is the function of speech to free men from the bondage of irrational fears. To justify suppression of free speech there must be reasonable ground to fear that serious evil will result if free speech is practiced. There must be reasonable ground to believe that the danger apprehended is imminent. There must be reasonable ground to believe that the evil to be prevented is a serious one. Every denunciation of existing law tends in some measure to increase the probability that there will be violation of it. Condonation of a breach enhances the probability. Expressions of approval add to the probability. Propagation of the criminal state of mind by teaching syndicalism increases it. Advocacy of law-breaking heightens it still further. But even advocacy of violation, however reprehensible morally, is not a justification for denying free speech where the advocacy falls short of incitement and there is nothing to indicate that the advocacy would be immediately acted on. The wide difference between advocacy and incitement, between preparation and attempt, between assembling and conspiracy, must be borne in mind. In order to support a finding of clear and present danger it must be shown either that immediate serious violence was to be expected or was advocated, or that the past conduct furnished reason to believe that such advocacy was then contemplated.[68]

In perhaps oversimplified form, we might portray Holmes' conception of a range of activity as a continuum stretching from "speech" to "action," which in their purest forms occupy the polar positions, with various intermediate behaviors arranged sequentially in between. See Figure 3. The notion of a contin-

67. 250 U.S. at 627, 40 S.Ct. at 21;   68. 274 U.S. at 376, 47 S.Ct. at 648.
Whitney v. California, 274 U.S.
357, 376, 47 S.Ct. 641, 648 (1927).

uum implies that a particular point or behavior along the spectrum differs from its neighbor in degree only. Above all, this scheme suggests considerable relativity in judgment. The judge's task in a given case is, of course, to decide on the basis of the facts whether the relative line that divides those behaviors associated with "speech" from those that are a part of "action" has been breached.

FIGURE 3.   SPEECH AND ACTION AS A CONTINUUM
OF BEHAVIORS

Speech ├┼┼┼┼┼┼┼┼┼┼┼┼┼┼┼┼┼┼┼┼┼┤ Action

Holmes' source for the "clear and present danger" concept was the doctrine of criminal attempts which long recognized government's legitimate interest in intervening to thwart injurious activity prior to the completion of a substantive crime. A continuum of behaviors seems a helpful way to picture what Holmes had in mind. Not only does it graphically show proximity to completion of a substantive crime, which is the heart of "action," but it helps us to understand proof of specific intent. Intent, of course, must usually be inferred from behavior since individuals rarely announce their criminal designs in advance. The further one moves from "speech" to "action," the more confidence we will have in assessing his intentions because of the pattern of previous behavior. To intervene too early in the process, before a criminal intent has crystalized or before it can be discerned with sufficient accuracy, heightens the risk that perfectly legitimate expression will be punished. "Clear and present danger" with respect to any sequence of behaviors is a point sufficiently along the spectrum with high enough risk of serious enough damage by an individual who, unless interrupted, would finish the steps to a substantive crime.

Aside from the fact that such an approach requires situational judgments—a matter of understandable anathema to the absolutists who insist on fixed standards and adequate forewarning —the relationship between "speech" and "action" in Holmes' formulation stands in obvious contrast to the relation espoused by Black: For Holmes, the difference between "speech" and "action" is essentially a matter of degree; and it is advocacy which connects the two. If the consequences of advocacy are of sufficient magnitude, then what was once "speech" becomes "action." And this is a variable proposition, because, as we know from *Schenck*, what passes muster as protected speech in some circumstances may not prove passable in a more volatile climate. For Black, on the other hand, the difference between "speech" and "action," or "conduct" as he refers to it, is, at bottom, a difference in kind. Speech is "speech" and can only become "conduct" when nonspeech elements are added; speech does not become "conduct" because of its content, or the speaker's intent, or the agitated response it may evoke from an audience.[69]

What emerges from a comparison of Black's and Holmes' conceptions of "speech" and "action" is a parallel quite striking to that encountered in the discussion of dual federalism. In both instances, the ideals of the Rule of Law concept are reflected in the efforts of the absolutists to achieve certainty in constitutional interpretation by finding rules of law that seem to be capable of deductive, almost mechanical, application. Invariably, these absolute rules are associated with the creation of rigid dichotomies in law, which are predicated on a difference in kind, so that two mutually exclusive pigeonholes are created into which the facts of subsequent cases can be sorted. The exercise of discretion by judges, that is inescapable in a flexible approach

---

69. I have intentionally refrained from adding "or its volume." Apparently, Justice Black would have distinguished between the loudness one could achieve with his own voice and the use of sound amplification equipment. He explicitly recognized the right of government to regulate the use of such devices both in terms of time and volume by narrowly-drawn statutes. Kovacs v. Cooper, 336 U.S. 77, 104, 69 S.Ct. 448, 462 (1949) (dissenting opinion). In both *Kovacs* and a previous loudspeaker case, Saia v. New York, 334 U.S. 558, 68 S.Ct. 1148 (1948), however, Justice Black voted to hold ordinances unconstitutional because they placed an absolute ban on the use of sound amplification equipment and failed to set out specific standards for licensing the use of such equipment, respectively.

which recognizes distinctions in degree among a given range of behaviors dealt with by law, seems to disappear.

3. Total Incorporation

The debate over whether and to what extent guarantees contained in the Bill of Rights bind the states as well as the federal government provides the context from which a third illustration of the absolutist mode of constitutional interpretation can be drawn. By way of introduction, it might be helpful to recall that, following the Supreme Court's decision in *Barron* v. *Baltimore* [70] in 1833, which held that provisions of the Bill of Rights operated only as limitations upon the federal government, the guarantee of civil liberties at the state level rested with provisions of the various state constitutions. With the ratification of the Fourteenth Amendment in 1868, the Court, once again turning its attention to the question in the *Slaughterhouse Cases*,[71] rejected the argument that the purpose or effect of the Privileges and Immunities Clause in section 1 of the Amendment was to impose certain substantive guarantees of personal liberties on the states. Instead, the Court gutted the clause by reading it only to impose a guarantee of equal treatment of residents and nonresidents alike under existing state constitutional protections. This did not spell an end to the efforts of those who sought to expand personal liberties at the state level through federal constitutional protection, but it did inspire them to look elsewhere within section 1 of the Fourteenth Amendment. The object of this refocused concern came to be the Due Process Clause. This, of course, is not the place to review in detail the various approaches which guided different Justices as they broached the question of incorporating provisions of the Bill of Rights into the Fourteenth Amendment (by equating such guarantees with the words "liberty" or "due process" in the Due Process Clause) and thus making them applicable also as re-

---

70. 32 U.S. (7 Pet.) 243, 8 L.Ed. 672.   **71.** 83 U.S. (16 Wall.) 36, 21 L.Ed. 394 (1873).

straints on state action.[72] Suffice it to say that the Justices were split: Some Justices favored incorporating all of the provisions of the first eight amendments; some opted for picking and choosing within the amendments, incorporating only those thought to be "fundamental" rights; some wanted to go beyond the amendments to include other "fundamental" rights; some, adhering to time-honored precedents and finding no warrant either in the text of the Fourteenth Amendment or in the debates surrounding its proposal and ratification, rejected any notion of incorporation.

Until the post-World War I era, not merely a majority, but, in fact, virtually all of the Justices who had sat on the Court, could be counted as members of the nonincorporation camp. As Justice Frankfurter later wrote, "[O]nly one, who may respectfully be called an eccentric exception, ever indicated the belief that the Fourteenth Amendment was a shorthand summary of the first eight amendments theretofore limiting only the Federal Government, and that due process incorporated those eight amendments as restrictions upon the powers of the States." [73] That exception, of course, was Justice John Harlan, Sr., who, in three cases before his tenure on the Court ended with his death in 1911, filed dissenting opinions each of which espoused the total incorporation view. On one of those occasions, after quoting the Due Process Clause of the Fifth Amendment, Harlan wrote: "The language is similar to that of the clause of the fourteenth amendment now under examination. That similarity was not accidental, but evinces a purpose to impose upon the states the same restrictions, in respect of proceedings involving life, liberty, and property, which had been imposed upon the general government." [74] In those cases, he voted to incorporate the guarantee of indictment by grand jury (and against California's

72. Chase and Ducat, Constitutional Interpretation 912–917 (1974); Abraham, Freedom and the Court, Ch. 3 (3d ed. 1977).

73. Adamson v. California, 332 U.S. 46, 62, 67 S.Ct. 1672, 1680 (1947) (concurring opinion).

74. Hurtado v. California, 110 U.S. 516, 541, 4 S.Ct. 111, 293 (1884).

practice of indicting by an information),[75] to incorporate the guarantee against self-incrimination (and against New Jersey's practice of allowing a trial judge to comment on the failure of the defendants to testify in their own behalf),[76] and to incorporate the right to a jury trial in a criminal case before a panel of 12 jurors as at common law (and against Utah's practice of trying cases to eight-man juries).[77]

Harlan's ideological successor was Justice Black. Announcing his views for the first time in a dissent to the Court's decision in 1947 in *Adamson* v. *California,* Black declared:

> My study of the historical events that culminated in the Fourteenth Amendment, and the expressions of those who sponsored and favored, as well as those who opposed its submission and passage, persuades me that one of the chief objects that the provisions of the Amendment's first section, separately, and as a whole, were intended to accomplish was to make the Bill of Rights, applicable to the states. With full knowledge of the import of the *Barron* decision, the framers and backers of the Fourteenth Amendment proclaimed its purpose to be to overturn the constitutional rule that case had announced. This historical purpose has never received full consideration or exposition in any opinion of this Court interpreting the Amendment.[78]

His dissenting opinion was followed by an extensive appendix in which he presented what seemed to him conclusive evidence of the framers' intent. The material presented by Black, which is a composite of his own research and the work of others,[79] has been roundly criticized, however.[80] Nonetheless, Black stands as

75. 110 U.S. at 538, 4 S.Ct. at 292.

76. Twining v. New Jersey, 211 U.S. 78, 114, 29 S.Ct. 14, 26 (1908).

77. Maxwell v. Dow, 176 U.S. 581, 605, 20 S.Ct. 448, 494 (1900).

78. 332 U.S. 46, 71-72, 67 S.Ct. 1672, 1686 (1947). See also Yarbrough, *Justice Black, the Fourteenth Amendment and Incorporation,* 30 U.Miami L.Rev. 231 (1976).

79. Particularly, Flack, The Adoption of the Fourteenth Amendment (1908). Black's Appendix appears at 332 U.S., 92, 67 S.Ct., 1696.

80. See, especially, Fairman, *Does the Fourteenth Amendment Incorporate the Bill of Rights? The*

the fullest and most enthusiastic exponent of total incorporation to date. It would not be unfair, then, to take Black's opinions as representative of the total incorporation position for the purpose of illuminating the connection with absolutism.

In the first place, total incorporation is absolute simply because it is *total*. Unlike advocates of selective incorporation, who sought to distinguish important from unimportant guarantees for the purpose of limiting incorporation only to the former, Black rejected the permissibility of such discretion. Total incorporation thus possesses the requisite all-or-nothing quality. Moreover, just as it is impermissible to incorporate less than all of the provisions of the first eight amendments, it is equally wrong to incorporate more. Black *concurred* with the majority on the Warren Court as it incrementally incorporated most of the guarantees in the first eight amendments, reasoning that, "If the choice must be made between the selective process of the *Palko* decision applying some of the Bill of Rights to the States, or the *Twining* rule applying none of them, I would choose the *Palko* selective process. But rather than accept either of these choices, I would follow what I believe was the original purpose of the Fourteenth Amendment—to extend to all the people of the nation the complete protection of the Bill of Rights." [81] When, however, in 1965, the majority reached out to incorporate

Original Understanding, 2 Stan.L. Rev. 5 (1949); Morrison, *Does the Fourteenth Amendment Incorporate the Bill of Rights? The Judicial Interpretation*, 2 Stan.L.Rev. 140 (1949). See also tenBroek, Equal Under Law (1965).

81. Adamson v. California, 332 U.S. 46, 89, 67 S.Ct. 1672, 1695 (1947). Black wrote the opinion of the Court in Gideon v. Wainwright, 372 U.S. 335, 83 S.Ct. 792 (1963), and Pointer v. Texas, 380 U.S. 400, 85 S.Ct. 1065 (1965); he joined the opinion of the Court in Robinson v.

California, 370 U.S. 660, 82 S.Ct. 1417 (1962), Malloy v. Hogan, 378 U.S. 1, 84 S.Ct. 1489 (1964), Klopfer v. North Carolina, 386 U.S. 213, 87 S.Ct. 988 (1967), Washington v. Texas, 388 U.S. 14, 87 S.Ct. 1920 (1967), and Benton v. Maryland, 395 U.S. 784, 89 S.Ct. 2056 (1969); he wrote a separate concurring opinion in Mapp v. Ohio, 367 U.S. 643, 661, 81 S.Ct. 1684, 1694 (1961), Murphy v. Waterfront Com'n, 378 U.S. 52, 80, 84 S.Ct. 1594, 1610 (1964), and Duncan v. Louisiana, 391 U.S. 145, 162, 88 S.Ct. 1444, 1454 (1968).

a constitutional right to privacy purportedly located in the penumbras of several amendments, Black *dissented* and intoned:

> I get nowhere in this case by talk about a constitutional "right or privacy" as an emanation from one or more constitutional provisions. I like my privacy as well as the next one, but I am nevertheless compelled to admit that government has a right to invade it unless prohibited by some specific constitutional provision. For these reasons I cannot agree with the Court's judgment and the reasons it gives for holding this Connecticut law unconstitutional.[82]

And total incorporation was equally absolute in its insistence that once a right was incorporated, the standards governing its interpretation would be identical at both the national and state levels.[83] Incorporation, therefore, governed not simply the rights contained in the first eight amendments, but all of the past and future *constitutional* constructions of those rights by the Supreme Court.[84]

82. Griswold v. Connecticut, 381 U. S. 479, 510–511, 85 S.Ct. 1678, 1695–1696 (1965).

83. Justice Black was careful to distinguish constitutional from common law requirements. Thus, in the debate that followed the incorporation of the Sixth Amendment's jury trial guarantee, in Duncan v. Louisiana, 391 U.S. 145, 88 S.Ct. 1444 (1968), as to what aspects of trial by jury were included, Justice Black voted to extent the guarantee to all state misdemeanor trials, Baldwin v. New York, 399 U.S. 66, 74, 90 S.Ct. 1886, 1891 (1970) (concurring opinion), but not to hold the states to the common law figure of 12 jurors, Williams v. Florida, 399 U.S. 78, 106, 90 S.Ct. 1893, 1909 (1970) (concurring and dissenting opinion). Nor, hypothesized Justice Douglas, would Black have agreed to later developments modi-

fying that guarantee by permitting conviction by less than a unanimous vote of the jurors, Johnson v. Louisiana, 406 U.S. 356, 380, 92 S. Ct. 1620, 1643 (1972) (dissenting opinion).

84. It is worth emphasizing that, in criminal procedure cases, care has to be taken to see whether the Court's ruling rests on interpretation of a constitutional provision or on the Court's statutory authority to supervise federal law enforcement; only the former extend to the states. Ker v. California, 374 U.S. 23, 30–34, 83 S.Ct. 1623, 1628–1630 (1963). For examples of the latter, see Nardone v. United States, 302 U.S. 379, 58 S.Ct. 275 (1937), McNabb v. United States, 318 U S. 332, 63 S.Ct. 608 (1943), Mallory v. United States, 354 U.S. 449, 77 S.Ct. 1356 (1957).

Total incorporation, in sum, offered a refuge from the exercise of discretion; it was an oasis of certainty in a desert of otherwise shifting sands. It is worth emphasizing at this point just what Black found so objectionable in the other incorporation alternatives; what is significant is the uniformity of the criticism. All of the other alternatives presented the inescapable problem of justifying an act of choice: for the selective incorporationists, how to explain which provisions of the Bill of Rights were "in" and which were "out"; for those who looked beyond the text of the Constitution, how to explain which additional rights were significant. And for the nonincorporationists, the discretionary problem was especially great because they proceeded case by case asking whether the facts of a given case demonstrated such a transgression of standards of "fairness" and "decency" with respect to state action that the canon of due process was breached. To Black, couching constitutional judgments in natural law terms—as the alternative approaches made inevitable—converted the Court into a super-legislature with no checks on the arbitrary and shifting sentiments of a temporary majority of sitting judges. As Justice Black wrote in his dissenting opinion in *Rochin* v. *California,* " * * * I believe that faithful adherence to the specific guarantees in the Bill of Rights insures a more permanent protection of individual liberty than that which can be afforded by the nebulous standards stated by the majority." He continued, "I long ago concluded that the accordion-like qualities of this philosophy must inevitably imperil all the individual liberty safeguards specifically enumerated in the Bill of Rights." [85]

4. Absolutism and the Benign Quota

Because it is both an illuminating example and a timely topic as well, it may prove useful to look at the absolutist approach as it grapples with the constitutionality of racial quotas used for the purpose of promoting integration in society by advancing

85. 342 U.S. 165, 175, 177, 72 S.Ct. 205, 209–210 (1952).

disadvantaged minorities in employment and admission to educational institutions. While we need not review here all of the ramifications of such quotas,[86] it is sufficient perhaps to note that the controversy surrounding the practice of reserving a certain number of spots for minorities in the context of a very limited number of openings often results in the selection of less skilled minority individuals than a sizable number of excluded whites, thus provoking the charge that benign quotas constitute reverse discrimination. As of this writing, the Supreme Court has never reached the merits of the question,[87] and, though it is expected to do so shortly,[88] it is somewhat doubtful, what with the absence of any absolutists from the present Court, that it will resolve the issue by recourse to that mode of constitutional interpretation.[89] Nonetheless, there is a ready supply of illustra-

86. For instance, see Kaplan, *Equal Justice in an Unequal World: Equality for the Negro—The Problem of Special Treatment*, 61 Nw. U.L.Rev. 363 (1966); O'Neil, Discriminating Against Discrimination (1975); Glazer, Affirmative Discrimination (1975); United Jewish Organizations of Williamburgh, Inc. v. Carey, 430 U.S. 144, 167, 97 S.Ct. 996, 1011 (1977) (concurring opinion of Brennan, J.). See also note 89, *infra*.

87. DeFunis v. Odegaard, 416 U.S. 312, 94 S.Ct. 1704 (1974) (judgment vacated on grounds of mootness). The Washington Supreme Court subsequently reinstated its judgment, 84 Wash.2d 617, 529 P.2d 438 (1974).

88. Bakke v. Regents of the University of California, 18 Cal.3d 34, 132 Cal.Rptr. 680, 553 P.2d 1152 (1976), *cert. granted* 429 U.S. 1090, 97 S. Ct. 1098.

89. In addition to the two examples discussed in this section, the absolutist approach is also illustrated by Lige v. Town of Montclair, 72 N.J. 5, 367 A.2d 833 (1976), Posner, *The DeFunis Case and the Constitutionality of Preferential Treatment of Racial Minorities*, 1974 Sup. Ct.Rev. 1. Among the alternative frameworks of analysis from which the Court might choose are: (1) an assessment that the purpose of the Fourteenth Amendment was to advance the Negro in society and benign quotas are a reasonable instrument toward that end, Bittker, *infra*, note 98 (opinion of Judge Everett), Alevy v. Downstate Medical Center, 39 N.Y.2d 326, 384 N.Y.S.2d 82, 348 N.E.2d 537 (1976), Lige v. Town of Montclair, 72 N.J. 5, 27, 367 A.2d 833, 845 (1976) (dissenting opinion of Pashman, J.), Bakke v. Regents of the University of California, 18 Cal.3d 34, 64, 132 Cal.Rptr. 680, 700, 553 P.2d 1152, 1172 (1976) (dissenting opinion of Tobriner, J.), Greenawalt, *Judicial*

tions from other sources, and it is far less important for our purposes that we have a Supreme Court opinion than that we have a good illustration. Before taking up two such examples, however, we should begin with the opinion that has become the touchstone of absolutist analysis in benign quota cases, the dissenting opinion of Justice John Harlan, Sr., in *Plessy* v. *Ferguson*.[90]

Still lumbering under the spirit of 1876, which historian C. Vann Woodward so aptly characterized as "reunion and reaction,"[91] the Court, in *Plessy* sustained the constitutionality of a Louisiana statute requiring that railroad companies provide segregated coaches for black and white passengers. Distinguishing away past precedents,[92] the Court held that this was a "reasonable" exercise of legislative power, so long as the facilities provided were "separate but equal." For reasons which are in-

---

Scrutiny of "Benign" Racial Preference in Law School Admissions, 75 Colum.L.Rev. 559 (1975), Ely, *The Constitutionality of Reverse Discrimination*, 41 U.Chi.L.Rev. 723, 742 (1974); (2) an analysis that assumes race is a suspect class and upholds benign quotas as necessary to further a compelling state interest, DeFunis v. Odegaard, 82 Wash.2d 11, 507 P.2d 1169 (1973), O'Neil, *Preferential Admissions: Equalizing the Access of Minority Groups to Higher Education*, 80 Yale L.J. 699 (1971), O'Neil, *Racial Preference in Higher Education: The Larger Context*, 60 Va.L.Rev. 925 (1974), O'Neil, Discriminating Against Discrimination (1975), Karst and Horowitz, *Affirmative Action and Equal Protection*, 60 Va. L.Rev. 955 (1974); (3) an evaluation that assumes race is a suspect class but strikes down benign quotas as failing to further a compelling state interest or unnecessarily trenching upon the right to equal treatment by

whites, Bakke v. Regents of the University of California, 18 Cal.3d 34, 132 Cal.Rptr. 680, 553 P.2d 1152 (1976).

A different approach, but one somewhat like (1) above, is Sandalow, *Racial Preferences in Higher Education: Political Responsibility and the Judicial Role*, 42 U.Chi.L.Rev. 653 (1975). He argues that affirmative action programs, adopted without explicit legislative sanction, can be sustained, but the reasons are a good deal less compelling than if the policies had received explicit legislative approval.

90. 163 U.S. 537, 552, 16 S.Ct. 1138, 1144 (1896).

91. Reunion and Reaction (1951).

92. Slaughterhouse Cases, 83 U.S. (16 Wall.) 36, 21 L.Ed. 394 (1873); Strauder v. West Virginia, 100 U.S. 303, 25 L.Ed. 664 (1880).

comprehensible as a matter of text, but probably best explained in terms of the efforts of segregationists to derive what benefits they could by clothing *Plessy* with the mantle of law—especially in the wake of its overruling by the Warren Court in *Brown* v. *Board of Education* [93]—the majority opinion in *Plessy* came to be characterized in some quarters as an opinion based on law, while Harlan's dissent was disparaged—along with *Brown*—as so much sociology.[94] In fact, precisely the reverse was true. Stripping away much of the Court's rhetoric in *Plessy,* language which was insensitive at best, the conclusion with respect to segregation as reasonable public policy was premised on three propositions, which together reflect a sort of nineteenth century sociology (as distinguished from twentieth century sociology's emphasis on environment as the dominant force in shaping attitudes) coupled with what later came to be called "social engineering": [95]

> 1. Racial prejudice is instinctive and, like physical differences between the races, inborn.

93. Brown v. Board of Education, 347 U.S. 483, 74 S.Ct. 686 (1954).

94. The closest the dissent comes to talking in sociological terms is Harlan's uncanny reference to that sort of public policy thinking articulated by the majority and ascribed to the statute as something like the self-fulfilling prophecy: "What can more certainly arouse race hate, what more certainly create and perpetuate a feeling of distrust between these races, than state enactments which, in fact, proceed on the ground that colored citizens are so inferior and degraded that they cannot be allowed to sit in public coaches occupied by white citizens?" 163 U.S. at 560, 16 S.Ct. at 1147. Equally astute was Harlan's prophetic parting shot at the largely cosmetic effect of the word "equal" in the Court's command of "separate but equal": "The thin disguise of 'equal' accommodations for passengers in railroad coaches will not mislead any one, nor atone for the wrong this day done." 163 U.S. at 562, 16 S.Ct. at 1147.

95. Though they have been restated in my own words, I am indebted to Professor Harry Ball for the gist of these propositions and for the notion of *Plessy* as embodying a kind of nineteenth century sociology. These observations were made in his Sociology of Law seminar at the 1968 Summer Institute for Behavioral Sciences and Law at the University of Wisconsin.

2. It is impossible to legislate changes in attitude (or, in the exact words of the opinion, to attain social equality "by an enforced commingling of the two races").

3. Segregation constitutes a viable method of peaceful co-existence.

In response to this, Justice Harlan wrote:

Is it meant that the determination of questions of legislative power depends upon the inquiry whether the statute whose validity is questioned is, in the judgment of the courts, a reasonable one, taking all the circumstances into consideration? A statute may be unreasonable merely because a sound public policy forbade its enactment. But I do not understand that the courts have anything to do with the policy or expediency of legislation. A statute may be valid, and yet, upon grounds of public policy, may well be characterized as unreasonable. Mr. Sedgwick correctly states the rule when he says that, the legislative intention being clearly ascertained, "the courts have no other duty to perform than to execute the legislative will, without any regard to their views as to the wisdom or justice of the particular enactment." Sedg.St. & Const. Law, 324. There is a dangerous tendency in these latter days to enlarge the functions of the courts, by means of judicial interference with the will of the people as expressed by the legislature. Our institutions have the distinguishing characteristic that the three departments of government are co-ordinate and separate. Each must keep within the limits defined by the constitution. And the courts best discharge their duty by executing the will of the lawmaking power, constitutionally expressed, leaving the results of legislation to be dealt with by the people through their representatives. Statutes must always have a reasonable construction. Sometimes they are to be construed strictly, sometimes literally, in order to carry out the legislative will. But, however construed, the intent of the legislature is to be respected if the particular statute in question is valid, although the courts, looking at the public interests, may conceive the statute to be both unreasonable and impolitic. If the power exists to enact a statute, that ends the matter so far as the courts are concerned. The adjudged cases in which statutes have been held to be void, because unreasonable, are those in which the means em-

ployed by the legislature were not at all germane to the end
to which the legislature was competent.[96]

Pushing on to the constitutional question, whether racial classifications in law were permissible and not whether they were reasonable, he found in the purpose behind the Civil War amendments and in the Court's own precedents interpreting them, particularly *Strauder* v. *West Virginia,* which he quoted at length,
the relevant constitutional rule:

> In respect of civil rights, common to all citizens, the consti-
> tution of the United States does not, I think, permit any pub-
> lic authority to know the race of those entitled to be protect-
> ed in the enjoyment of such rights. Every true man has
> pride of race, and under appropriate circumstances, when the
> rights of others, his equals before the law, are not to be af-
> fected, it is his privilege to express such pride and to take
> such action based upon it as to him seems proper. But I
> deny that any legislative body or judicial tribunal may have
> regard to the race of citizens when the civil rights of those
> citizens are involved. Indeed, such legislation as that here in
> question is inconsistent not only with that equality of rights
> which pertains to citizenship, national and state, but with the
> personal liberty enjoyed by every one within the United
> States.
>
> * * *
>
> The white race deems itself to be the dominant race in this
> country. And so it is, in prestige, in achievements, in educa-
> tion, in wealth, and in power. So, I doubt not, it will contin-
> ue to be for all time, if it remains true to its great heritage,
> and holds fast to the principles of constitutional liberty. But
> in view of the constitution, in the eye of the law, there is in
> this country no superior, dominant, ruling class of citizens.
> There is no caste here. Our constitution is color-blind, and
> neither knows nor tolerates classes among citizens. In re-
> spect of civil rights, all citizens are equal before the law.
> The humblest is the peer of the most powerful. The law re-
> gards man as man, and takes no account of his surroundings
> or of his color when his civil rights as guarantied by the su-
> preme law of the land are involved. It is therefore to be re-

96. 163 U.S. at 558–559, 16 S.Ct. at
1146.

gretted that this high tribunal, the final expositor of the fundamental law of the land, has reached the conclusion that it is competent for a state to regulate the enjoyment by citizens of their civil rights solely upon the basis of race.[97]

The constitutional rule enunciated by Harlan was both clear and absolute: Race is never a permissible basis for the construction of classifications in law. With this behind us, we now turn to take up the benign quota.

The earliest and—given its clarity—much the best illustration of the absolutist approach to the benign quota can be found in Professor Boris Bittker's seminal article of a decade and a half ago presenting a mythical circuit court with the hypothetical case of the checkerboard ordinance.[98] Though the article is composed of several opinions which present alternative ways of resolving the constitutional question, for our purposes we will focus on the opinion of the imaginary Judge Adams.

The facts in the case can be summarized briefly as follows: The town of New Harmony, seeking to promote better social relationships between whites and Negroes and avoid the divisiveness of *de facto* segregation, adopted an ordinance which classified all residential building lots in the town as W or N respectively. Not included in this scheme are public buildings, schools, parks, businesses, churches, and other nonresidential land. It is the alternating classification of residential lots as W or N throughout the town that gives the ordinance its name. Owners of property designated as W or N may sell that property only to a member of the race for which that particular lot is zoned; real estate classified as N, for example, could not be sold to a white and vice versa. The ordinance accommodates persons who are neither Negro or white by allowing them initially to acquire property under either classification but, after making the purchase, forbidding that person from acquiring any real estate

97. 163 U.S. at 554–555, 559, 16 S.Ct. at 1145–1146.

98. *The Case of the Checker-Board Ordinance: An Experiment in* *Race Relations*, 71 Yale L.J. 1387 (1962) [hereafter referred to as Bittker].

under the other classification.   Multi-family dwellings follow this same scheme with the apartments being alternately designated as W or N.   The ordinance also contains appropriate provisions to prevent subversion of the integration policy by land acquisition through corporations or dummies.   Jones, who is white, contracted to sell property zoned W to Smith, a Negro. When the town clerk refused to record the deed, since the transaction was in violation of the ordinance, Jones and Smith sued the town alleging that the ordinance violated the Equal Protection and Due Process Clauses of the Fourteenth Amendment.

Judge Adams begins with a discussion of two Supreme Court decisions, *Buchanan* v. *Warley* [99] and *Shelley* v. *Kraemer*.[100] *Buchanan* held unconstitutional a Louisville ordinance which prohibited blacks from moving into houses on residential blocks predominantly occupied by whites and vice versa.   Said the Court:

> It is the purpose of such enactments, and, it is frankly avowed it will be their ultimate effect, to require by law, at least in residential districts, the compulsory separation of the races on account of color.   *   *   *
>
> *   *   *
>
> It is urged that this proposed segregation will promote the public peace by preventing race conflicts.   Desirable as this is, and important as is the preservation of the public peace, this aim cannot be accomplished by laws or ordinances which deny rights created or protected by the Federal Constitution.
>
> It is said that such acquisitions by colored persons depreciate property owned in the neighborhood by white persons. But property may be acquired by undesirable white neighbors or put to disagreeable though lawful uses with like results.
>
> We think this attempt to prevent the alienation of the property in question to a person of color was not a legitimate exercise of the police power of the State, and is in direct violation of the fundamental law enacted in the Fourteenth Amendment of the Constitution preventing state interference

99.   245 U.S. 60, 38 S.Ct. 16 (1917).   100.   334 U.S. 1, 68 S.Ct. 836 (1948).

with property rights except by due process of law. That
being the case the ordinance cannot stand. * * * [101]

In *Shelley*, the Court ruled that, while racially-restrictive cove-
nants among neighborhood property-owners were not in themselves constitutionally *verboten*, when such restrictions on the
sale of real estate were enforced by state courts, it constituted
discriminatory state action in violation of the Equal Protection
Clause. From these decisions, Judge Adams drew the conclusion
that both "establish an absolute prohibition on the use of race or
color as a criterion of state action, at least in the area of land
tenure and occupancy." [102]

Adams found this conclusion "reinforced by *Brown* v. *Board
of Education* * * *." [103] Though Adams noted that the
Court in *Brown* had remarked on the feelings of inferiority generated by the practice of racial segregation, he found a rule similar to that articulated in *Buchanan* and *Shelley*:

> I conclude that *Brown* v. *Board of Education* decided that
> race is an improper criterion for the assignment of school
> children, regardless of the consequences of such a classifica-
> tion. This conclusion is supported by the Supreme Court's
> later decisions outlawing racial segregation in public parks,
> buses, and golf courses in per curiam opinions that cited the
> *Brown* case without suggesting that adverse consequences
> would be generated by discrimination in these other public
> facilities. * * * In short, I construe *Brown* as endorsing
> Mr. Justice Harlan's famous statement that the "Constitution
> is color-blind." [104]

The impact of this clear constitutional rule cannot be modified
in the present case, wrote Adams, on the theory that the constitutionally objectionable practices at issue in *Buchanan*, *Shelley*,
and *Brown* were designed to, and did, in fact, separate the races,
whereas New Harmony's checkerboard ordinance is aimed at integration. Reiterating that the Louisville ordinance was also

101. 245 U.S. at 81–82, 38 S.Ct. at
20.

102. Bittker, 1391.

103. *Ibid.*

104. *Ibid.*, 1391–1392.

justified on the grounds that it was enacted "to prevent conflict and ill-feeling between the white and colored races," [105] Adams continued:

> Publicly announced purposes, to be sure, may be exercises in deception, or even in self-deception, but I have no tools for probing below the surface of either Louisville's or New Harmony's announced purpose; and our courts, whether from fear or humility, have traditionally refused to inquire into the motives of legislators. And if we are to confine our inquiry to the results of the state's action, I am not equipped as a judge to decide whether New Harmony's ordinance will contribute more than Louisville's zoning scheme to racial amity or whether either would be more efficacious than complete freedom of movement—and I would not know whether to compare their results, even if I had the tools to predict them, on a short-run or long-run basis, on a local or national scale, or in terms of outward behavior or inward attitude. The one fixed star that I can make out in this area is that the Supreme Court did not hesitate in *Shelley* v. *Kraemer* to prohibit judicial enforcement of a covenant that may have been, and probably was, the principal reason why an area that had enjoyed mixed Negro and white occupancy for a generation had not become a Negro ghetto. And in doing so, the Court used language that admits of no distinction between high-minded and low-minded covenantors.[106]

The same conclusion and style mark the opinion written by Chief Justice Hale of the Washington Supreme Court dissenting in *DeFunis* v. *Odegaard*.[107] In that case, Marco DeFunis, who had applied for admission to the University of Washington Law School, was denied admission, and brought suit against university officials. He charged that the procedures and criteria employed by the law school admissions committee invidiously discriminated against him in violation of both federal and state constitutions. While a numerical scale, the Predicted First Year Average (based on Law School Aptitude Test results and the

105. Quoted from the title of the ordinance, 245 U.S. at 70, 38 S.Ct. at 17.

106. Bittker, 1392.

107. 82 Wash.2d 11, 45, 507 P.2d 1169, 1189 (1974).

junior-senior grade point average) was used to screen non-minority applicants, very different standards were applied in the decision to admit candidates who indicated on their applications that they were Black, Chicano, American Indian, or Filipino. As a consequence of applying differential criteria, 37 minority applicants were admitted, 36 of whom had PFYA's lower than DeFunis and 30 of whom had scale scores below the figure which otherwise would have spelled automatic rejection. The trial court found this bifurcated admissions policy unconstitutional. This judgment was subsequently reversed by decision of the state supreme court, a decision to which Chief Justice Hale, joined by Justice Hunter, took the following exception:

> If this be constitutional, then, of course, the constitutions are not color blind; one racial group may be given political or economic preferment over another solely because of race or ethnic origin. Yet, this was the very thing that the Fourteenth Amendment was designed to prevent. All races, and all individuals, are entitled to equal opportunity to enter the law school. To admit some solely because of race or ethnic origin is to deny others that privilege solely for the same reasons, which in law amounts to a denial of equal protection to the one while granting special privileges and immunities to the other.[108]

He went on to point out that the Supreme Court, in *Brown,* had, with respect to equal educational opportunity, specifically declared, "Such an opportunity, where the state has undertaken to provide it, is a right which must be made available to all on equal terms." [109] Citing Supreme Court rulings since *Brown* which struck down segregation in public parks and playgrounds, in public transportation, in public swimming areas, and in public restaurants, and which invalidated anti-miscegenation statutes and laws specially punishing interracial fornication, Chief Justice Hale concluded, "If the Fourteenth Amendment stands for anything at all, it should be clear from these decisions that it stands for the principle that all discrimination based on race, re-

108. 82 Wash.2d at 60–61, 507 P.2d   109. 347 U.S. 483, 493, 74 S.Ct. 686,
  at 1197.   691.

ligion, creed, color or ethnic background by any state, its constitutions, its subdivisions, or its agencies, is prohibited." [110]   Finally, the influence of Justice John Harlan, Sr.'s initial formulation of the constitutional rule is particularly evident in Hale's
opening paragraph, which, for our purposes, might also serve as
a concise summation:

> Racial bigotry, prejudice and intolerance will never be end-
> ed by exalting the political rights of one group or class over
> that of another. The circle of inequality cannot be broken by
> shifting the inequities from one man to his neighbor. To
> aggrandize the first will, to the extent of the aggrandizement,
> diminish the latter. There is no remedy at law except to
> abolish all class distinctions heretofore existing in law. For
> that reason, the constitutions are, and ever ought to be, color
> blind. Now the court says it would hold the constitutions col-
> or conscious that they may stay color blind. I do not see how
> they can be both color blind and color conscious at the same
> time toward the same persons and on the same issues, so I
> dissent.[111]

Critique

These illustrations and the general sketch of the absolutist approach presented earlier raise some serious, perhaps even fatal
objections to its adequacy as a framework for constitutional interpretation. Only a comparative assessment of its contributions and limitations as against other modes of interpretation
can, of course, tell whether it is more or less acceptable than its
rivals. But this is likely to be an uneasy, even a tentative, judgment. One of the reasons why this is likely to be so is that the
arguments for and against these modes of constitutional interpretation are remarkably intertwined; some of the criticisms
mentioned below will surface in subsequent chapters as the
strong points of alternative frameworks, while several of the arguments for absolutism may later appear to be cogent reasons
for rejecting interest balancing and preferred freedoms.

110. 82 Wash.2d at 62, 507 P.2d at   111. 82 Wash.2d at 45, 507 P.2d at
    1198.   1189.

1. *Rules and Principles*

One of absolutism's most serious difficulties lies in its definition of law as a system of *rules*. The possibility of deductive adjudication hinges substantially on the identification of law as a collection of if-then propositions, conditional clauses to which are attached specific consequences. The clarity of rules simultaneously functions to constrain the judge's discretion and to adequately apprise the citizen. Though our focus is on constitutional law, not law in general, the above illustrations provide substantial support for the conclusion that absolutists read constitutional provisions as statements of rules. And many provisions of the Constitution—I should hasten to add—do state a rule, such as that allowing each state two senators, or that prescribing a four year term for the President.

But many do not. The Constitution's guarantees of equal protection, or due process, or against the imposition of cruel and unusual punishments state *principles* not rules. In Professor Ronald Dworkin's words:

> The difference between legal principles and legal rules is a logical distinction. Both sets of standards point to particular decisions about legal obligation in particular circumstances, but they differ in the character of direction they give. Rules are applicable in an all-or-nothing fashion. If the facts a rule stipulates are given, then either the rule is valid, in which case the answer it supplies must be accepted, or it does not, in which case it contributes nothing to the decision.[112]

112. *Is Law a System of Rules?* in Summers, ed., Essays in Legal Philosophy 37 (1968). Dworkin continues, "The first difference between rules and principles entails another. Principles have a dimension that rules do not—the dimension of weight or importance." *ibid.*, 39. And he observes:

[W]e cannot say that one rule is more important than another within the system of rules, so that when two rules conflict one supersedes the other by virtue of its greater weight. If two rules conflict, one of them cannot be a valid rule. The decision as to which is valid, and which must be abandoned or recast, must be made by appealing to considerations beyond the rules themselves. A legal system might regulate such conflicts by other rules, which prefer the rule enacted by the higher authority, or the rule enacted later, or the more specific rule, or something of

Absolutists time and again have insisted on reading clauses which state principles as though they stated rules. In large part, this accounts for the difference between Justice Black's reading of the First Amendment and that given it by Justices Holmes and Brandeis, or the reading of the Commerce Clause by the dual federalists, on the one hand, and the cooperative federalists, such as Chief Justice Hughes, on the other.

Perhaps the effect of attempting to read a constitutional provision stating a principle as if it were one of the "black-and-white clauses," as Judge Edgerton called them,[113] is best illustrated when the Court comes to unploughed ground. Consider *Olmstead* v. *United States,* for example. The year is 1928; the question is whether evidence obtained by employing the new technology of the wiretap is admissible in federal court. On the basis of such evidence, Roy Olmstead and his associates, rum runners on Puget Sound, have been indicted and convicted for violating the Volstead Act. Compare the approaches of Chief Justice Taft, speaking for the Court, and Justice Brandeis, dissenting. Chief Justice Taft:

> There is no room in the present case for applying the Fifth Amendment, unless the Fourth Amendment was first violated. There was no evidence of compulsion to induce the defendants to talk over their many telephones. They were continually and voluntarily transacting business without knowledge of the interception. Our consideration must be confined to the Fourth Amendment.
>
>   *   *   *
>
> The well-known historical purpose of the Fourth Amendment, directed against general warrants and writs of assistance, was to prevent the use of governmental force to search a man's house, his person, his papers, and his effects, and to prevent their seizure against his will. *   *   *
>
>   *   *   *

that sort. A legal system may also prefer the rule supported by the more important principles.
* * *

Ibid., 40. This is another way of casting the discussion that begins *infra*, at p. 111.

113. See Chapter 1, note 52.

The amendment itself shows that the search is to be of material things—the person, the house, his papers, or his effects. The description of the warrant necessary to make the proceeding lawful is that it must specify the place to be searched and the person or *things* to be seized.

* * *

* * * The amendment does not forbid what was done here. There was no searching. There was no seizure. The evidence was secured by the use of the sense of hearing and that only. There was no entry of the houses or offices of the defendants.

* * *

The language of the amendment cannot be extended and expanded to include telephone wires, reaching to the whole world from the defendant's house or office. The intervening wires are not part of his house or office, any more than are the highways along which they are stretched.

* * *

Congress may, of course, protect the secrecy of telephone messages by making them, when intercepted, inadmissible in evidence in federal criminal trials, by direct legislation, and thus depart from the common law of evidence. But the courts may not adopt such a policy by attributing an enlarged and unusual meaning to the Fourth Amendment. The reasonable view is that one who installs in his house a telephone instrument with connecting wires intends to project his voice to those quite outside, and that the wires beyond his house, and messages while passing over them, are not within the protection of the Fourth Amendment. Here those who intercepted the projected voices were not in the house of either party to the conversation.

* * *

We think, therefore, that the wire tapping here disclosed did not amount to a search or seizure within the meaning of the Fourth Amendment.[114]

Justice Brandeis:

When the Fourth and Fifth Amendments were adopted, "the form that evil had theretofore taken" had been neces-

114.   277 U.S. 438, 462–466, 48 S.Ct.
564, 567–568 (1928).

sarily simple. Force and violence were then the only means known to man by which a government could directly effect self-incrimination. It could compel the individual to testify —a compulsion effected, if need be, by torture. It could secure possession of his papers and other articles incident to his private life—a seizure effected, if need be, by breaking and entry. Protection against such invasion of "the sanctities of a man's home and the privacies of life" was provided in the Fourth and Fifth Amendments by specific language. Boyd v. United States, 116 U.S. 616, 630, 6 S.Ct. 521. But "time works changes, brings into existence new conditions and purposes." Subtler and more far-reaching means of invading privacy have become available to the government. Discovery and invention have made it possible for the government, by means far more effective than stretching upon the rack, to obtain disclosure in court of what is whispered in the closet.

Moreover, "in the application of a Constitution, our contemplation cannot be only of what has been, but of what may be." The progress of science in furnishing the government with means of espionage is not likely to stop with wire tapping. Ways may some day be developed by which the government, without removing papers from secret drawers, can reproduce them in court, and by which it will be enabled to expose to a jury the most intimate occurrences of the home. Advances in the psychic and related sciences may bring means of exploring unexpressed beliefs, thoughts and emotions. * * * Can it be that the Constitution affords no protection against such invasions of individual security?

* * *

Time and again this court, in giving effect to the principle underlying the Fourth Amendment, has refused to place an unduly literal construction upon it. * * *

* * *

The protection guaranteed by the amendments is much broader in scope. The makers of our Constitution undertook to secure conditions favorable to the pursuit of happiness. They recognized the significance of man's spiritual nature, of his feelings and of his intellect. They knew that only a part of the pain, pleasure and satisfactions of life are to be found in material things. They sought to protect Americans in their beliefs, their thoughts, their emotions and their sensations. They conferred, as against the government, the right to be let alone—the most comprehensive of rights and the right most valued by civilized men. To protect, that right, every unjustifiable intrusion by the government upon the privacy of the individual, whatever the means employed, must be deemed a violation of the Fourth Amendment. And the use, as evidence in a criminal proceeding, of facts ascertained by such intrusion must be deemed a violation of the Fifth.[115]

It would be difficult to imagine a clearer illustration of the difference in constitutional interpretation between reading a clause as embodying a rule and reading it as embodying a principle. It took the Court nearly four decades, but eventually, of course, the principle triumphed over the rule. Also, it is worth noting as a postscript, that when the Court finally overruled *Olmstead* and its progeny,[116] which had protected eavesdropping as well, Justice Black, dissenting, endorsed Taft's view.[117]

---

115.   277 U.S. at 473–479, 48 S.Ct. at 570–572.

116.   Katz v. United States, 389 U.S. 347, 88 S.Ct. 507 (1967), overruled both *Olmstead* and Goldman v. United States, 316 U.S. 129, 62 S. Ct. 993 (1942), which had applied the same reasoning to evidence obtained by electronic eavesdropping. The Court had questioned the viability of *Olmstead* earlier in the year in Berger v. New York, 388 U.S. 41, 87 S.Ct. 1873.

117.   In *Berger*, Justice Black summed up his views as follows:

While the electronic eavesdropping here bears some analogy to the problems with which the Fourth Amendment is concerned, I am by no means satisfied that the Amendment controls the constitutionality of such eavesdropping. As pointed out, the Amendment only bans searches and seizures of "persons, houses, papers, and effects." This literal language imports tangible things, and it would require an expansion of the language used by the framers, in the interest of "privacy" or some equally vague judge-made goal, to hold that it applies to the spoken word. It simply requires an imaginative transformation of the English language to say that conversations can be searched and words seized. * * *

388 U.S. at 78, 87 S.Ct. at 1893. The following excerpt from his dissent in *Katz* is also worth noting:

Tapping telephone wires, of course, was an unknown possibility at the time the Fourth Amendment was adopted. But eavesdropping (and wiretapping is nothing more than eavesdropping by telephone) was, as even the majority opinion in *Berger*, supra, recognized, "an ancient practice which at common law was condemned as a nuisance.

Principles often underlie rules, or are sometimes contained in rules (as when rules contain words such as "reasonable," "unjust," or "negligent"),[118] or directly interact with the facts when courts are asked to determine hard cases.[119] The failure of the absolutists to acknowledge principles in law, in addition to rules, is not only a serious flaw in itself, but contributes to additional difficulties.

2. Misrepresenting the Decisional Process

If principles are an integral part of the law and they are ambiguous, the chances for a deductive procedure that will produce

IV Blackstone, Commentaries § 168. In those days the eavesdropper listened by naked ear under the eaves of houses or their windows, or beyond their walls seeking out private discourse." 388 U.S., at 45, 87 S.Ct., at 1876. There can be no doubt that the Framers were aware of this practice, and if they had desired to outlaw or restrict the use of evidence obtained by eavesdropping, I believe that they would have used the appropriate language to do so in the Fourth Amendment. They certainly would not have left such a task to the ingenuity of language-stretching judges. No one, it seems to me, can read the debates on the Bill of Rights without reaching the conclusion that its Framers and critics well knew the meaning of the words they used, what they would be understood to mean by others, their scope and their limitations. Under these circumstances it strikes me as a charge against their scholarship, their common sense and their candor to give to the Fourth Amendment's language the eavesdropping meaning the Court imputes to it today.

* * *

Since I see no way in which the words of the Fourth Amendment can be construed to apply to eavesdropping, that closes the matter for me. In interpreting the Bill of Rights, I willingly go as far as a liberal construction of the language takes me, but I simply cannot in good conscience give a meaning to words which they have never before been thought to have and which they certainly do not have in common ordinary usage. I will not distort the words of the Amendment in order to "keep the Constitution up to date" or "to bring it into harmony with the times." It was never meant that this Court have such power, which in effect would make us a continuously functioning constitutional convention.

389 U.S. at 366, 373, 88 S.Ct. 519, 522–523. See Landynski, *In Search of Justice Black's Fourth Amendment*, 45 Fordham L.Rev. 453 (1976).

118. Dworkin, *Is Law a System of Rules?* 41.

119. See note 123, *infra.*

certainty in adjudication have been substantially reduced. There are other reasons as well for concluding that judicial decision-making cannot accurately be described as the deductive application of rules, a process which is then faithfully reported in Court opinions. It is important to clarify at the outset the claim which is being made; namely, that the process of decision has been *explained*, not merely that an opinion has been written which adequately *justifies* the decision.[120] Even if we conclude that judges do not reach their decisions deductively—if, indeed, we can accurately say very much to describe that process at all —it can still be argued that an acceptable justification can or must assume the form of deductive logic,[121] or of reasoning by analogy,[122] or of principle over policy.[123] It is also quite possible —in fact, probable—that the form, in which the justification can or must be cast to be regarded as acceptable or functional, exercises some influence both over the content of the opinion written and over the decision itself. But these, of course, are much reduced claims.

The reason why the text of a well-written opinion cannot explain the process of thinking that led up to the decision is simply that the opinion presents reconstructed logic, not the logic, or even the illogic, of reaching the decision. People simply do not reach a decision through neat, ordered thought patterns such as complex analogies; and much less do they think in syllogisms. The decision may be the product of a hunch,[124] or the process of judging may be tentative and fluid for it

> begins   *   *   *   with a conclusion more or less vaguely formed; a man ordinarily starts with such a conclusion and afterwards tries to find the premises which will substantiate

120. Wasserstrom, 25–31.

121. Miller, Principles, Rules, and Cases: The Logic of Judicial Decisions. Unpublished Ph.D. thesis, Case Western Reserve University, 1970.

122. Levi, An Introduction to Legal Reasoning (1948).

123. Dworkin, *Hard Cases*, 88 Harv.L.Rev. 1057 (1975).

124. Hutcheson, *The Judgment Intuitive:—The Function of the "Hunch" in Judicial Decision*, 14 Cornell L.Q. 274 (1929).

it. If he cannot, to his satisfaction, find proper arguments to link up his conclusion with premises which he finds acceptable, he will, unless he is arbitrary or mad, reject the conclusion and seek another.[125]

Nor does the opinion reflect—at least in a way readily identifiable to all but the judicial participants—the impact of collegial interaction, the discussion and compromise necessary to reach a decision in an appellate court composed of several judges of varied backgrounds, personalities, and political outlooks.

Even if the observations made earlier with respect to the existence and importance of principles had not already discredited the simplistic assumption that for each and every legal problem, there is a rule which furnishes the single correct answer, the deductive method itself contains no guarantee that the correct answer would be found. Syllogisms, after all, have no way of testing the truth of their premises. In the words of Justice Holmes, "You can give any conclusion a logical form." [126] That a premise may, indeed, be highly controversial—even the product of some manipulation—is reasonably well demonstrated by our previous discussion of the minor premise in Chief Justice Marshall's syllogism (pp. 22–26).

Nor is deductive logic any guide to the classification of facts in legal categories, the critical step preceding rule application and without which the latter would not be possible.[127] Yet without the guarantee that facts would be unerringly classified in the future, the treatment of like cases alike would be frustrated, no matter how clear the pre-existing rule. The fact is that no two cases are ever exactly alike; a generalization as to the likeness of their facts is a conclusion which has to be drawn.

Equally illusory is the belief that ambiguities in critical constitutional provisions can be settled by divining the intent of the framers (either of the original Constitution or of the amend-

125. Frank, Law and the Modern Mind 108 (1930).

126. Holmes, *The Path of the Law*, 10 Harv.L.Rev. 457, 466 (1897).

127. Wasserstrom, 32–33.

ments). By this means, absolutists, such as Justice Black, hope to discover clear rules imminent in the document. But as Professor William Anderson has shown,[128] this is a dubious enterprise for more than one reason: the difficulty of identifying whom we will count as framers; the incompleteness of records or other evidence of intent; the lack of a monolithic intent among those framers whose views could be identified; and the likelihood that one's perception of intent would be skewed in favor of the views of those who talked or wrote a lot. As with conclusions judges draw in regard to the classification of facts, conclusions they draw with respect to things as nebulous as the intentions of the framers can easily be made to effect their policy preferences. In the extreme case, this exercise reduces to the charade of "pick your framer" in which the judge casts about for like-minded framers to conceal what would otherwise stand out as a straight-forward value statement. Even if the process retains a detached, scholarly quality and successfully avoids the pitfalls mentioned above, there remains the ultimate objection that the framers, after all, are dead, and, in the contemporary world, their views are neither relevant nor morally binding.[129]

It is one thing to argue that rules and precedents constitute parameters within which judicial choice operates, that rules are rather like bench marks beyond which no justification could be deemed persuasive; it is quite something else to argue that there is a correct answer out there waiting to be discovered. Whether the mechanism devised is the syllogism of deductive

128. *The Intention of the Framers: A Note on Constitutional Interpretation*, 49 Am.Pol.Sci.Rev. 340 (1955).

129. The relevance of the framers' intentions pales quickly in light of the argument proffered in Rawls, A Theory of Justice (1971), for example. Though Rawls does not mention the Court, application of the principles of justice he enunci- ates would clearly reinforce Woodrow Wilson's characterization of the Court as a "constitutional convention in continuous session." For the traditional allegation of class bias in the Constitution and founding—the historical "original position"—see Beard, An Economic Interpretation of the Constitution of the United States (1913); but *cf.* Brown, Charles Beard and the Constitution (1956).

logic or the intention of the framers, the fallacy is the same: the attempt to create a judicial process in which there is no exercise of judgment.

3. *Rigidity and Unreality*

Law, anyway, has a certain unreality about it. Regardless of how one chooses to characterize the width of the principle that sufficiently justifies the instant decision or adequately reconciles it with a precedent, the fact is that it is an abstract creation. And simply because the categories created by legal principles are themselves abstract, there is an irreducible amount of unreality to them. Absolutism, however, intensifies this gap between abstraction and reality. Doubtless, it was this penchant for reification in law to the point where rules became formalistic stupidities that evoked from Dickens' Mr. Bumble the classic retort, "If the law supposes that, the law is a ass—a idiot." [130]

As the illustrations of dual federalism and Justice Black's First Amendment views show, absolute principles postulate a difference in kind which separates categories in law. Yet what seems clearest about reality is that things merge into one another; shades of gray predominate and things are rarely black or white. Process, not essence, seems to characterize real life.[131] Distinctions far more often seem to be differences in degree, and rarely in kind. But distinctions in degree move us toward seem-

---

130. Oliver Twist, Ch. 51. 1 Works of Charles Dickens 110 (1880). The legal presumption, which was the object of Mr. Bumble's scorn, was that "if a wife commits a crime in the presence of her husband she is presumed to have done it under his coercion." Holdsworth, Charles Dickens As a Legal Historian 7 (1929). The rest of what Mr. Bumble has to say is also to the point: "If that's the eye of the law, the law's a bachelor; and the worst I wish the law is, that his eye may be opened by experience—by experience." Certainly, this was the fondest wish of Holmes, too; *cf.* note 126, *supra.*

131. A good illustration of this surfaces in the abortion debate when attention is focused on the question "When does life begin?" See Justice Blackmun's discussion in Roe v. Wade, 410 U.S. 113, 159–163, 93 S.Ct. 705, 730–731 (1973). For a discussion of this continuity in process in the context of economics, see note 134, *infra.*

ingly more arbitrary, less defensible, judgments—judgments which can and will be eroded by future developments. The persuasiveness of principled decision-making lies in the fact that it looks toward the creation of distinctions in kind. Absolutism seeks certainty and therefore aims at the imposition of a static order in the midst of continuous change.

The consequences that flow from an uncompromising commitment to justice defined as adherence to the application of fixed, absolute, legal principles are both several and significant. Beyond a point, this singular characterization of justice and the attendant social benefit of stability are overserved. Insistence on absolutism is counterproductive to the political system. At the least, it cuts off experimentation and innovation in public policy without which it is difficult, if not impossible, to address new public problems.[132] By demanding that problems be approached only in terms of generalized rules, it frustrates dealing with problems which demand *particular* solutions (*i. e.,* responses to demands which are unique and where the approach taken has to be groomed to the specifics of the problem).[133] At its worst, of course, blind devotion to fixed principles may forestall a response to pressing public problems to the point where a genuine crisis results jeopardizing the entire political system. Surely, this is one of the lessons to be learned from the Court's preoccupation with constitutional doctrines such as dual federalism and substantive due process which allowed it to dictate the country's economic policy not only before but through much of the Great

132. See, *e. g.,* Duncan v. Louisiana, 391 U.S. 145, 193, 88 S.Ct. 1444, 1472 (1968) (dissenting opinion of Harlan, J.); Shapiro v. Thompson, 394 U.S. 618, 677, 89 S.Ct. 1322, 1354 (1969) (dissenting opinion of Harlan, J.); Powell v. Texas, 392 U.S. 514, 535–537, 88 S.Ct. 2145, 2155–2156 (1968).

133. Menninger, The Crime of Punishment, Chs. 1–2, 4 (1969). See also the Court's decisions attempting to strike a balance between rights and rehabilitation in the disposition of cases involving juvenile offenders, In re Gault, 387 U.S. 1, 87 S.Ct. 1428 (1967); In re Winship, 397 U.S. 358, 90 S.Ct. 1068 (1970); McKeiver v. Pennsylvania, 403 U.S. 528, 91 S.Ct. 1976 (1971); Breed v. Jones, 421 U.S. 519, 95 S. Ct. 1779 (1975).

Depression, when it impeded legislative efforts, both national and state, to conform public policy to the belatedly-recognized realities of an interdependent economic system.[134]

As the same chapter in our national history showed, the cost of absolutism was also heavy for the Court. While it is more than likely that public nostalgia and reverence for the Rule of Law concept saved the Court by prompting an overwhelmingly Democratic Congress to turn thumbs down on FDR's Court-packing proposal, still, the Court would not have had to face the whirlwind in the first place had it leavened its decisions with a bit more sophisticated jurisprudence. In any case, if it is true, as has been speculated,[135] that public acceptance of the traditional mythology has seriously eroded, absolutism may no longer blunt political criticism.

4. Considering the Consequences

The steadfast refusal of absolutists to address the immediate consequences of the decision at hand presents additional problems. This unwillingness to consider the possible or probable effects of a decision before making it is motivated both by a desire to avoid what is thought to be arbitrary adjudication in the chronic fitting of rulings to the unique features of each new dispute and to avoid the possibility of partiality to either of the affected parties. This means that absolutists are obliged either to

134. For opinions which note or discuss the interrelationship of component parts of the economic process, see Schechter Poultry Corp. v. United States, 295 U.S. 495, 554–555, 55 S.Ct. 837, 853 (1935) (concurring opinion of Cardozo, J.); United States v. Butler, 297 U.S. 1, 78, 56 S.Ct. 312, 324 (1936) (dissenting opinion of Stone, J.); Carter v. Carter Coal Co., 298 U.S. 238, 324–330, 56 S.Ct. 855, 879–881 (1936) (dissenting opinion of Cardozo, J.); National Labor Relations Board v. Jones & Laughlin Steel Corp., 301 U.S. 1, 57 S.Ct. 615 (1937); Steward Machine Co. v. Davis, 301 U.S. 548, 57 S.Ct. 883 (1937); United States v. Darby, 312 U.S. 100, 61 S.Ct. 451 (1941); Wickard v. Filburn, 317 U.S. 111, 63 S.Ct. 82 (1942).

135. Shapiro, *Stability and Change in Judicial Decision-Making: Incrementalism or Stare Decisis,* 2 Law in Transition Q. 135, 136 (1965); see also Shapiro, *Neutral Principles,* 600.

reach decisions without regard for their consequences, or else to examine all of the possible consequences, anticipating a sizable number of future like cases in order to frame a rule that will cover all of them. Pursuit of these strategies, however, tends either to produce disturbing results or to make unreasonable demands.

The easiest place to begin is with the total disregard for the consequences of a decision. Precisely because there is no feedback of possible consequences on making the decision, there is no way in which the demands of conflicting interests can be taken into account and a compromise achieved. The result is that the application of rules, which have about them an all-or-nothing quality, yields the total satisfaction of some interests to the total exclusion of others. Disregard for the consequences, therefore, has not infrequently produced results generally regarded as absurd. Under Justice Black's reading of the First Amendment, for example, there will be *no* libel laws, no matter how savage and irresponsible the attacks on people's reputations; the freedom of the press and media to report criminal proceedings will go totally unregulated, no matter how frenzied, biased, or intrusive the coverage. And, drawing an illustration from dual federalism, the E. C. Knight Company will go completely unregulated by the federal government, despite the fact that the sprawling conglomerate controlled 98 per cent of the sugar refining capacity of the country. Indeed, the proposition that anyone, much less high government officials, should regularly make important decisions without regard to their consequences is absurd in itself.

Because decisions justified by recourse to absolute principles, instead of those more narrowly drawn to the particular contours of the case at hand, are more likely to have a broader impact on the rest of society, sometimes there is an attempt to retreat from the full impact of a rule in the face of its increasing absurdity, its high cost, or its disruptive effects, while, at the same time, maintaining doctrinal purity. A classic example, in the eyes of Justice John Harlan, Jr., was the Court's treatment of the jury trial guarantee in criminal cases following its incorporation in *Duncan* v. *Louisiana*.[136] A perennial critic of incorporation, anyway, Justice Harlan proceeded to blow the whistle in *Williams* v. *Florida,* as the Court, in his view, watered down the meaningfulness of the jury trial guarantee after it had found that blind imposition of the Sixth Amendment requirement on the states threatened dire consequences for an already overloaded criminal justice system:

> The historical argument by which the Court undertakes to justify its view that the Sixth Amendment does not require 12-member juries is, in my opinion, much too thin to mask the true thrust of this decision. The decision evinces, I think, a recognition that the "incorporationist" view of the Due Process Clause of the Fourteenth Amendment, which underlay *Duncan* and is now carried forward * * * must be tempered to allow the States more elbow room in ordering their own criminal systems. With that much I agree. But to accomplish this by diluting constitutional protections within the federal system itself is something to which I cannot possibly subscribe. Tempering the rigor of *Duncan* should be done forthrightly, by facing up to the fact that at least in this area the "incorporation" doctrine does not fit well with our federal structure, and by the same token that *Duncan* was wrongly decided.[137]

His conclusion appeared to receive further verification with the Court's subsequent rulings in *Johnson* v. *Louisiana* and *Apodaca* v. *Oregon*,[138] allowing for conviction by less than a unanimous vote. The jury trial guarantee remained incorporated, but it had been substantially diluted.

The reason why Justice Black could afford to overlook considering the consequences in his First Amendment decisions—the reason why, in other words, he could appear to abdicate

136. 391 U.S. 145, 88 S.Ct. 1444 (1968).

137. 399 U.S. 78, 118, 90 S.Ct. 1893, 1915 (1970) (concurring in the result).

138. 406 U.S. 404, 92 S.Ct. 1628 (1972).

judgment [139]—and not be subjected generally to the kind of criticism he received for his position on the unconstitutionality of libel laws, for example, is that principles can be both absolute *and narrow.* The fact of the matter is that Black's First Amendment precepts, in areas other than libel, obscenity, fair trial-free press, and association, provide much less protection for expression generally than may appear at first glance, or than may be connoted by Justice Black's repeated declarations that "freedom of speech is absolute." The cumulative effect of his time, place, and manner qualifications on speech—the factors which add something to "speech" so that it becomes "conduct"—shrink the scope of protected expression to a remarkable degree.[140] If Black did not need to involve himself in the intricate line-drawing that separates "symbolic speech" from unprotected expression, for example, it is equally true that he did not vote to uphold the civil liberties claim there either, unlike Douglas or even Harlan, Jr.[141]

139. I say "appears to" because the deductive application of such an integrated system of rules as Black purports to discover in the First Amendment tends to camouflage the exercise of discretion. In fact, the exercise of discretion on a case-by-case basis, one could argue, has simply been replaced by inventing an entire interpretive framework which is then rigidly followed. This is no less an exercise of discretion, though, from one standpoint, it is perhaps more consistent. See Mendelson, *Hugo Black and Judicial Discretion,* 85 Pol.Sci.Q. 17 (1970). But the absolutist interpretive structure did not spring full-blown from the Constitution even for Justice Black, and the discretionary element is more clearly revealed when we see the emergence of these rules over time. Further, it has been suggested, the absolutist stance is less a reflection of sober reason than a headiness resulting from the nonresponsibility implicit in writing dissenting opinions. Resnick, *Black, Douglas, and Absolutes: Some Suggestions for a New Perspective on the Supreme Court,* 47 J. Urban L. 765 (1970).

140. See Yarbrough, *Justice Black and His Critics on Speech-Plus and Symbolic Speech,* 52 Texas L.Rev. 257 (1974); see also Yarbrough, *Justice Black, the First Amendment, and the Burger Court,* 46 Miss.L.J. 203 (1975).

141. Two of the most interesting examples are Street v. New York, 394 U.S. 576, 89 S.Ct. 1354 (1969), and Cohen v. California, 403 U.S. 15, 91 S.Ct. 1780 (1971). In both cases Black dissented *and Harlan wrote the Court's opinion.*

The alternative to justice which is literally blind is justice which is calculatedly blind. Thus Professor Wechsler would not have judges eschew discretion, but instead would direct their ingenuity toward resolving the present case by formulating a generalized solution, one that "transcend[s] the immediate result that is achieved" because it is "tested not only by the instant case but by others that the principles imply." Whatever other problems inhere in this prescription—how this instruction can be squared with the canon of judicial practice that admonishes judges to decide only the case before them,[142] for instance—it is clear that the decisional process required to take into account all of the consequences would be demanding—indeed, too demanding.

The ultra-rational, comprehensive calculation essential to the process Wechsler has in mind has been convincingly rejected in the political science literature.[143] Among other things, the systematic canvass and evaluation of all possible consequences prior to reaching final decision is a procedure not adapted to man's limited problem-solving capabilities, or to the inadequacy of available information; and it is far too costly to be worthwhile. The ranking of priorities and the discrete evaluation of the effects of each decision alternative, steps essential to such rational decision-making, fail to take into account the necessary continuous reciprocal adjustment of ends and means in the making of decisions,[144] and are ill-suited to the decision-maker's frequent need to make strategic political moves.[145] Far from strengthen-

---

142. Deutsch, 197–198.

143. Lindblom, *The Science of "Muddling Through,"* 19 Pub.Admin.Rev. 79 (1959); Braybrooke and Lindblom, A Strategy of Decision (1963); Lindblom, the Intelligence of Democracy (1965). A review of the "neutral principles" literature in decision-making terms, linking it with the rational-comprehensive or synoptic approach, appears in Snortland and Stanga, *Neutral Principles and Decision-Making Theory: An Alternative to Incementalism,* 41 Geo.Wash.L.Rev. 1006 (1973).

144. Fuller, *An Afterword: Science and the Judicial Process,* 79 Harv. L.Rev. 1604, 1626–1627 (1966); see also Shapiro, *supra,* note 135.

145. Shapiro, Law and Politics in the Supreme Court, Chs. 2–6; Shapiro, The Supreme Court and

ing the Court, some observers have suggested that insistence upon judicial adherence to the rational-comprehensive approach to decision-making, implicit in the call for "neutral principles," would most likely result in paralysis through analysis, ultimately forcing the Court into an insignificant role in the political system because its reasoning would always be less than the optimum.[146]

5. Conflicting Constitutional Guarantees

Another serious flaw in the absolutist approach lies in the faulty assumption that constitutional principles would not collide with one another. As indicated earlier (p. 56), this structural feature of the absolutist framework was essential to avoid forcing the judge into a position where he would have to strike a balance between conflicting constitutional values. The difficulties with such interest balancing are, of course, that it repudiates a balance ostensibly already struck in the Constitution itself, and it denies the possibility of a deductive application of what were also assumed to be clear constitutional provisions.

It is obvious that the amendments that make up the Bill of Rights contain clearly conflicting guarantees: the First Amendment's freedom of the press can collide with the Fifth Amendment's requirement of due process and the Sixth Amendment's protection of trial before an impartial jury; [147] the First Amendment's freedom of speech can collide with the Fifth

Administrative Agencies, Chs. 3–4 (1968).

146. Rostow, *American Legal Realism and the Sense of the Profession*, 34 Rocky Mt.L.Rev. 123, 145 (1962).

147. See Irvin v. Doud, 366 U.S. 717, 81 S.Ct. 1639 (1961); Rideau v. Louisiana, 373 U.S. 723, 83 S.Ct. 1417 (1963); Estes v. Texas, 381 U.S. 532, 85 S.Ct. 1628 (1965); Sheppard v. Maxwell, 384 U.S. 333,

86 S.Ct. 1507 (1966); Times-Picayune Pub. Corp. v. Schulingkamp, 419 U.S. 1301, 95 S.Ct. 1 (1974); Murphy v. Florida, 421 U.S. 794, 95 S.Ct. 2031 (1975); Nebraska Press Ass'n v. Stuart, 427 U.S. 539, 96 S.Ct. 2791 (1976); Oklahoma Pub. Co. v. District Court, 430 U.S. 308, 97 S.Ct. 1045 (1977); Dobbert v. Florida, 432 U.S. 282, 97 S.Ct. 2290 (1977). See also Calley v. Callaway, 382 F.Supp. 650 (1974), *reversed* 519 F.2d 184 (1975).

Amendment's guarantee that private property not be taken for public use without due process;[148] the First Amendment's freedom of the press can interfere with the right to privacy which the Court has found in the penumbras of several amendments.[149] Examples of this sort abound. Indeed, such contradictions may surface within the same amendment, as with the First Amendment's ban on the establishment of religion and its simultaneous assurance of the free exercise of religious belief.[150] Probably the most concise statement of why an absolutist approach is therefore impossible appears in Chief Justice Burger's opinion for the Court in *Walz* v. *Tax Commission of the City of New York*:

> The Establishment and Free Exercise Clauses of the First Amendment are not the most precisely drawn portions of the Constitution. The sweep of the absolute prohibitions in the Religion Clauses may have been calculated; but the purpose

148. See note 59, *supra*.

149. In addition to the libel cases cited in note 47, *supra*, see Gertz v. Robert Welch, Inc., 418 U.S. 323, 94 S.Ct. 2997 (1974); Cantrell v. Forest City Pub. Co., 419 U.S. 245, 95 S.Ct. 465 (1974); Cox Broadcasting Co. v. Cohn, 420 U.S. 469, 95 S.Ct. 1029 (1975); Time, Inc. v. Firestone, 424 U.S. 448, 96 S.Ct. 958 (1976); Zacchini v. Scripps-Howard Broadcasting Co., 433 U.S. 562, 97 S.Ct. 2849 (1977). See also Dionisopoulos and Ducat, The Right to Privacy (1976).

150. A classic illustration is Braunfeld v. Brown, 366 U.S. 599, 81 S.Ct. 1144 (1961). See also Everson v. Board of Education, 330 U.S. 1, 67 S.Ct. 504 (1947); McCollum v. Board of Education, 333 U.S. 203, 68 S.Ct. 461 (1948); Zorach v. Clauson, 343 U.S. 306, 72 S.Ct. 679 (1952); McGowan v. Maryland, 366 U.S. 420, 81 S.Ct. 1101 (1961); Engel v. Vitale, 370 U.S. 421, 82 S.Ct. 1261 (1962); Abington Township School District v. Schempp, 374 U.S. 203, 83 S.Ct. 1560 (1963); Sherbert v. Verner, 374 U.S. 398, 83 S.Ct. 1790 (1963); Board of Education v. Allen, 392 U.S. 236, 88 S.Ct. 1923 (1968); Walz v. Tax Commission of City of New York, 397 U.S. 664, 90 S.Ct. 1409 (1970); Lemon v. Kurtzman, 403 U.S. 602, 91 S.Ct. 2105 (1971); Tilton v. Richardson, 403 U.S. 672, 91 S.Ct. 2091 (1971); Wisconsin v. Yoder, 406 U.S. 205, 92 S.Ct. 1526 (1972); Committee for Public Education and Religious Liberty v. Nyquist, 413 U.S. 756, 93 S.Ct. 2955 (1973); Meek v. Pittenger, 421 U.S. 349, 95 S.Ct. 1753 (1975); Roemer v. Board of Public Works of Maryland, 426 U.S. 736, 96 S.Ct. 2337 (1976); Wolman v. Walter, 433 U.S. 229, 97 S.Ct. 2593 (1977).

was to state an objective not to write a statute. In attempting to articulate the scope of the two Religion Clauses, the Court's opinions reflect the limitations inherent in formulating general principles on a case-by-case basis. The considerable internal inconsistency in the opinions of the Court derives from what, in retrospect, may have been too sweeping utterances on aspects of these clauses that seemed clear in relation to the particular cases but have limited meaning as general principles.

The Court has struggled to find a neutral course between the two Religion Clauses, both of which are cast in absolute terms, and either of which, if expanded to a logical extreme, would tend to clash with the other. *   *   *

*   *   *

The course of constitutional neutrality in this area cannot be an absolutely straight line; rigidity could well defeat the basic purpose of these provisions, which is to insure that no religion be sponsored or favored, none commanded, and none inhibited. The general principle deducible from the First Amendment and all that has been said by the Court is this: that we will not tolerate either governmentally established religion or governmental interference with religion. Short of those expressly proscribed governmental acts there is room for play in the joints productive of a benevolent neutrality which will permit religious exercise to exist without sponsorship and without interference.

Each value judgment under the Religion Clauses must therefore turn on whether particular acts in question are intended to establish or interfere with religious beliefs and practices or have the effect of doing so. Adherence to the policy of neutrality that derives from an accommodation of the Establishment and Free Exercise Clauses has prevented the kind of involvement that would tip the balance toward government control of churches or governmental restraint on religious practice.[151]

Nor, as the discussion in Chapter 3 shows (pp. 136–145), is absolutism likely to be any more tenable when dealing with principles of the constitutional scheme outside the Bill of Rights.

151. 397 U.S. 664, 668–670, 90 S.Ct.
1409, 1411–1412 (1970).

Symptomatic of the dilemma in which Justice Black found himself in this regard was his behavior in *Sheppard* v. *Maxwell*.[152] That case, you may recall, constituted one of the Warren Court's most important encounters with the conflict between fair trial and free press. The Court voted to overturn Sam Sheppard's murder conviction because of the prejudicial impact of press and media coverage on the trial; Justice Black dissented *without opinion*.[153] This does not mean that it would be impossible to break the stalemate between competing constitutional guarantees by prioritizing them through a set of interlocking principles.[154] Certainly it would not have been possible for Justice Black, however, since the Constitution itself contains no such hierarchy of rights.

6. *Justice and the Like Treatment of Like Cases*

Especially serious is the inadequate notion of justice implicit in the absolutist approach. For the fact is that people may be treated equally under the law and be treated with equal wretchedness. Great deprivation of freedom can coexist with the treatment of like cases alike because equal treatment is a hedge against arbitrariness, not repression.[155] Consider, for example, the following oft-quoted excerpt from Justice Jackson's dissent in *Shaughnessy* v. *United States ex rel. Mezei*:

> Only the untaught layman or the charlatan lawyer can answer that procedures matter not. Procedural fairness and regularity are of the indispensable essence of liberty. Severe substantive laws can be endured if they are fairly and impartially applied. Indeed, if put to the choice, one might well prefer to live under Soviet substantive law applied in good faith by our common law procedures than under our substantive law enforced by Soviet procedural practices. * * * [156]

152. 384 U.S. 333, 86 S.Ct. 1507 (1966).

153. 384 U.S. at 363, 86 S.Ct. at 1523.

154. Miller, *supra*, note 121, resolves the difficulty of two conflicting principles by selecting the principle supporting the greater number of extant rules. Principles, Rules, and Cases 170.

155. Shklar, 15, 17.

156. 345 U.S. 206, 224, 73 S.Ct. 625, 635 (1953).

To ask which we would prefer is not to show that our choice is just, but simply that there are degrees of injustice. Surely, Justice Jackson is right when he argues that equal, regularized treatment is necessary to a free society, but that is not all there is to it. It may be a necessary, but it is not a sufficient, condition. That we would make the same choice Justice Jackson thought we would seemed apparent to de Tocqueville too, though he put it in harsher terms:

> I think democratic peoples have a natural taste for liberty; left to themselves, they will seek it, cherish it, and be sad if it is taken from them. But their passion for equality is ardent, insatiable, eternal, and invincible. They want equality in freedom, and if they cannot have that, they still want equality in slavery. They will put up with poverty, servitude, and barbarism, but they will not endure aristocracy.[157]

Equality, then, may be the bottom line, but we need not set our sights so low. And to do so is to take the "if" clause in de Tocqueville's next to the last sentence as a statement of reality, which it is not. A framework of constitutional interpretation, therefore, must not only address the equal sharing of rights and obligations, but the substance of those liberties and responsibilities as well.

The preference of absolutists for the narrow, almost brittle, conception of justice as something akin to equal protection is a reflection of the wall that has been built between law and morals. To broach the *substance* of constitutional liberties is to risk a discussion of what is a "fundamental" right, of what is a "fair" trial, and so on. And it is precisely because there is no authoritative definition for such terms that makes such discussions so distasteful to them.

157. Democracy in America 506 (Mayer, ed. 1969).

Chapter 3

The Balancing of Interests

Absolutism, as we saw in Chapter 2, justifies the claim to judicial review for reasons of both the substance and style of Chief Justice Marshall's opinion in *Marbury* v. *Madison*. If the Court's unique function consists of doing justice through the application of rules, the exercise of judicial review is thought to be implicit in the adjudicative function. However, to the extent that the criticisms laid against absolutism cast doubt upon the decision-making distinctiveness of the judicial process,[1] the capacity to justify the review power depreciates accordingly. Once the commonality of the judicial process with other governmental processes is recognized, the focus of discussion shifts abruptly to considerations of prudence in judicial intervention and the relation of courts to quite a different concept of justice.[2]

1. Consider, for example, the distinction between courts and other institutions of government implicit in the following paragraph:

The distinction, then, between a legal and a political issue turns on the amount and intensity of the contention about the interest that is being furthered rather than any distinction in the reasoning process or the methods used to dispose of the issue. What will be "legal" and what will be "political" can be determined only by looking at the entire field of activity. The distinction is analogous to that between policy and administration. These terms continue to be useful, but we no longer insist upon discussing administration as though it existed outside the process of policy-making nor do we insist that administrative behavior cannot be discussed as part of that process.

Peltason, *A Political Science of Public Law*, 34 Sw.Soc.Sci.Q. 51, 52 (1953).

2. Arguments for the supremacy of one or another branch of government are implicitly, if not explicitly, linked to assertions that a particular brand of justice is justifiably dominant. Thus the unique function fulfilled by the judiciary to justify its dominance is the treatment of like cases alike (Chapter 2) or the guarantee of substantive equality (Chapter 4). Since the argument for judicial self-restraint is a concession to legislative supremacy, the argument is transformed into judicial respect for justice defined as majority

Toward Balance: The Weighing of Interests

Sensitive to the flaws in absolutism, a second mode of constitutional interpretation, which I will call the balancing of interests,[3] focuses on the function of judges as allocators of rights and resources in society. In the course of rendering decisions, judges are thought to aim at an accommodation or balance of society's conflicting interests.[4]

The litigants who appear in court personify more than individual claims; behind them lurk larger social interests.[5] That

rule. Likewise, those who assert that the executive should dominate argue that the President is uniquely endowed with some capacity to discern the public interest in a corporate sense. Theodore Roosevelt "declined to adopt the view that what was imperatively necessary for the Nation could not be done by the President unless he could find some specific authorization to do it." Rather, according to his Stewardship Theory, Roosevelt "acted for the public welfare, * * * for the common well-being of all our people, whenever and in whatever manner was necessary, unless prevented by direct constitutional or legislative prohibition." An Autobiography 388–389 (1913). Woodrow Wilson asserted that the President "is the representative of no constituency, but of the whole people. When he speaks in his true character, he speaks for no special interest." This was so, Wilson observed, because "[t]he nation as a whole has chosen him, and is conscious that it has no other political spokesman. His is the only national voice in affairs." Constitutional Government in the United States 68 (1908). The executive is similarly imbued with a

special understanding of what is in the public interest in Lippmann, The Public Philosophy (1955).

3. Known in legal philosophy as "sociological jurisprudence." See Chapter 1, note 54.

4. In addition to the works cited in Chapter 1, note 54, the discussion of interest balancing which follows draws substantially on the contributions of Dean Pound; see also his Jurisprudence (5 vols. 1959); *A Survey of Social Interests*, 57 Harv.L.Rev. 1 (1943); *The Theory of Judicial Decision*, 36 Harv.L. Rev. 641 (1923); *Interests of Personality*, 28 Harv.L.Rev. 343 (1915). For an excellent summary of Pound's thought and a presentation of his theory that, in fact, is better than Pound himself, see McLean, *Roscoe Pound's Theory of Interests and the Furtherance of Western Civilization*, 41 Il Politico 5 (1976).

5. From this notion that litigants represented "group interests" developed the later idea of "litigation pressure" in the political science literature, that litigants were the tools of "interest groups." Because of the prohibitive expense of

judges are expected to be significantly influenced by precedent in the disposition of future cases reinforces the notion that the judgment is not merely for the plaintiff or the defendant in a civil case, or for the state or the defendant in a criminal case, but for the satisfaction of some social interest at the expense of another social interest. Since each of the contending social interests cannot be entirely satisfied, political choice is inescapable, whether judges choose to openly acknowledge it or not. However, since court opinions which adopt the interest balancing framework usually address claims in the form of social interests, as distinct from the depoliticizing tendency of absolutists to frame cases in terms of the rights (or interests) of individuals, judicial opinions are much more likely to be seen for what they really are; that is, as statements of policy.[6]

An approach to constitutional interpretation which structures court opinions in terms of the interests likely to be touched by the decision in a case is unlikely to promote the view that a judge stands helpless to affect the result. This proposition seems hardly contestable once one recognizes that most judges —certainly those on the federal bench, at least—have spent years in the political process prior to their appointment and whose selection itself was often a highly-charged political act.[7]

the legal process, these interest groups, it was alleged, generated and managed "test cases," supported parties to suits which were conductive to the making of policy by furnishing funding and legal aid, and even exerted a gate-keeping function over the cases that came before the courts. See Truman, The Governmental Process, Ch. 15 (1951); Vose, *Litigation as a Form of Pressure Group Activity*, 319 Annals Am.Acad.Pol.Soc.Sci. 20 (1958); Vose, Caucasians Only (1959); N.A.A.C.P. v. Button, 371 U.S. 415, 429–430, 83 S.Ct. 328, 336 (1963); Birkby and Murphy, *Interest Group Conflict in the Judicial*

Arena: The First Amendment and Group Access to the Courts, 42 Texas L.Rev. 1018 (1964). *But cf.* Hakman, *Lobbying the Supreme Court—An Appraisal of "Political Science Folklore*," 35 Fordham L. Rev. 15 (1966); Hakman, *The Supreme Court's Political Environment: The Processing of Noncommercial Litigation*, in Grossman and Tanenhaus, eds., Frontiers of Judicial Research, Ch. 7 (1969).

6. Pound, *A Survey of Social Interests*, 4–5.

7. See Chase, Federal Judges: The Appointing Process (1972); Danel-

It would be naive of us to expect judges to check their political values and experiences at the door when they don their black robes. If all we were interested in when we selected them was their adeptness at the mechanics of legal research, we would have hired their law clerks instead, or chosen judges on the basis of their bar examination scores, not through a process of political appointment.[8]

Yet, if awareness of the opportunity for judicial discretion gives rise to its exercise, it is equally true that the perception is usually accompanied by a sense of responsibility for the decision and thus an appreciation of the consequences of that decision. It is not surprising, then, to find that the approach to judicial decision-making, taken by interest balancers, is much like that taken by political actors staffing coordinate institutions of government who must themselves choose between rival group interests on issues of the day.[9]

ski, A Supreme Court Justice Is Appointed (1964); Grossman, Lawyers and Judges: The ABA and the Politics of Judicial Selection (1965); Harris, Decision (1971); Shogan, A Question of Judgment: The Fortas Case and the Struggle for the Supreme Court (1972); Todd, Justice on Trial: The Case of Louis D. Brandeis (1968).

8. Despite this, debates over the alternative methods of judicial selection proceed as if technical expertise were the only relevant variable. In fact, campaigns at the state level to "take the judges out of politics" by introducing what is euphemistically called "merit selection" do nothing of the sort; the process is simply converted to one of subterranean politics. Watson and Downing, The Politics of the Bench and the Bar (1969). Though much has been written about the

methods of judicial selection, the topic remains one of the least *researched* areas of public law. The literature abounds in endless speculations, wishful thinking, generalizing from bizarre examples, and self-serving promotion by the bar associations. Ducat and Flango, *In Search of Qualified Judges: An Inquiry Into the Relevance of Judicial Selection Research,* paper presented at the annual meeting of the American Political Science Ass'n, Sept., 1975. Describing the astounding repetitiveness that characterizes half a century of judicial selection "research," Professor Sheldon Goldman observed that the literature largely "goes in one era and out the other."

9. Shapiro, *Stability and Change in Judicial Decision-Making: Incrementalism or Stare Decisis?* 2 Law in Transition Q. 134 (1965);

The decision-making literature in political science describes this common approach as incrementalism or "muddling through." [10] Due to time, cost, informational, and political constraints, decision-makers focus on the margins of public policy, attempting to understand how several alternative proposals for change differ in potential impact from each other and from the *status quo*. Resolution of a conflict at hand between competing social values is not effected by formulation of clear guidelines which preempt recurring clashes in the future, but is instead phrased in terms of "how much of one value is worth sacrificing at the margin * * * to achieve an increment of another." [11] Such an approach to decision-making is marked by restricted focus on the alternatives to be considered, limited examination of the consequences (to those that are reasonably foreseeable), adjustment of objectives and policies over a string of decisions, and recognized interaction between facts and policies such that data can change policy alternatives. As political institutions in a political system, courts, no less than other agencies of government, must also temper their decisions with a consideration of the need for making strategic political moves.[12] The upshot of all this is the generation and evaluation of public policy by fits and starts. It is a process geared toward moving away from ills and discomfitures rather than striving toward goals. This characterization of the decision-making process fits well with our perception of the American system as decentralized and pluralistic, an arrangement that frequently gives us "government by crisis." In fact, the process by which the whole political system operates appears to be a magnification of the approach which describes how individual policy-makers work, what Reinhold Niebuhr

see also Weiler, *Two Models of Judicial Decision-Making*, 46 Can. Bar Rev. 406 (1968).

10. See Chapter 2, note 143.

11. Braybrooke and Lindblom, A Strategy of Decision 88 (1962)

[hereafter referred to as Braybrooke and Lindblom].

12. Shapiro, *Political Jurisprudence*, 52 Ky.L.J. 294 (1964); see also Chapter 2, note 145.

called "a process of finding proximate solutions for insoluble problems." [13]

This decision-making strategy is epitomized by the common law tradition of adjudication [14] according to which principles and rules of law developed incrementally through the decision of discrete cases. Interest balancing appears firmly rooted in this inductive approach. Interest balancers are people who say "first courts, then rules." [15] Law becomes a statement of a trend in the accumulated solutions to problems. The process proceeds case by case so that a string of decisions emerges. From these decisions are gathered common principles as to how rival interests will be treated. These precepts are continually tested and refined in the adjudication of future cases. From chronic replication, some of the principles and rules harden over time, while others fall into disuse. Surviving rules and principles also come to be qualified as varying fact situations in cases provoke modifications as to how certain interests will be treated under peculiar conditions. New cases call forth new principles or further expand or chop away at old ones. Since courts have little control over the kind, rate, or order of problems brought before them, the development of these propositions of law will often proceed in an uneven, disjointed, frequently a hit-or-miss fashion. Professor Rostow sums it up this way:

> Any lawyer who has worked through a line of cases about easements or trust or bills and notes or any other legal subject, knows that no court has ever achieved perfection in its reasoning in its first, or indeed in its twentieth opinion on the same subject. Law professors make their modest livings

13. The Children of Light and the Children of Darkness 118 (1944).

14. See Llewellyn, The Common Law Tradition (1960). It is no coincidence that critics of the formalistic, mechanical jurisprudence that dominated American law in the late nineteenth and early twentieth centuries presented their discussions of the judicial function in the context of the development of the common law; see Holmes, The Common Law (1881); Gray, The Nature and Sources of the Law (1909); Pound, An Introduction to the Philosophy of Law (1922).

15. Fuller, *Adjudication and the Rule of Law*, 54 Proc.Am.Soc.Int.L. 1, 6 (1960).

in large part by dissecting judicial opinions, and helping their students to see how imperfectly most of them satisfy Professor Wechsler's rule, and other, even more important standards for the evaluation of judicial action. In the nature of law as a continuing process, constantly meeting the shocks of social change, and of changes in people's ideas of justice, this characteristic of law must be true, even for our greatest and most insightful judges. They grapple with a new problem, deal with it over and over again, as its dimensions change. They settle one case, and find themselves tormented by its unanticipated progeny. They back and fill, zig and zag, groping through the mist for a line of thought which will in the end satisfy their standards of craft and their vision of the policy of the community they must try to interpret. The opinions written at the end of such a cycle rarely resemble those composed at the beginning. Exceptions emerge, and new formulations of what once looked like clear principle. If we take advantage of hindsight, we can see in any line of cases and statutes a pattern of growth, and of response to changing conditions and changing ideas. There are cases that lead nowhere, stunted branches and healthy ones. Often the judges who participated in the process could not have described the tree that was growing. Yet the felt necessities of society have their impact, and the law emerges, gnarled, asymmetrical, but very much alive—the product of a forest, not of a nursery garden, nor of the gardener's art.[16]

Precedent in such a scheme serves several useful functions: guidance, stability, efficiency, and equality.[17] As the crystalization of experience it is certainly entitled to great weight. Even so, precedents do not apply themselves. They form the perimeter which usually marks the outer boundary of discretion. But considerable leeway often remains within, for it is possible, perhaps probable, that more than one precedent or line of precedents will surface as plausible avenues along which to dispose of a given case, particularly if it is a novel dispute. If so,

16. Rostow, *American Legal Realism and the Sense of the Profession*, 34 Rocky Mt.L.Rev. 123, 141–142 (1962) [now University of Colorado Law Review]. Reprinted by permission.

17. Wasserstrom, The Judicial Decision 60–73 (1961) [hereafter referred to as Wasserstrom].

determination of which road to take will be a matter for the judge's discretion. Usually, the justification for choosing one precedent or line of precedents will be presented in the form of an analogy [18] like that rather simply sketched in Figure 4. A typical opinion may layer several analogies supported by reasoning which grows quite complex. The opinion, if it is well written, elaborates the factual similarities between the precedent(s) viewed as controlling and the instant case. The choice may be bolstered by evidence drawn from the social sciences or other empirical research.[19] Other precedents are distinguished away

FIGURE 4. SIMPLIFIED VERSION OF REASONING BY
ANALOGY FROM PRECEDENTS

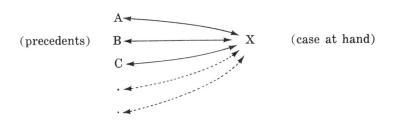

(precedents)   A   B   C   X   (case at hand)

The pattern of facts in A (B, C, . . .) is sufficiently like the pattern of facts in X (in certain respects which are then specified) such that the holding in A(B, C, . . .) should also be the holding in X. (Implicit in the analogy is a rule or principle which connects a common fact pattern with a particular consequence).

18. Levi, An Introduction to Legal Reasoning (1948); Levi, *The Nature of Judicial Reasoning*, in Hook, ed., Law and Philosophy 263–281 (1964).

19. See Rosen, The Supreme Court and Social Science (1972); Simon, ed., Sociology of Law, Pts. I, III (1968). Because of the tentative nature of social science findings, judicial opinions which lean heavily on them become equally precarious; see Stell v. Savannah-Chatham County Board of Education, 220 F.Supp. 667 (S.D.Ga.1963), *reversed* 333 F.2d 55 (5th Cir. 1964). Further, increased reliance upon empirical findings requires that the judges themselves become experts

by the examination of critical differences that weaken their analogy to the case at hand or discredit their principles as viable policies. Depending upon the intricacy of the present case and the number and ambiguity of available precedents, cases can be easy or hard; that is, the analogies can be more or less obvious. And to some extent, judges can make hard cases seem easy and easy cases seem hard by the way they choose to portray the facts. Suffice it to say, in the absence of compelling precedents which yield unshakable analogies to the instant case, judges retain leeway to affect the decision and—by extending the principle(s) implicit in one precedent as opposed to another—to color the future growth of the law; in a word, judges can manipulate precedents to achieve policy goals in ambiguous cases.

But opinions, as we have already noted, do not explain the process of decision, though it might plausibly be argued that opinions structured along the lines of interest balancing stand a better chance of drawing closer to it than opinions framed in syllogisms. Be that as it may, in fact the criteria for choosing among competing interests have never been stated with precision, or even reasonable clarity, for that matter. Proponents of the framework maintain that the balance should be struck so as to maximize as many interests as possible [20] consistent with the political and ethical postulates that form the society's creed; that is, the collection of commonly-held values and traditions that make for a community.[21] (In American society, such val-

---

in research design, a role for which they may be ill-suited by training.

It is important to differentiate the "sociology in law" (i. e., the use of social science evidence in the making of legal decisions) one finds in interest balancing from the "sociology of law" which is the empirical study of how legal institutions function and change. For examples of the latter, see ibid., Pts. II, IV; Friedman and Macaulay, Law

and the Behavioral Sciences (1969); Schwartz and Skolnick, Society and the Legal Order (1970).

20. Pound, A Survey of Social Interests, 14, 39.

21. Ibid., 17. Cardozo writes: "It is the customary morality of right-minded men and women which he [the judge] is to enforce by his decree." The Nature of the Judicial Process 106 (1921). "The judge interprets the social conscience, and

ues would presumably include equal opportunity, fair play, private property, decentralization and local control, democracy, and individuality, among others). Despite the findings of contemporary political science which have shown significant correlation between judicial decisions and the personal political attitudes of the judges making them,[22] practitioners of interest balancing have repeatedly affirmed that judges' decisions ought to mirror society's values, not their own.[23] Perhaps the following excerpt

gives effect to it in law, but in doing so he helps to form and modify the conscience he interprets. Discovery and creation react upon each other." The Growth of the Law 96–97 (1924). See also Devlin, The Enforcement of Morals (1965); *but cf.* Hart, Law, Liberty, and Morality (1966); Dworkin, *Lord Devlin and the Enforcement of Morals*, 75 Yale L.J. 986 (1966).

22. For instance, see Pritchett, The Roosevelt Court (1948); Pritchett, Civil Liberties and the Vinson Court (1954); Schubert, Quantitative Analysis of Judicial Behavior, Chs. 3, 5 (1959); Tanenhaus, *Supreme Court Attitudes Toward Federal Administrative Agencies*, 22 J.Politics 502 (1960); Ulmer, *The Analysis of Behavior Patterns on the United States Supreme Court*, 22 J.Politics 629 (1960); Nagel, *Political Party Affiliation and Judges' Decisions*, 55 Am.Pol.Sci. Rev. 843 (1961); Spaeth, *Warren Court Attitudes Toward Business: The "B" Scale*, in Schubert, ed., Judicial Decision-Making 79–108 (1963); Schubert, The Judicial Mind (1965); Danelski, *Values as Variables in Judicial Decision-Making: Notes Toward a Theory*, 19 Vanderbilt L.Rev. 721 (1966); Howard, *On the Fluidity of Judi-*

cial Choice, 62 Am.Pol.Sci.Rev. 43 (1968); Schubert, The Judicial Mind Revisited (1974).

23. "[A] judge, I think, would err if he were to impose upon the community as a rule of life his own idiosyncracies of conduct or belief." Cardozo, The Nature of the Judicial Process 108. Still, "[i]n the present state of our knowledge, the estimate of the comparative value of one social interest and another, when they come two or more of them, into collision, will be shaped for the judge, as it is for the legislator, in accordance with an act of judgment in which many elements cooperate. It will be shaped by his experience of life; his understanding of the prevailing canons of justice and morality; his study of the social sciences; at times, in the end, by his intuitions, his guesses, even his ignorance or prejudice." Cardozo, The Growth of the Law 85–86.

Perhaps the most poignant illustration of the effort by a judge to divorce his personal views from the decision at hand is provided by the following excerpt from the opening paragraph of Justice Frankfurter's dissenting opinion in West Virginia State Board of Education v. Bar-

from Justice Holmes' essay, "The Path of the Law," sums up the process best:

> The language of judicial decision is mainly the language of logic. And the logical method and form flatter that longing for certainty and for repose which is in every human mind. But certainty generally is illusion, and repose is not the destiny of man. Behind the logical form lies a judgment as to the relative worth and importance of competing legislative grounds, often an inarticulate and unconscious judgment, it is true, and yet the very root and nerve of the whole proceeding. You can give any conclusion a logical form. You always can imply a condition in a contract. But why do you

nette, 319 U.S. 624, 646–647, 63 S. Ct. 1178, 1189 (1943):

One who belongs to the most vilified and persecuted minority in history is not likely to be insensible to the freedoms guaranteed by our Constitution. Were my purely personal attitude relevant I should wholeheartedly associate myself with the general libertarian views in the Court's opinion, representing as they do the thought and action of a lifetime. But as judges we are neither Jew nor Gentile, neither Catholic nor agnostic. We owe equal attachment to the Constitution and are equally bound by our judicial obligations whether we derive our citizenship from the earliest or the latest immigrants to these shores. As a member of this Court I am not justified in writing my private notions of policy into the Constitution, no matter how deeply I may cherish them or how mischievous I may deem their disregard. The duty of a judge who must decide which of two claims before the Court shall prevail, that of a State to enact and enforce laws within its general competence or that of an individual to refuse

obedience because of the demands of his conscience, is not that of the ordinary person. It can never be emphasized too much that one's own opinion about the wisdom or evil of a law should be excluded altogether when one is doing one's duty on the bench. The only opinion of our own even looking in that direction that is material is our opinion whether legislators could in reason have enacted such a law. In the light of all the circumstances, including the history of this question in this Court, it would require more daring than I possess to deny that reasonable legislators could have taken the action which is before us for review. Most unwillingly, therefore, I must differ from my brethren with regard to legislation like this.
* * *

You will recall that the case presented the question of whether the state could constitutionally compel children attending public school to salute the flag each morning; the act of allegiance required, it should be remembered, was a stiff arm salute.

imply it? It is because of some belief as to the practice of the community or of a class, or because of some opinion as to policy, or, in short, because of some attitude of yours upon a matter not capable of exact quantitative measurement, and therefore not capable of founding exact logical conclusions. Such matters really are battle grounds where the means do not exist for determinations that shall be good for all time, and where the decision can do no more than embody the preference of a given body in a given time and place. We do not realize how large a part of our law is open to reconsideration upon a slight change in the habit of the public mind. No concrete proposition is self-evident, no matter how ready we may be to accept it * * *.[24]

Understandably, several aspects of this problem-solving, "result-oriented jurisprudence" [25] (case-by-case adjudication, disposition of cases on the narrowest ground, subordination of individual claims to social aims, awareness of the leeway in applying precedent, recognition of the judge's function as an allocator of rights and resources, and the injection of the judge's own values and attitudes into decision-making) combine to provoke concern

24. Holmes, *The Path of the Law*, 10 Harv.L.Rev. 457, 465–466 (1897).

25. The term is Professor Shapiro's. *The Supreme Court and Constitutional Adjudication: Of Politics and Neutral Principles*, 31 C⁻⁻ Wash.L.Rev. 587, 592 (1963). Cardozo says of it:

Not the origin, but the goal, is the main thing. There can be no wisdom in the choice of a path unless we know where it will lead. The teleological conception of his function must be ever in the judge's mind. This means, of course, that the juristic philosophy of the common law is at bottom the philosophy of pragmatism. Its truth is relative, not absolute. The rule that functions well produces a title deed to recognition. Only in deter-

mining how it functions we must not view it too narrowly. We must not sacrifice the general to the particular. We must not throw to the winds the advantages of consistency and uniformity to do justice in the instance. We must keep within those interstitial limits which precedent and custom and the long and silent and almost indefinable practice of other judges through the centuries of the common law have set to judge-made innovations. But within the limits thus set, within the range over which choice moves, the final principle of selection for judges, as for legislators, is one of fitness to an end. * * *

The Nature of the Judicial Process 102–103.

among critics as to whether the principled quality of the judicial process can be sustained at all with interest balancing. In large part, these were the things that bothered Professor Wechsler. And it is not difficult to see why; for the potential impact of these variables could be such as to produce adjudication which is preconceived, manipulative, and arbitrary—"political," in the pejorative sense one uses the term to characterize "show" trials.[26] But it need not be.

---

26. A "political trial" I take to mean a criminal proceeding in which there is no risk that the defendant will be acquitted. Kirchheimer, Political Justice 339 (1961). The predetermined results are the product of subordinating the proceedings to government policy.

Illustrative in this respect are the following excerpts from a speech by Senator Robert A. Taft in which he criticized the International War Crimes Trials then taking place at Nuremberg:

Unfortunately, the philosophy of equal justice under law, and acceptance of decisions made in accordance with respected institutions, has steadily lost strength during recent years. It is utterly denied in totalitarian states. There the law and the courts are instruments of state policy. It is inconceivable to the people of such a state that a court would concern itself to be fair to those individuals who appear before it when the state has an adverse interest. Nor do they feel any need of being fair between one man and another. Therefore they see no reason for presenting logical argument to justify a position. Nothing is more typical of the Communist or the Fascist than to assert and re-assert an argument which has been completely answered and disproved, in order to create public opinion by propaganda to the ignorant.

* * *

The trial of the vanquished by the victors cannot be impartial no matter how it is hedged about with the forms of justice. I question whether the hanging of those, who, however despicable, were the leaders of the German People, will ever discourage the making of aggressive war, for no one makes war unless he expects to win. About this whole judgment there is the spirit of vengeance, and vengeance is seldom justice. * * *

In these trials we have accepted the Russian idea of the purpose of trials—government policy and not justice—with little relation to Anglo-Saxon heritage. By clothing policy in the forms of legal procedure, we may discredit the whole idea of justice in Europe for years to come. * * *

Equal Justice Under Law, 13 Vital Speeches 44, 45, 47 (1946); for background to the speech, see Kennedy, Profiles in Courage, Ch. 9 (1956). But *cf.* Shklar, Legalism, Pt. II (1964).

It is probably true that perversion of the judicial process is inversely proportional to the number of cases against which the ruling in the case at hand is analogized and tested. But, as we observed before, the more extensive this comparison, the greater the cost, the greater the time consumed, and the less capable are human beings of undertaking it. The truth of the matter is, as Justice Brandeis said, that "in most matters it is more important that the applicable rule of law be settled than that it be settled right." [27]

Where does this leave us, then? Hopefully, it should leave us with the conclusion that one need not be forced to the choice between absolutism, on the one hand, and *ad hoc* adjudication, on the other, which looks only to the result in the instant case. The mutually exclusive choice between principle and policy is a false choice because principles state policy too. The argument, then, reduces to how many cases shall be canvassed to test out the ruling in the present case; and how wide should the principle be that justifies it? An alternative that appears consistent with Wechsler's call for thoroughly reasoned opinions is interest balancing justified by analogical reasoning such that the present decision is justified as an extension of the principle(s) implicit in the precedent selected.[28] The comprehensiveness of the analogy will probably vary somewhat from case to case, but this is surely distinguishable from adjudication on a one-shot basis where the judge juggles the competing interests to effect a particular result in the instant case.

27. Burnet v. Colorado Oil & Gas Co., 285 U.S. 393, 406, 52 S.Ct. 443, 447 (1932) (dissenting opinion).

28. This appears to be what is suggested by Nimmer in his notion of "definitional balancing" as distinguished from "*ad hoc* balancing," *The Right to Speak from* Times *to* Time: *First Amendment Theory Applied to Libel and Misapplied to Privacy*, 56 Cal.L.Rev. 935 (1968); and by Fried in his distinction between the adjudication of "interests" as opposed to "wants," *Two Concepts of Interests: Some Reflections on the Supreme Court's Balancing Test*, 76 Harv.L.Rev. 755 (1963). See also Dworkin, *Hard Cases*, 88 Harv.L.Rev. 1057 (1975).

The Ethos of Judicial Self-Restraint

Starting from the premise that judicial review is "an undemocratic aspect of our scheme of government" which "prevents the full play of the democratic process," proponents of interest balancing, while "not call[ing] for its rejection or its disuse," have time and again counseled "the greatest caution in its use." [29] Self-conscious about the prospect that ready exercise of the review power will convert the Court into a "super-legislature," [30] they see the remedy for unwise legislation in the hands of "an informed, civically militant electorate" [31] which articulates its demands through the ballot box.

They deny what others assert, that judicial supremacy is justified by the Court's fulfillment of a unique function. Its function in a system of checks and balances, they argue, is little different than that exercised by the other two branches of government. The Court is unmistakably a political institution. Judges are not distinguished from legislators either by the values they hold (or do not hold), by the way they reach their decisions, or by the content or form of their policies.[32] As an equally political third branch of government, the Court is caught in a perilous dilemma. After the *tour de force* scored by Chief Justice Marshall when he seized for the Court the power of judicial review, the balancers find no way to square it with democratic theory. In short, while not wanting to give the power back, they cannot justify its use in a democratic system.

---

29. West Virginia State Board of Education v. Barnette, 319 U.S. 624, 650, 63 S.Ct. 1178, 1191 (dissenting opinion of Frankfurter, J.).

30. Jay Burns Baking Co. v. Bryan, 264 U.S. 504, 534, 44 S.Ct. 412, 421 (1924) (dissenting opinion of Brandeis, J.).

31. Baker v. Carr, 369 U.S. 186, 270, 82 S.Ct. 691, 739 (1962) (dissenting opinion of Frankfurter, J.).

32. Not only are legislators, political executives, and administrators also compelled to justify their policies to either their constituents or their superiors, but other governmental processes besides those of the courts operate on the basis of precedent. See Wildavsky, The Politics of the Budgetary Process (1964).

Prudence in decision-making is matched by prudence in intervention. If, in Hamilton's words, the Court is "the least dangerous branch," it is so because it is least powerful. Acutely aware of the Court's inability to force compliance with its own decisions, convinced that the Court's slim arsenal holds only "public confidence in its moral sanction" which "must be nourished by the Court's complete detachment, in fact and in appearance, from political entanglements and by abstention from injecting itself into the clash of political forces in political settlements," [33] the balancers assume a low constitutional profile. The risks of intervention are to be chanced only on rare and auspicious occasion. Only in an instance of an obviously capricious, unreasonable, or arbitrary exercise of legislative or executive power should the Court invoke its power to nullify policy.[34]

33. Baker v. Carr, 369 U.S. 186, 267, 82 S.Ct. 691, 737–738 (dissenting opinion of Frankfurter, J.).

34. But this reason for exercising the review power would seem itself unjustified for the following reason articulated by Judge Hand:

* * * I do not see how a court can invalidate them [the choices among competing interests embodied in a statute] without putting itself in the same position and declaring whether the legislature's substitute is what the court would have coined to meet the occasion. True, courts might, and indeed they always do, disclaim authority to intervene unless they are sure beyond doubt that the compromise imposed is wrong; but that does not disguise the fact that their choice is an authentic exercise of the same process that produced the statute itself. On the other hand, if a court goes so far as that, surely it may not say that it is doing no more than keeping the legislature within its accredited authority, and that it is not assuming power itself to review the legislative choice de novo. How would it do then to avoid this antinomy by saying that the limits of a legislature's power are determined by the rightness of the adjustments it prescribes between the conflicting values and sacrifices before it? Why not exclude as not legislative at all any compromises that are too flagrantly wrong? In accord with some such vague principle it seems to have satisfied judicial scruples for a season to say that the extent of legislative authority was measured by that curiously inept phrase, the "Police Power."

The Bill of Rights 39–40 (1958). The fact that one does not intervene very often can hardly be said to furnish a reason for intervening at all. By expanding the principle behind interest balancing to "the limit of its logic," to use Justice Cardozo's words (The Nature of the Judicial Process 51), it would ap-

The ethos of restraint also follows logically from the precept, mentioned before, that in a democratic society interest-balancing judges should seek to maximize as many claims as possible. Legislative policy, after all, is the product of majority rule.[35] When legislation comes to the Court for review and interpretation, presumption should be in its favor because, having been passed by the majority, it is assumed to maximize more claims and satisfy more interests. The only alternative would be to thwart democratic rule and extol minority interests.[36] Only on rare and unusual occasion, as when the majority has gone patently beyond the bounds of fair play, explicitly abridged constitutional provisions, or acted arbitrarily or irrationally, should the judiciary intervene.

pear that Justice Gibson's argument in *Eakin v. Raub* (p. 32) is correct: either the use of judicial review is justified by a court's claim of a unique function or the justification of the review power collapses.

35. This breezy assertion, which forms so much of the case for judicial self-restraint is, in fact, predicated on at least five separate assumptions of varying doubtfulness: (1) that majority rule is a decision-making rule of some special significance; (2) that the legislative seats have been equally apportioned; (3) that legislators were elected by a majority rather than a plurality vote; (4) that legislators assume the delegate role and reflect the wishes of their constituency; and (5) that the legislative body is itself a democratic institution.

36. This was clearly Justice Frankfurter's view. West Virginia State Board of Education v. Barnette, 319 U.S. 624, 662, 63 S.Ct. 1178, 1196. It has also been argued by Professor Commager: (1) that the checks and balances of the American system sufficiently check majority rule without adding judicial review; (2) that, with the exception of blacks, minorities have not been exploited or abused by the system; (3) that judicial review has usually spelled Court intervention on the side of well-to-do minorities; (4) that judicial review has been relatively unimportant in sustaining civil liberties; and (5) that most judicial nullifications of federal legislation have been overturned by amendment, legislation, or Court reversal. Majority Rule and Minority Rights (1943). The developments of the last three and a half decades, I submit, would refute all, or virtually all, of these statements.

A concise statement of what it is the Court should be doing and why surfaces in Justice Frankfurter's concurring opinion in *Dennis* v. *United States*:

> But how are competing interests to be assessed? Since they are not subject to quantitative ascertainment, the issue necessarily resolves itself into asking, who is to make the adjustment?—who is to balance the relevant factors and ascertain which interest is in the circumstances to prevail? Full responsibility for the choice cannot be given to the courts. Courts are not representative bodies. They are not designed to be a good reflex of a democratic society. Their judgment is best informed, and therefore most dependable, within narrow limits. Their essential quality is detachment, founded on independence. History teaches that the independence of the judiciary is jeopardized when courts become embroiled in the passions of the day and assume primary responsibility in choosing between competing political, economic and social pressures.
>
> Primary responsibility for adjusting the interests which compete in the situation before us of necessity belongs to the Congress. * * * We are to set aside the judgment of those whose duty it is to legislate only if there is no reasonable basis for it. * * *[37]

But if "reasonableness" is to be the test, we need to understand more exactly how it is to be assessed within the narrow parameters of adjudication. In short, we need to know how the technique of judicial review differs from legislative interest balancing. The difference is as follows: Suppose that the legislature is confronted with a problem and that there are, say, half a dozen different policy alternatives (which we will denote by the letters A through F) that comprise the range of possible responses. For whatever reason(s) (it was the choice of the political establishment, it cost less, it was the product of compromise, it provided the most political plums, etc.), let us assume the legislature chose Alternative B. The constitutionality of B is then challenged by the disaffected parties in court. The judges, in

37. 341 U.S. 494, 525, 71 S.Ct. 857, 875 (1951).

the balancers' view, must confine their focus to the alternative selected by the legislature, B in this case, and they must ask only whether a body of reasonable persons could have selected this policy as a response to the problem. They may not ask whether B was the *best* alternative as compared with A, C, D, E, and F, only whether B was a reasonable response. Surveying the full range of alternatives is the function of the legislature. The difference between assessing a policy alternative in terms of its "reasonableness," on the one hand, and its "bestness," on the other, is what Justice Brandeis and other restraintists meant when they talked about distinguishing judgments about the constitutionality of legislative policy from judgments about its wisdom.[38]

38. Jay Burns Baking Co. v. Bryan, 264 U.S. 504, 519–520, 44 S.Ct. 412, 416 (dissenting opinion of Brandeis, J.); United States v. Butler, 297 U.S. 1, 78, 87, 56 S.Ct. 312, 325, 329 (1936) (dissenting opinion of Stone, J.); West Virginia State Board of Education v. Barnette, 319 U.S. 624, 661–662, 63 S.Ct. 1178, 1196 (dissenting opinion of Frankfurter, J.); Dennis v. United States, 341 U.S. 494, 552, 71 S.Ct. 857, 889 (concurring opinion of Frankfurter, J.).

As we shall see in Chapter 4, there is a body of opinion which holds that it is wrong to judge legislation affecting civil liberties, particularly First Amendment rights, by the same standard (of reasonableness) used to assess the constitutionality of statutes regulating other interests. Its proponents argue that certain civil liberties are in a "preferred position" and that legislation directly impinging upon them should be judged by some criterion of "bestness" in the sense

that the regulatory policy chosen must be the least restrictive alternative. Rejecting this, Justice Frankfurter wrote that he saw no grounds in the text of the Constitution supporting such different treatment:

Judicial self-restraint is equally necessary whenever an exercise of political or legislative power is challenged. There is no warrant in the constitutional basis of this Court's authority for attributing different roles to it depending upon the nature of the challenge to the legislation. Our power does not vary according to the particular provision of the Bill of Rights which is invoked. The right not to have property taken without just compensation has, so far as the scope of judicial power is concerned, the same constitutional dignity as the right to be protected against unreasonable searches and seizures, and the latter has no less claim than freedom of the press or freedom of speech or religious free-

A final word should be added as to the scope of adjudication. The exercise of judicial self-restraint entails not only avoiding constitutional questions where possible,[39] but also avoiding as much of a constitutional question as possible. This calls for settling the matter on the narrowest possible ground. Prudence in decision-making and intervention alike counsel it.

But these restraintist canons of constitutional practice are provoked by more than mere circumspection in making decisions, or feelings of political vulnerability, or qualms of democratic theory. They are at least as much inspired by a belief that the judicial process is too poor a mechanism for the generation of coherent public policy.[40] These misgivings are concisely summed up in the following conclusion of Professor Bickel:

> The lesson, rather, is that in dealing with problems of great magnitude and pervasive ramifications, problems with complex roots and unpredictably multiplying offshoots—in dealing with such problems, the society is best allowed to develop its own strands out of its tradition; it moves forward most effectively, perhaps, in empirical fashion, deploying its full tradition, in all its contradictions, not merely one or another self-contained aspect of it, as it retreats and advances, shifts and responds in accordance with experience, and with pressures brought to bear by the political process. The only abiding thing, as Brandeis liked to say, is change, and in those broad realms of social policy where that is so, judicial supremacy, we must conclude, is not possible.
>
> The judicial process is too principle-prone and principle-bound—it has to be, there is no other justification or explanation for the role it plays. It is also too remote from condi-

dom. In no instance is this Court the primary protector of the particular liberty that is invoked. * * *

West Virginia State Board of Education v. Barnette, 319 U.S. 624, 648, 63 S.Ct. 1178, 1190 (dissenting opinion).

39. See Bickel, The Least Dangerous Branch (1962); *but cf.* Gunth-er, *The Subtle Vices of the "Passive Virtues"—A Comment on Principle and Expediency in Judicial Review*, 64 Colum.L.Rev. 1 (1964).

40. For a wide-ranging examination of the limitations on courts as institutions for the formulation of public policy, see Horowitz, The Courts and Social Policy (1977).

tions, and deals, case by case, with too narrow a slice of reality. It is not accessible to all the varied interests that are in play in any decision of great consequence. It is, very properly, independent. It is passive. It has difficulty controlling the stages by which it approaches a problem. It rushes forward too fast, or it lags; its pace hardly ever seems just right. For all these reasons, it is, in a vast, complex, changeable society, a most unsuitable instrument for the formation of policy.[41]

(Discussion of judicial self-restraint as a strategy perhaps encouraging a greater degree of political change than that likely to be achieved by judicial policy-making appears on pp. 278–279).

Illustrations

That the balancing of interests presents a mode of interpretation applicable to the full range of constitutional claims is apparent from the breadth of the following illustrations. The examples below have been selected because they also highlight some of the ambiguities and disparities in the criteria for maximizing the greatest number of claims and/or resolving conflicts among interests consistent with the underlying values of society.

1. *Executive Privilege: The Two* Nixon *Cases*

The Court's decision in *United States* v. *Nixon* [42] was as significant for its contribution to constitutional doctrine as for its strategic importance as an event hastening the downfall of a particular President. Our purpose in examining that decision, and another subsequent to it, is neither to examine the pros and cons of executive privilege, or even to assess whether the decision showed the Court to be an effective check on the accretion of executive power,[43] but rather to consider the form in which

41. Bickel, The Supreme Court and the Idea of Progress 175 (1970). Reprinted by permission.

42. 418 U.S. 683, 94 S.Ct. 3090 (1974).

43. In the long view of American history, it would be difficult to conclude that the Court has been a very effective check on the Presidency. Corwin, Total War and the Constitution (1947); Corwin, The President: Office and Powers (1957); Randall, Constitutional Problems Under Lincoln (Rev. ed.

1951); Schubert, The Presidency in the Courts (1957); Scigliano, The Supreme Court and the Presidency (1970).

It could be argued, however, that this trend has been reversed since the 1950s, and that the Court has become much more assertive. The principal cases in support of this thesis would seem to be Youngstown Sheet & Tube Co. v. Sawyer, 343 U.S. 579, 72 S.Ct. 863 (1952), and United States v. Nixon, supra, note 42. But even these cases may serve less as illustrations of significant limits fastened on the presidential office than as sharp rebuffs administered to vulnerable incumbents (both Truman and Nixon had recorded the lowest and next lowest Gallup Poll readings respectively on presidential popularity at about the time these decisions were handed down). As such, these decisions may not serve so much to limit the presidential office as to illustrate Professor Neustadt's concept of presidential leeway, Presidential Power 90 (1960); that is, that the President is freest to act when his public prestige is highest and other officeholders think twice about risking a challenge to his authority, but when his prestige falls others are encourage to contest his power. While it is true that both Youngstown and Nixon were decisions which ran against the exercise of presidential power, it is open to question whether either significantly limited the executive office. To a considerable extent, of course, any assessment of this kind turns on exactly how one defines defeat for the Presidency. Though President Truman's seizure of the steel mills was rejected in Youngstown, I would argue that that decision was not a significant defeat for the presidential office: (1) because of the Court's deep division, something not only reflected in the three dissenting votes, but, more significantly, in the fact that each Justice in the majority wrote a separate opinion; (2) because of the circumscription of the holding pretty much to the circumstances at hand, in which Congress' defeat of a proposed seizure authorization amendment to the Taft-Hartley Act figured prominently; (3) because of the Justices' complete disregard for the literalist conception of the Presidency which the district judge below attempted to rivet on the Constitution; (4) because of the explicit disclaimer of any attempt to sketch any constitutional theory of the executive (notably in Justice Frankfurter's concurring opinion); and (5) because of the sympathy exhibited (principally by Justice Jackson) for the problems of presidential leadership, the understanding shown for why the Presidency had grown strong, and the conclusion announced that any viable check on the further accretion of power in the executive would have to come from Congress, if, in fact, it would come at all. In much the same vein, I would contend that, though the Court rejected the absolute claim of executive privilege asserted by the President in Nixon, and did so by a unanimous vote, still the Court: (1) raised executive privilege to constitutional status; (2) affirmed an absolute privilege for military plans and state secrets; (3) accorded the President a presumptive privilege, thus placing a substantial burden of proof

the Court cast its decision and how the framework of the Court's opinion seemed a natural outgrowth of its perception of the relationship among the coordinate branches of government.

In *United States* v. *Nixon,* the Court was asked to decide whether the Watergate Special Prosecutor could constitutionally compel the President by subpoena to produce certain tape-recorded conversations with specifically-identified advisors and aides on particular dates, together with other memoranda then in his possession, relevant to the upcoming trial of six former employees of the executive branch on conspiracy and obstruction of justice charges. Rejecting at the outset the "contention * * * that the separation of powers doctrine precludes judicial review of a President's claim of privilege," the Court, per Chief Justice Burger, began by reaffirming the holding in *Marbury* v. *Madison* that "it is emphatically the province and duty of the judicial department to say what the law is." [44]

The Court went on to consider two interests put forth by the administration to defend its claim of "an absolute, unqualified presidential privilege": (1) "the valid need for protection of communications between high government officials and those who advise and assist them in the performance of their manifold duties"; and (2) "the independence of the Executive Branch within its own sphere * * * [which] insulates a president from judicial subpoena in an ongoing criminal prosecution, and thereby protects confidential presidential communications." [45]

on one seeking to gain access to executive materials (proof both of specifying the materials and demonstrating their relevance to the matter at hand); and (4) restricted screening to *in camera* inspection of the materials by a federal judge who would excise all nonrelevant matter and hold it in utmost confidence appropriate to "that high degree of respect due the President of the United States."

But see Dionisopoulos, *New Patterns in Judicial Control of the Presidency,* 10 U.Akron L.Rev. 1 (1976), which argues that several categories of recent Court decisions, in addition to the *Youngstown* and *Nixon* cases, manifest a significant change in the Court's attitude toward containing executive power.

44. 418 U.S. at 703, 94 S.Ct. at 3105.

45. 418 U.S. at 705–706, 94 S.Ct. at 3106.

Recognizing the "constitutional underpinnings" of the privilege as implicit in the enumerated powers given the President by the Constitution, the Court agreed that "[t]he President's need for complete candor and objectivity from advisers calls for great deference from the courts." [46] The Court, however, rejected any *absolute* claim of privilege "[a]bsent a claim of need to protect military, diplomatic or sensitive national security secrets." [47] Noting that "when the privilege depends solely on the broad, undifferentiated claim of public interest in the confidentiality of such conversations, a confrontation with other values arises," [48] the Court observed:

> The impediment that an absolute, unqualified privilege would place in the way of the primary constitutional duty of the Judicial Branch to do justice in criminal prosecutions would plainly conflict with the function of the courts under Art. III. In designing the structure of our Government and dividing and allocating the sovereign power among three coequal branches, the Framers of the Constitution sought to provide a comprehensive system, but the separate powers were not intended to operate with absolute independence.
>
> "While the Constitution diffuses power the better to secure liberty, it also contemplates that practice will integrate the dispersed powers into a workable government. It enjoins upon its branches separateness but interdependence, autonomy but reciprocity." Youngstown Sheet & Tube Co. v. Sawyer, 343 U.S. 579, 635, 72 S.Ct. 863, 870 (1952) (Jackson, J., concurring).[49]

46. 418 U.S. at 706, 94 S.Ct. at 3106–3107.

47. 418 U.S. at 706, 94 S.Ct. at 3107.

48. *Ibid.*

49. 418 U.S. at 707, 94 S.Ct. at 3107. Professor Neustadt sets out a similar observation in the following passage:

The limits on command suggest the structure of our government. The constitutional convention of 1787 is supposed to have created a government of "separated powers." It did nothing of the sort. Rather, it created a government of separated institutions *sharing* powers.
* * *

Presidential Power 33. The "power to command" would typify presidential power only in an institutional arrangement where governmental powers were completely independent of one another and neatly compartmentalized, a political

An absolutist approach "would upset the constitutional balance of 'a workable government' and gravely impair the role of courts

framework on the order of what Professor Shapiro described as the discredited "all-Gaul" theory of American government. See Chapter 1, note 2. Only in such a scheme could executive privilege, or any other executive power for that matter, be absolute. Once the reality of interdependent branches is seen, balancing the competing interests of institutions in conflict logically follows.

The relationship between an individual's perception of the structure of American government and his mode of constitutional interpretation is strikingly illustrated in the case of Chief Justice Taft. Students of constitutional interpretation often find it difficult to reconcile, on the one hand, Taft's opinion for the Court in Myers v. United States, 272 U.S. 52, 47 S.Ct. 21 (1926), a decision which asserted the unfettered power of the President to remove political appointees of the executive branch and struck down legislation that had required Senate concurrence in the matter, and, on the other hand, the former President's view of the presidential office, expressed a decade earlier, as follows:

The true view of the Executive function is, as I conceive it, that the President can exercise no power which cannot be fairly and reasonably traced to some specific grant of power or justly implied and included within such express grant as proper and necessary to its exercise. Such specific grant must be either in the Federal Con-

stitution or in an act of Congress passed in pursuance thereof. There is no undefined residuum of power which he can exercise because it seems to him to be in the public interest * * *. The grants of Executive power are necessarily in general terms in order not to embarrass the Executive within the field of action plainly marked for him, but his jurisdiction must be justified and vindicated by affirmative constitutional or statutory provision, or it does not exist.

Our Chief Magistrate and His Powers 139–140 (1916). There is a seeming conflict here between advocacy of first greater and then lesser executive power. In fact, there is no contradiction at all. What these views reflect is an absolutist view of constitutional interpretation: a bias toward negative government coupled with a rigid categorization of governmental powers. This is no surprise given that Taft embraced dual federalism as well. But the fit here is particularly snug, for the executive responsibility rationale expressed in *Myers* is precisely the notion of presidential power as the "power to command." Taft's espousal of the command theory of presidential power is matched by his allegiance to the command theory of law. As we noted before (Chapter 2, notes 1 and 2), absolutists are also known as analytical positivists, and it was John Austin, one of their earliest and most influential exponents, who defined law as "the command of the sovereign."

under Art. III." [50] Given this, the framework of the Court's opinion becomes clear: "Since we conclude that the legitimate needs of the judicial process may outweigh presidential privilege, it is necessary to resolve those competing interests in a manner that preserves the essential functions of each branch." [51] The Court then proceeds to balance the interests as follows:

> In this case we must weigh the importance of the general privilege of confidentiality of presidential communications in performance of his responsibilities against the inroads of such a privilege on the fair administration of criminal justice. The interest in preserving confidentiality is weighty indeed and entitled to great respect. However we cannot conclude that advisers will be moved to temper the candor of their remarks by the infrequent occasions of disclosure because of the possibility that such conversations will be called for in the context of a criminal prosecution.
>
> On the other hand, the allowance of the privilege to withhold evidence that is demonstrably relevant in a criminal trial would cut deeply into the guarantee of due process of law and gravely impair the basic function of the courts. A President's acknowledged need for confidentiality in the communications of his office is general in nature, whereas the constitutional need for production of relevant evidence in a criminal proceeding is specific and central to the fair adjudication of a particular criminal case in the administration of justice. Without access to specific facts a criminal prosecution may be totally frustrated. The President's broad interest in confidentiality of communications will not be vitiated by disclosure of a limited number of conversations preliminarily shown to have some bearing on the pending criminal cases.
>
> We conclude that when the ground for asserting privilege as to subpoenaed materials sought for use in a criminal trial is based only on the generalized interest in confidentiality, it cannot prevail over the fundamental demands of due process of law in the fair administration of criminal justice. The generalized assertion of privilege must yield to the demonstrated, specific need for evidence in a pending criminal trial.[52]

50. *Ibid.*

51. *Ibid.*

52. 418 U.S. at 711–713, 94 S.Ct. at 3109–3110.

The Court found that the procedures employed by the district court conformed to this balance of interests. It affirmed a "presumptive privilege" accorded the President, which had been rebutted by the Special Prosecutor in the case at hand, and upheld *in camera* inspection of the material for the purpose of excising nonrelevant parts so that only germane portions would be available at trial. The Court took special pains to point out the great deference due the President in maintaining the confidentiality of the excised portions pending their return to him.

Three years later, the Court affirmed much of this reasoning in *Nixon* v. *Administrator of General Services*.[53] In that case the former President, suing for injunctive and declaratory relief, challenged the constitutionality of the Presidential Recordings and Materials Preservation Act. The Act had been passed following disclosure of the fact that Nixon had entered into a depository agreement with the General Services Administration for the storage of some 42 million documents and 880 tape recordings. The agreement spelled out conditions of access to the materials and provided for the eventual destruction of the tape recordings. Three months after the terms of the agreement became public, Congress passed the legislation which directed the Administrator of the GSA to: (1) take custody of the materials; (2) screen the materials and return to the former President those which were personal and private in nature; (3) preserve materials of historical value; and (4) maintain the availability of any materials for use in judicial proceedings conditional upon "any rights, defenses, or privileges which the Federal Government or any person may invoke." The Administrator was also directed to draw up regulations regarding public access to the materials, taking into account guidelines specified in the Act, but such regulations had not yet been promulgated.

Reviewing Nixon's contentions that the legislation trenched upon the independence of the executive branch and infringed ex-

53. 433 U.S. 425, 97 S.Ct. 2777 (1977).

ecutive privilege,[54] the Court, speaking through Justice Brennan, announced:

> We reject the argument that only an incumbent President may assert such claims and hold that appellant, as a former President, may also be heard to assert them. We further hold, however, that neither his separation of powers claim nor his claim of breach of constitutional privilege has merit.[55]

Specifically, the former President argued: (1) that by "delegat[ing] to a subordinate officer of the Executive Branch the decision whether to disclose Presidential materials and to prescribe the terms that govern any disclosure," Congress had "impermissibl[y] interfere[d] * * * [in] matters inherently the business solely of the Executive Branch"; (2) that the balancing test as employed by the lower court (as a result of which it "conclud[ed] that, notwithstanding the fact that some of the materials might legitimately be included within a claim of Presidential confidentiality, substantial public interests outweighed and justified the limited inroads on Presidential confidentiality necessitated by the Act's provision for government custody and screening of the materials"), failed to sufficiently weight the former President's "presumptive privilege"; and (3) that the process for screening materials, set up by the Act, "will chill the future exercise of constitutionally protected executive functions, thereby impairing the ability of future Presidents to obtain the candid advice necessary to the conduct of their constitutionally imposed duties."[56]

The Court disposed of the separation of powers argument by noting: (1) that screening and control of the materials pursuant to the Act still remained with an officer of the executive branch; (2) that the former President's view of the separation

---

54. The former President also argued that the legislation violated his right to privacy, infringed his First Amendment right to association, and constituted a bill of attainder. The Court rejected all of these contentions.

55. 433 U.S. at 439, 97 S.Ct. at 2788.

56. 433 U.S. at 440–441, 97 S.Ct. at 2788–2789.

of powers reflected the notion of watertight compartmentalization of powers among the three coordinate branches explicitly rejected in *United States* v. *Nixon;* and (3) that the Act contained clear guidelines and conditions regulating access as protection against reckless and indiscriminate disclosure.[57] Both Nixon's separation-of-powers contention and his argument for executive privilege, the Court concluded, were materially weakened by "the fact that neither President Ford nor President Carter supports appellant's claim * * *."[58] Moreover, the Court found the screening process not unlike that which takes place anyway when former Presidents leave office and deposit their papers in presidential libraries, for, as the Court observed, "The expectation of the confidentiality of executive communications thus has always been limited and subject to erosion over time after an administration leaves office." [59] Finally, the Court concluded that "adequate justifications are shown for this limited intrusion into executive confidentiality comparable to those held to justify *in camera* inspection of the District Court sustained in *United States* v. *Nixon* * * *." [60] Among those purposes which legitimately moved Congress to pass the legislation, the Court mentioned the public's interest in, among other things: (1) insuring a complete and accurate historical record; (2) "rectify[ing] the hit-or-miss approach that has characterized past attempts to protect these substantial interests by entrusting the materials to expert handling by trusted and disinterested professionals"; (3) "restor[ing] public confidence in our political processes by preserving the materials as a source for facilitating a full airing of the events leading to appellant's resignation"; (4) enhancing "Congress' need to understand how those political processes had in fact operated in order to gauge the necessity for remedial legislation"; and (5) "shed[ding] light upon issues in civil or criminal litigation, a social interest

57. 433 U.S. at 441–446, 97 S.Ct. at 2789–2791.

58. 433 U.S. at 441, 449, 97 S.Ct. at 2789, 2793.

59. 433 U.S. at 451, 97 S.Ct. at 2794.

60. 433 U.S. at 452, 97 S.Ct. at 2794.

that cannot be doubted." [61] Summing up, Justice Brennan said, "In short, we conclude that the screening process contemplated by the Act will not constitute a more severe intrusion into Presidential confidentiality than the *in camera* inspection by the District Court approved in *United States* v. *Nixon* * * *." [62]

2. *The State Police Power, the Commerce Clause, and the Truck and Train Cases*

Though the Court for a time had difficulty settling on a definition of what activities were encompassed in the phrase "interstate commerce," it has long held that when Congress exercises its authority in accordance with Article I, section 8, clause 3 of the Constitution, its power to do so is plenary. [63] If manufacturing, mining, and agriculture temporarily eluded Congress' jurisdiction, surely the railroads and other interstate carriers did not. But Congress does not always act, and the Court has never accepted the proposition that, even when dormant, the commerce power necessarily precludes the exercise of state authority. [64] Even when Congress has legislated and the states have sought to exercise concurrent jurisdiction, the Court has attempted to resolve the matter only after assessing whether Congress intended to occupy the entire field, whether the federal interest was so dominant as to preclude the exercise of state power, and whether state regulation presented a serious conflict with what Congress had enacted. [65] This decision to leave some play in the

---

61. 433 U.S. at 452–454, 97 S.Ct. at 2794–2796.

62. 433 U.S. at 455, 97 S.Ct. at 2796.

63. Gibbons v. Ogden, 22 U.S. (9 Wheat.) 1, 6 L.Ed. 23 (1824).

64. Even Chief Justice Marshall intimated that there might be a limited role for the states in filling gaps left by the absence of congressional legislation, provided the states did not infringe interstate interests. See Willson v. Black

Bird Creek Marsh Co., 27 U.S. (2 Pet.) 245, 7 L.Ed. 412 (1829).

65. The tripartite test is set out in Pennsylvania v. Nelson, 350 U.S. 497, 76 S.Ct. 477 (1956). For applications of the supersession doctrine in commerce cases, see, *e. g.*, Huron Portland Cement Co. v. Detroit, 362 U.S. 440, 80 S.Ct. 813 (1960); City of Burbank v. Lockheed Air Terminal, 411 U.S. 624, 93 S.Ct. 1854 (1973); Northern States Power Co. v. Minnesota, 447 F.2d 1143 (8th Cir. 1971).

joints of federalism has marked out a role for the Court as umpire of the federal system and inescapably involved it in the methodology of interest balancing. While this conclusion is evident in the following discussion of cases involving the state police power, this political role and the attendant constitutional framework mark as well the Court's treatment of constitutional issues in state taxation of interstate business and full faith and credit.[66]

Consistent with the constitutional posture of the Taney Court in affording greater recognition of the scope of state regulatory power, the Court in 1852 accepted the principle that, under some conditions, the regulation of commerce could be a concurrent power of the national and state governments. In the words of Justice Curtis, who spoke for the Court in *Cooley* v. *Board of Wardens of the Port of Philadelphia,* the national government would exercise exclusive control only over "subjects of this power [which] are in their nature national, or admit only of one uniform system, or plan of regulation * * *."[67] Though the Court has often affirmed since then its recognition that the state has a legitimate interest in protecting the health, safety, and welfare of its people, particularly in this age of positive government, it has been equally conscious that regulation toward these ends frequently burdens interstate commerce. Assessments of constitutionality in the exercise of the state police power involve questions, then, of striking a balance between burdens imposed by the state and the justifications it offers, in the context of a particular economic activity. And, of course, it goes without saying that, where the purpose of a state's regulatory policy reflects an attempt to gain a competitive economic advantage over her sister states, such a policy is *per se* unconstitutional.[68]

A particularly informative illustration of the Court's effort to strike such a balance is its decision in *South Carolina State*

---

66. Chase and Ducat, Constitutional Interpretation, Chs. 7, 8 (1974).

67. 53 U.S. (12 How.) 299, 319, 13 L.Ed. 996, 1005 (1855).

68. H. P. Hood & Sons v. DuMond, 336 U.S. 525, 532–539, 69 S.Ct. 657, 662–665 (1949).

Highway Dept. v. *Barnwell Bros.*[69] In that case an interstate trucking firm challenged the constitutionality of a state statute which prohibited trucks weighing more than 20,000 lbs. and wider than 90 inches from using state highways. The state offered as twin justifications, the protection of public safety and the conservation of its roads.[70] A federal district court concluded that the state's regulations unreasonably burdened interstate commerce, and, in effect, substituted its own restrictions, increasing the width limitation to 96 inches and eliminating altogether the weight restriction with the exception of bridges which were either too narrow or of insufficient strength.

The Supreme Court, per Justice Stone, began by reviewing the reasoning of the trial court which prompted its finding of unconstitutionality:

> To reach this conclusion the court weighed conflicting evidence and made its own determinations as to the weight and width of motortrucks commonly used in interstate traffic and the capacity of the specified highways of the state to accommodate such traffic without injury to them or danger to their users. It found that interstate carriage by motortrucks has become a national industry; that from 85 to 90 per cent of the motortrucks used in interstate transportation are 96 inches wide and of a gross weight, when loaded, of more than 10 tons; that only four other states prescribe a gross load weight as low as 20,000 pounds; and that the American Association of State Highway Officials and the National Conference on Street and Highway Safety in the Department of Commerce have recommended for adoption weight and width limitations in which weight is limited to axle loads of 16,000 to 18,000 pounds and width is limited to 96 inches.

---

69. 303 U.S. 177, 58 S.Ct. 510 (1938).

70. Though justifications for a state's regulatory policies are necessarily cast in such terms, clearly these choices are the product of the political process. As such, the determination of truck width and weight limitations may be critically influenced by a political struggle between rival modes of transportation to secure whatever competitive advantage is to be had. See, *e. g.*, Hacker, *Pressure Politics in Pennsylvania: The Truckers vs. the Railroads*, in Westin, ed., The Uses of Power, Ch. 7 (1962).

It found in detail that compliance with the weight and width limitations demanded by the South Carolina act would seriously impede motortruck traffic passing to and through the state and increase its cost; that 2,417 miles of state highways, including most of those affected by the injunction, are of the standard construction of concrete or concrete base with asphalt surface, 7½ or 8 inches thick at the edges and 6 or 6½ inches thick at the center; that they are capable of sustaining without injury a wheel load of 8,000 to 9,000 pounds or an axle load of double those amounts, depending on whether the wheels are equipped with high-pressure or low-pressure pneumatic tires; that all but 100 miles of the specified highways are from 18 to 20 feet in width; that they constitute a connected system of highways which have been improved with the aid of federal money grants, as a part of a national system of highways; and that they constitute one of the best highway systems in the southeastern part of the United States.

It also found that the gross weight of vehicles is not a factor to be considered in the preservation of concrete highways, but that the appropriate factor to be considered is wheel or axle weight; that vehicles engaged in interstate commerce are so designed and the pressure of their weight is so distributed by their wheels and axles that gross loads of more than 20,000 pounds can be carried over concrete roads without damage to the surface; that a gross weight limitation of that amount, especially as applied to semitrailer motortrucks, is unreasonable as a means of preserving the highways; that it has no reasonable relation to safety of the public using the highways; and that the width limitation of 90 inches is unreasonable when applied to standard concrete highways of the state, in view of the fact that all other states permit a width of 96 inches, which is the standard width of trucks engaged in interstate commerce.[71]

Observing that "South Carolina has built its highways and owns and maintains them," [72] the Court went on to bring the legislation in question within the ambit of the *Cooley* rule:

Few subjects of state regulation are so peculiarly of local concern as is the use of state highways. There are few, local

71. 303 U.S. at 182–184, 58 S.Ct. at   72. 303 U.S. at 184, 58 S.Ct. at 513.
512–513.

regulation of which is so inseparable from a substantial effect on interstate commerce. Unlike the railroads, local highways are built, owned, and maintained by the state or its municipal subdivisions. The state has a primary and immediate concern in their safe and economical administration. The present regulations, or any others of like purpose, if they are to accomplish their end, must be applied alike to interstate and intrastate traffic both moving in large volume over the highways. The fact that they affect alike shippers in interstate and intrastate commerce in large number within as well as without the state is a safeguard against their abuse.[73]

The Court found support for the conclusion that the legislature had "acted within its province" in several past decisions of the Court "that a state may impose nondiscriminatory restrictions with respect to the character of motor vehicles moving in interstate commerce as a safety measure and as a means of securing the economical use of its highways." [74]

Having established the permissibility of the end for which regulation was sought, the Court, implicitly criticizing the approach of the district court, described the judicial function in appraising the reasonableness of the means chosen by the legislature as follows:

[C]ourts do not sit as Legislatures, either state or national. They cannot act as Congress does when, after weighing all the conflicting interests, state and national, determines when and how much the state regulatory power shall yield to the larger interests of a national commerce. And in reviewing a state highway regulation where Congress has not acted, a court is not called upon, as are state Legislatures, to determine what, in its judgment, is the most suitable restriction to be applied of those that are possible, or to choose that one which in its opinion is best adapted to all the diverse interests affected. * * * When the action of a Legislature is within the scope of its power, fairly debatable questions as to

73. 303 U.S. at 187, 58 S.Ct. at 515. In view of the massive federal interstate highway program which has grown up over the last two and a half decades, it is at least somewhat open to question whether the Court would still stress the primacy of local responsibility for the building and upkeep of roads in a case such as this.

74. 303 U.S. at 190, 58 S.Ct. at 517.

its reasonableness, wisdom, and propriety are not for the determination of courts, but for the legislative body, on which rests the duty and responsibility of decision. * * * This is equally the case when the legislative power is one which may legitimately place an incidental burden on interstate commerce. It is not any the less a legislative power committed to the states because it affects interstate commerce, and courts are not any the more entitled, because interstate commerce is affected, to substitute their own for the legislative judgment. * * *

Since the adoption of one weight or width regulation, rather than another, is a legislative, not a judicial, choice, its constitutionality is not to be determined by weighing in the judicial scales the merits of the legislative choice and rejecting it if the weight of evidence presented in court appears to favor a different standard. * * * Being a legislative judgment it is presumed to be supported by facts known to the Legislature unless facts judicially known or proved preclude that possibility. Hence, in reviewing the present determination, we examine the record, not to see whether the findings of the court below are supported by evidence, but to ascertain upon the whole record whether it is possible to say that the legislative choice is without rational basis. * * * Not only does the record fail to exclude that possibility but it shows affirmatively that there is adequate support for the legislative judgment.[75]

For a number of reasons, summarized here, the Court concluded that the weight limitation was reasonably related to preventing destruction of the state's roadways: (1) there was no clear indication of the relative merit of "an axle or weight wheel limitation" over and above "a gross weight limitation"; (2) the weight limitation was more workable and less likely to be easily violated; (3) none of the engineering studies supporting "an axle or weight wheel limitation" had been performed on South Carolina roads; and (4) approximately 60 per cent of South Carolina's paved highways were built without a longitudinal center joint, common to more recent road construction, so that

---

75. 303 U.S. at 190–192, 58 S.Ct. at 517. Cf. Dean Milk Co. v. City of Madison, 340 U.S. 349, 71 S.Ct. 295 (1951).

those roads were thinner at the center than at the edges and, consequently, could not indefinitely support great weight.[76]

Given the presumption of constitutionality, the Court found these factors sufficient to sustain the legislature's choice of policy. South Carolina, the Court noted, had had experience with higher weight limitations, and the present policy followed from recommendations of a state commission and a report by the state engineer urging a lower limitation to preserve the roads. "The fact that other states have adopted a different standard is not persuasive," observed the Court. "The conditions under which highways must be built in the several states, their construction, and the demands made upon them, are not uniform. The road building art, as the record shows, is far from having attained a scientific certainty and precision, and scientific precision is not the criterion for the exercise of the constitutional regulatory power of the states." [77]

Sustaining the width limitation of 90 inches imposed by the state, as against that of 96 inches preferred by the district court, the Court observed that on a road 18 to 20 feet wide, the wider limitation left little room for passing, while on a 16 foot wide road, of which South Carolina had approximately 100 miles, it left no room at all.[78] "The record shows without contradiction," Justice Stone pointed out, "that the use of heavy loaded trucks on the highways tends to force other traffic off the concrete surface onto the shoulders of the road * * * and to increase repair costs materially." [79] Finally, the Court noted, "as the width of trucks is increased it obstructs the view of the highway, causing much inconvenience and increased hazard in its use." [80]

Seven years later, the Court had occasion to review the constitutionality of the Arizona Train Limit Law, a statute which pro-

76. 303 U.S. at 192–194, 58 S.Ct. at 517–518.

77. 303 U.S. at 195, 58 S.Ct. at 519.

78. 303 U.S. at 196, 58 S.Ct. at 519.

79. *Ibid.*

80. *Ibid.*

hibited passenger trains of more than 14 cars and freight trains of more than 70 cars from operating in the state. When challenged by a railroad company, the state offered the justification of public safety. Speaking through Chief Justice Stone, the Court, in *Southern Pacific Co.* v. *Arizona*,[81] struck down the state law as an unwarranted imposition on interstate commerce.

The Court began its analysis by noting that it was "standard practice over the main lines of the railroads of the United States" to operate passenger and freight trains of greater length than Arizona's statute allowed. Moreover, continued the Court, "if the length of trains is to be regulated at all, national uniformity in the regulation adopted, such as only Congress can prescribe, is practically indispensable to the operation of an efficient and economical national railway system." [82] The Court observed, "In Arizona, approximately 93% of the freight traffic and 95% of the passenger traffic is interstate." In order to comply with the statute, the Southern Pacific Company was "required to haul 30% more trains in Arizona than would otherwise have been necessary." The resulting burden on interstate commerce, the Court concluded, was "serious." The effect of the statute was such as to drive up operating costs for the two railroads traversing the state by about $1 million annually, to significantly increase the number of locomotives and the amount of manpower required, and to delay the traffic and diminish its volume due to "breaking up and remaking long trains upon entering and leaving the state * * *."[83] The alternative for any carrier to this process of breaking up and reconstituting trains, wrote the Chief Justice, "is * * * to conform to the lowest train limit restriction of any of the states through which its trains pass, whose laws thus control the carriers' operations both within and without the regulating state." [84]

---

81. 325 U.S. 761, 65 S.Ct. 1515 (1945).

82. 325 U.S. at 771, 65 S.Ct. at 1521.

83. 325 U.S. at 772, 65 S.Ct. at 1522.

84. 325 U.S. at 773, 65 S.Ct. at 1522.

The justification proffered by the state was simply not proportional to the burden imposed. Chief Justice Stone explained:

> We think, as the trial court found, that the Arizona Train Limit Law, viewed as a safety measure, affords at most slight and dubious advantage, if any, over unregulated train lengths, because it results in an increase in the number of trains and train operations and the consequent increase in train accidents of a character generally more severe than those due to slack action. [Slack action is the amount of free movement of one car before it transmits its motion to an adjoining coupled car.] Its undoubted effect on the commerce is the regulation, without securing uniformity, of the length of trains operated in interstate commerce, which lack is itself a primary cause of preventing the free flow of commerce by delaying it and by substantially increasing its cost and impairing its efficiency. In these respects the case differs from those where a state, by regulatory measures affecting the commerce, has removed or reduced safety hazards without substantial interference with the interstate movement of trains. Such are measures abolishing the car stove * * *; requiring locomotives to be supplied with electric headlights, * * * providing for full train crews, * * * and for the equipment of freight trains with cabooses * * *.[85]

The Court also rejected any analogy to South Carolina's regulation of truck traffic relying upon the distinction between truck and train regulation previously developed in *Barnwell Bros.* And the Court discounted too the similarity in impact of full train crew laws which it had upheld earlier, reasoning that while they "placed an added financial burden on the railroads in order to serve a local interest, they did not obstruct interstate transportation or seriously impede it. They had no effects outside the state beyond those of picking up and setting down the extra employees at the state boundaries; they involved no wasted use of facilities or serious impairment of transportation efficiency, which are among the factors of controlling weight here."[86]

85. 325 U.S. at 779, 65 S.Ct. at 1525.   86. 325 U.S. at 782, 65 S.Ct. at 1526.

A third and, for our purposes, final example of the Court's reliance on interest balancing in this area is provided by its decision in *Bibb* v. *Navajo Freight Lines, Inc.*[87] At issue in this case was the constitutionality of an Illinois law which made it illegal for trucks traveling the state's highways to be equipped with straight or conventional mudflaps (legal in at least 45 states and required in Arkansas), and instead required the use of a special, contoured mudguard.

The Court began by accepting the findings of the district court. That court had observed that since it was impossible for an interstate carrier to determine on exactly what days its trucks would be operating in Illinois, the effect of the law would be to force the carrier to equip all its trailers to conform with the Illinois law. With perhaps only two exceptions, "the mudflaps required in those States which have mudguard regulations would not meet the standards required by the Illinois statute." The district court also found the initial cost of installing the curved mudguards to be substantial, as was the cost of maintenance and replacement.[88] Though Illinois defended the contoured mudguards as superior in preventing debris from being thrown into the faces of drivers in passing cars and onto the windshields of a vehicle following behind, the lower court found the curved mudguards to possess no advantages over the straight mudflap.[89] Moreover, the court below observed that the curved mudguards presented two new safety hazards: (1) the tendency "to cause an accumulation of heat in the brake drum, thus decreasing the effectiveness of brakes"; and (2) "the fact that they were susceptible of being hit and bumped when the trucks were backed up and of falling off on the highway." [90]

The Supreme Court noted that the Illinois statute additionally burdened interstate commerce by obstructing the transportation of goods to and from any states which required straight mud-

87.   359 U.S. 520, 79 S.Ct. 962 (1959).   89.   359 U.S. at 525, 79 S.Ct. at 965.

88.   359 U.S. at 524–525, 79 S.Ct. at   90.   *Ibid.*
      965.

flaps, here Arkansas, and by interfering with the practice of "interlining." With respect to the former, the Court observed that changing mudguards would "caus[e] a significant delay in an operation where prompt movement may be of the essence," because "from two to four hours of labor are required to install or remove a contour mudguard" since they are attached by welding.[91] As to the second burden, the interference with "interlining" ("the interchanging of trailers between an originating carrier and another carrier when the latter serves an area not served by the former" such that the entire trailer is physically transferred without the loading or unloading of cargo), the Court pointed out that "if an interchanged trailer * * * were hauled to or through Illinois, the statute would require that it contain contour guards. Since carriers which operate in and through Illinois cannot compel the originating carriers to equip their trailers with contour guards, they may be forced to cease interlining with those who do not meet the Illinois requirements." [92]

In view of "the rather massive showing of burden on interstate commerce" [93] put forth by the interstate carrier here, Justice Douglas, speaking for the Court, concluded:

> This is one of those cases—few in number—where local safety measures that are nondiscriminatory place an unconstitutional burden on interstate commerce. This conclusion is especially underlined by the deleterious effect which the Illinois law will have on the "interline" operation of interstate motor carriers. The conflict between the Arkansas regulation and the Illinois regulation also suggests that this regulation of mudguards is not one of those matters "admitting of diversity of treatment, according to the special requirements of local conditions," to use the words of Chief Justice Hughes in Sproles v. Binford, * * * 286 U.S. at page 390, 52 S. Ct. at page 585. A State which insists on a design out of line with the requirements of almost all the other States may

91. 359 U.S. at 527, 79 S.Ct. at 966.   93. 359 U.S. at 528, 79 S.Ct. at 967.

92. 359 U.S. at 527–528, 79 S.Ct. at 966–967.

sometimes place a great burden of delay and inconvenience on those interstate motor carriers entering or crossing its territory. Such a new safety device—out of line with the requirements of the other States—may be so compelling that the innovating State need not be the one to give way. But the present showing—balanced against the clear burden on commerce—is far too inconclusive to make this mudguard meet that test.

We deal not with absolutes but with questions of degree. The state legislatures plainly have great leeway in providing safety regulations for all vehicles—interstate as well as local. Our decisions so hold. Yet the heavy burden which the Illinois mudguard law places on the interstate movement of trucks and trailers seems to us to pass the permissible limits even for safety regulations.[94]

3. Liberty and Security in the Balance: The Barenblatt Case

Since so much of the controversy over interest balancing has erupted in the context of constitutional adjudication involving the competing interests of national security and First Amendment rights, particularly freedoms of speech and association,[95] it would be unthinkable not to draw an illustration from that area. Though the following discussion revolves around the Court's de-

---

94. 359 U.S. at 529–530, 79 S.Ct. at 967–968.

95. See, e. g., Meiklejohn, *What Does the First Amendment Mean?* 20 U.Chi.L.Rev. 461 (1953); Kalven, *Mr. Alexander Meiklejohn and the Barenblatt Opinion,* 27 U.Chi. L.Rev. 315 (1960); Meiklejohn, *The Barenblatt Opinion,* 27 U.Chi.L. Rev. 329 (1960); Karst, *Legislative Facts in Constitutional Litigation,* 1960 Sup.Ct.Rev. 75; Meiklejohn *The Balancing of Self-Preservation Against Political Freedom,* 49 Cal. L.Rev. 4 (1961); Meiklejohn, *The First Amendment Is an Absolute,* 1961 Sup.Ct.Rev. 245; Frantz, *The First Amendment in the Balance,* 71 Yale L.J. 1424 (1962); Mendelson, *On the Meaning of the First Amendment: Absolutes in the Balance,* 50 Cal.L.Rev. 821 (1962); Fried, *Two Concepts of Interests: Some Reflections on the Supreme Court's Balancing Test,* 76 Harv.L.Rev. 755 (1963); Frantz, *Is the First Amendment Law?—A Reply to Professor Mendelson,* 51 Cal.L.Rev. 729 (1963); Mendelson, *The First Amendment and the Judicial Process: A Reply to Mr. Frantz,* 17 Vanderbilt L.Rev. 479 (1964); Alfange, Jr., *The Balancing of Interests in Free Speech Cases: In Defense of an Abused Doctrine,* 2 Law in Transition Q. 35 (1965).

cision in one case, *Barenblatt* v. *United States*,[96] there is no reason to believe that decision is atypical. Any number of other speech or association cases decided about the same time could have served the purpose;[97] *Barenblatt* is perhaps better than most, for, in addition to the clarity with which the Court deployed the balancing framework, the decision is pregnant with the suggestion of judicial self-restraint in response to political cues from Congress.

Under subpoena, Barenblatt appeared with counsel before a subcommittee of the House Un-American Activities Committee. After initially responding to a few preliminary inquiries, he subsequently refused to answer five questions concerning his present and past membership in the Communist Party (when he had been a graduate student at the University of Michigan) and his knowledge of others' membership in the Party. He was cited for contempt and convicted. Appealing his conviction, Barenblatt argued: (1) that the subcommittee's power to compel testimony was neither authorized by the House nor constitutionally permissible because of the vagueness of Rule XI, the parent committee's charter; (2) that he was not sufficiently apprised of the pertinency of the subcommittee's questions to the matter under investigation; and (3) that the questions which he refused to answer violated his First Amendment rights.[98]

---

96. 360 U.S. 109, 79 S.Ct. 1081 (1959).

97. N.A.A.C.P. v. Alabama, 357 U.S. 449, 78 S.Ct. 1163 (1958); Uphaus v. Wyman, 360 U.S. 72, 79 S.Ct. 1040 (1959); Wilkinson v. United States, 365 U.S. 399, 81 S.Ct. 567 (1961); Braden v. United States, 365 U.S. 431, 81 S.Ct. 584 (1961); Konigsberg v. State Bar of California, 366 U.S. 36, 81 S.Ct. 997 (1961); In re Anastaplo, 366 U.S. 82, 81 S.Ct. 978 (1961); Communist Party v. Subversive Activities Control Board, 367 U.S. 1, 81 S.Ct. 1357 (1961); Scales v. United States, 367 U.S. 203, 81 S.Ct. 1469 (1961). See also American Communications Ass'n v. Douds, 329 U.S. 382, 70 S.Ct. 674 (1950); Dennis v. United States, 341 U.S. 494, 71 S. Ct. 857 (1951).

98. Because the relevance of his First Amendment claim may not readily be apparent, it might be useful to explain the difference between invoking this ground for refusal to testify as opposed to that associated with the Fifth Amendment. The latter, which is a more common ground for refusal to testify, is predicated on the constitu-

Taking up the first of these objections, Justice John Harlan, Jr., speaking for the Court, rejected the proposition that vagueness in Rule XI, the authorizing resolution for the whole committee, was automatically determinative of the matter of apprising the witness adequately as to the subject of the subcommittee's investigation. The Court pointed out that an understanding of the purpose of the investigation could also be gathered from statements by the chairman and committee members, and from the nature of the proceedings themselves.[99] Further, the Court reasoned that, though Rule XI might be vague as to empowering the committee to compel testimony with respect to activities of the Communist Party, it had to be read in the light of its legislative history. That legislative history, the Court observed, adduced undeniable evidence that the House, pursuing its legitimate concern with national security, had "clothed the Un-American Activities Committee with pervasive authority to investigate Communist activities in this country."[100] In light of the House's actions continuing the life of the committee at the beginning of each new Congress, raising it to the status of a standing committee, and supporting its investigations with sub-

tional guarantee against compelled self-incrimination. The advantage of invoking it is obvious; a claim of Fifth Amendment privilege ends the matter, for the witness cannot be punished for refusing to answer. Against this, of course, has to be weighed the fact that, in invoking the privilege, the witness will have to say, "I refuse to answer on the grounds that my answer may tend to incriminate me," which carries with it the clear implication of criminal wrongdoing. A witness invoking First Amendment rights (*i. e.*, that the questions infringe protected rights of speech, thought, or association), on the other hand, does not assert his refusal under such a cloud. But the risk here is great, for if the investigation is later held to be legitimate, and the questions asked are found to be pertinent, then refusal to answer is punishable for contempt. As questions fly across the table to the witness, he and his counsel must decide in a matter of seconds whether or not he will answer. Clearly, any ambiguity or vagueness along the way heightens the risk that the witness may guess wrong about invoking the privilege.

99. 360 U.S. at 116–117, 79 S.Ct. at 1087–1088.

100. 360 U.S. at 118, 79 S.Ct. at 1088.

stantial appropriations, the Court concluded "it can hardly be seriously argued that the investigation of Communist activities generally, and the attendant use of compulsory process, was beyond the purview of the Committee's intended authority under Rule XI." [101]

Second, the Court held the questions were pertinent to the subject matter of the investigation. Observing at the outset that Barenblatt had failed to register any specific pertinency objection at the time he had been asked the questions,[102] the Court went on to conclude that he had been indisputably apprised of the topic under inquiry and the relationship between it and the questions asked of him. The questions were pertinent, said Harlan, given that the chairman had announced the topic of the investigation to be Communist infiltration of education, the chairman had indicated the specific line of inquiry to be pursued that day, and Barenblatt had been present to hear the testimony of the preceding witness who named him as a member of a Communist student organization.[103] Added Justice Harlan, "And lastly, * * * petitioner refused to answer questions as to his own Communist Party affiliations, whose pertinency of course was clear beyond doubt."[104]

As framed by the Court, the third issue was "whether the Subcommittee's inquiry into petitioner's past or present mem-

101. 360 U.S. at 120–121, 79 S.Ct. at 1089–1090.

102. 360 U.S. at 123, 79 S.Ct. at 1091. Though, in his opening statement at the hearing, Barenblatt indicated that he "might wish to * * * challenge the pertinency of the question to the investigation" and made other reference to situations where pertinency objections had been successfully asserted, the Court held that such statements "cannot * * * be accepted as the equivalent of a pertinency objection." Said Harlan, "At best they constituted but a contemplated objection to questions still unasked," and "buried as they were" in the witness' general challenge to the power of the committee, they were not sufficient "to trigger what would have been the Subcommittee's reciprocal obligation had it been faced with a pertinency objection." 360 U.S. at 123–124, 79 S.Ct. at 1091.

103. 360 U.S. at 124–125, 79 S.Ct. at 1091–1092.

104. 360 U.S. at 125, 79 S.Ct. at 1092.

bership in the Communist Party transgressed the provisions of the First Amendment, which of course reach and limit congressional investigations."[105]   Continued Justice Harlan, "Where First Amendment rights are asserted to bar governmental interrogation resolution of the issue always involves a balancing by the courts of the competing private and public interests at stake in the particular circumstances shown." [106]

"The first question is whether this investigation was related to a valid legislative purpose," wrote Harlan, "for Congress may not constitutionally require an individual to disclose his political relationships or other private affairs except in relation to such a purpose." [107]   Answering this question in the affirmative, the Court reasoned that Congress' "wide power to legislate in the field of Communist activity in this Country" stems from the nation's "right of self-preservation." [108]   The justification for this conclusion rested on the finding that "the tenets of the Communist Party include the ultimate overthrow of the Government of the United States by force and violence, a view which has been given formal expression by the Congress." [109]   The Communist Party, in short, was not simply "an ordinary political party" but a criminal conspiracy aimed at the destruction of the government.[110]

Because the Communist Party does more than advocate ideas, because it conducts programs of infiltration "furthering the alleged ultimate purpose of overthrow," [111] investigatory power in this domain is not to be denied Congress solely because the field

---

105. 360 U.S. at 126, 79 S.Ct. at 1092.

106. 360 U.S. at 126, 79 S.Ct. at 1093.

107. 360 U.S. at 127, 79 S.Ct. at 1093.

108. 360 U.S. at 127–128, 79 S.Ct. at 1093.

109. 360 U.S. at 128, 79 S.Ct. at 1093.

110. 360 U.S. at 128–129, 79 S.Ct. at 1094. On the other hand, Justice Black, dissenting, characterized the Party as a political organization that from time to time commits illegal acts, 360 U.S. at 149, 79 S.Ct. at 1105, something, perhaps, on the order of the Committee to Re-Elect the President of recent Watergate fame.

111. 360 U.S. at 132, 79 S.Ct. at 1096.

of education is involved." [112] The Court also declined to accept the contention that this investigation was conducted purely for the purpose of "exposure," citing numerous precedents in support of the view that "[s]o long as Congress acts in pursuance of its constitutional power, the Judiciary lacks authority to intervene on the basis of the motives which spurred the exercise of that power." [113] Continued Justice Harlan:

> Finally, the record is barren of other factors which in themselves might sometimes lead to the conclusion that the individual interests at stake were not subordinate to those of the state. There is no indication in this record that the Subcommittee was attempting to pillory witnesses. Nor did petitioner's appearance as a witness follow from indiscriminate dragnet procedures, lacking in probable cause for belief that he possessed information which might be helpful to the Subcommittee. And the relevancy of the questions put to him by the Subcommittee is not open to doubt.[114]

Following this review of the issues, the Court "conclude[d] that the balance between the individual and the governmental interests here at stake must be struck in favor of the latter, and that therefore the provisions of the First Amendment have not been offended." [115]

Throughout, Justice Harlan's opinion makes a point of distinguishing the facts in *Barenblatt* from those in *Watkins* v. *United States*,[116] decided two years before. Watkins, an active leader in the labor movement, appeared before a HUAC subcommittee to testify about the activities of himself and others in the Communist Party. He admitted that he had cooperated in Communist Party functions and volunteered to identify people whom he believed still to be active in that organization. He refused, however, to answer questions concerning the past activity of individuals that he thought were no longer participants in the Commu-

---

112. 360 U.S. at 129, 79 S.Ct. at 1094.

113. See note 111, *supra*.

114. 360 U.S. at 134, 79 S.Ct. at 1097.

115. *Ibid.*

116. 354 U.S. 178, 77 S.Ct. 1173 (1957).

nist movement on the grounds these questions were not relevant to the purpose of the investigation and amounted to exposure for exposure's sake. The Supreme Court overturned his conviction on contempt charges. Initially, the Supreme Court had vacated the judgment of the appeals court in *Barenblatt* when that case was first appealed, remanding it for reconsideration in light of the decision in *Watkins*.[117]

Despite some obvious overall similarities in the two cases, Justice Harlan, taking up the pertinency objection in *Barenblatt*, wrote that "the factors which led us to rest decision on this ground in Watkins were very different from those involved here." He elaborated:

> In Watkins the petitioner had made specific objection to the Subcommittee's questions on the ground of pertinency; the question under inquiry had not been disclosed in any illuminating manner; and the questions asked the petitioner were not only amorphous on their face, but in some instances clearly foreign to the alleged subject matter of the investigaion—"Communism in labor." * * * [118]

And furthermore, "unlike Watkins," Barenblatt "refused to answer questions as to his own Communist Party affiliations, whose pertinency of course was clear beyond doubt." [119]

Some observers of the Court, however, argue that these are marginal distinctions, that the vagueness of Rule XI remained unchanged from the time it was so severely criticized by Chief Justice Warren speaking for the Court in *Watkins*,[120] and that the different outcomes of the two cases are better explained by looking to the political context of the Court's decision in *Barenblatt*. In this view, the decision in the later case represents the third phase of a recurring model of confrontations between the Court and Congress. An initial phase of judicial activism in the use of the review power is followed by a congressional response

117. 354 U.S. 930, 77 S.Ct. 1394 (1957).

118. 360 U.S. at 123, 79 S.Ct. at 1091.

119. See note 104, *supra*.

120. See Justice Black's discussion of the vagueness of Rule XI in his dissenting opinion, 360 U.S. at 137–140, 79 S.Ct. at 1098–1100.

of considering but not necessarily completing action against the Court (*e. g.,* impeachment and removal of some of the Justices, expanding the size of the Court, cutting the Court's appellate jurisdiction, etc.), which in turn prompts the Court to retreat (by simply forgetting the offending precedents in the decision of later cases, by overruling them, or by distinguishing them away).[121]

In the context of the mid to late 1950s, the first phase of this Court-curbing model was characterized by a number of Warren Court decisions involving racial segregation,[122] state sedition laws,[123] congressional and state investigations,[124] criminal procedure,[125] and constitutional safeguards in the dismissal of government employees alleged to be subversives.[126] Congress responded by considering and narrowly defeating two serious proposals in its 1958 session (H.R. 3 and S. 2646 [the Jenner-Butler Bill]) to restrict the Court's appellate jurisdiction.[127] Whereupon the Court, beginning with its October, 1958 Term, pulled the teeth of several of the offensive rulings, particularly those deal-

121. Nagel, *Court-Curbing Periods in American History*, 18 Vanderbilt L.Rev. 925 (1965), reprinted as *Curbing the Court: The Politics of Congressional Reaction*, in his The Legal Process from a Behavioral Perspective, Ch. 21 (1969).

122. Brown v. Board of Education, 347 U.S. 483, 74 S.Ct. 686 (1954); Bolling v. Sharpe, 347 U.S. 497, 74 S.Ct. 693 (1954); Brown v. Board of Education, 349 U.S. 294, 75 S.Ct. 753 (1955).

123. Pennsylvania v. Nelson, 350 U. S. 497, 76 S.Ct. 477 (1956). Also offensive to the conservative coalition that dominated Congress was the Court's decision interpreting the Smith Act in Yates v. United States, 354 U.S. 298, 77 S.Ct. 1064 (1957).

124. Watkins v. United States, 354 U.S. 178, 77 S.Ct. 1173 (1957); Sweezey v. New Hampshire, 354 U.S. 234, 77 S.Ct. 1203 (1957).

125. Mallory v. United States, 354 U.S. 449, 77 S.Ct. 1356 (1957).

126. Cole v. Young, 351 U.S. 536, 76 S.Ct. 861 (1956); Jencks v. United States, 353 U.S. 657, 77 S.Ct. 1007 (1957); Service v. Dulles, 354 U.S. 363, 77 S.Ct. 1152 (1957).

127. For the gist of the bills, see Congressional Quarterly's outline of the proposed legislation in *Court-Curb Proposals Stimulated by Controversial Decisions*, 1 Congress and the Nation 1442 (1965). An extraordinarily good account of the Court-curbing fight is Professor Murphy's Congress and the Court (1962).

ing with legislative investigations into alleged subversive activities.

Apart from the asserted unpersuasiveness of the distinctions developed by Justice Harlan, support for this thesis emerges from an examination of the votes cast in the *Watkins* and *Barenblatt* cases. As Figure 5 shows, only two Justices recorded a change in votes between the two cases, *i. e.,* in the second case they supported a set of interests different from that which they

FIGURE 5. COMPARING THE VOTING PATTERNS IN THE WATKINS AND BARENBLATT CASES

Watkins (1957)		*Barenblatt* (1959)	
Pro-Security	Pro-Liberty	Pro-Security	Pro-Liberty
Clark	Warren	Clark	Warren
	Black	Whittaker	Black
	Douglas	Stewart	Douglas
	Frankfurter	Frankfurter	Brennan
	Harlan	Harlan	
	Brennan		
Not Participating			
Burton			
Whittaker			

Pro-Liberty: For the petitioner (and the claim of First Amendment rights) and against the government (and the claim of national security)

Pro-Security: For the government (and the claim of national security) and against the petitioner (and the claim of First Amendment rights)

† Justice Burton retired October 13, 1958; Justice Stewart took office the following day.

voted for in the first, —Frankfurter and Harlan. What makes this interesting, of course, is the fact that both men are apostles of the interest-balancing, self-restraint viewpoint on the Court, and the direction of their change in heart coincides perfectly with the gist of Congress' dissatisfaction. This change in emphasis was neither temporary nor without effect. On a closely-divided Court, where these two Justices held swing votes,[128] the activism of the early Warren Court flickered and dimmed perceptibly. Not until 1962, when Justices Whittaker and Frankfurter retired and were replaced respectively by the appointments of Justices White and Goldberg, did the vigorous libertarian and equalitarian spirit of the later Warren years assert itself.

4. "Social Engineering" and Criminal Justice: Narrowing the Reach of the Suppression Doctrine

In order to understand contemporary law, Dean Pound explained, it should be seen as "a picture of satisfying as much of the whole body of human wants as we may with the least sacrifice." In the pursuit of this function of law, he saw evolving "a continually more efficacious social engineering," that is "a continually wider recognizing and satisfying of human wants or claims or desires through social control; a more embracing and more effective securing of social interests; a continually more complete and effective elimination of waste and precluding of friction in human enjoyment of the goods of existence

---

128. A simple illustration will suffice: Taking those 8 cases cited in notes 123–126, *supra*, decided in 1956 or 1957, *i. e.*, immediately preceding the Court-curbing effort, two were decided by a unanimous vote (*Mallory* and *Service*), three with only one dissent (*Jencks*, *Yates*, and *Watkins*), and three with more than one dissenting vote (*Cole*, *Nelson*, and *Sweezey*) thus capable of being reversed by a change in the votes of Justices Frankfurter and Harlan who sided with the pro-liberty interest majority in every case. If we take the seven cases cited in note 97, *supra*, decided between 1959 and 1961, *i. e.*, following the session of Congress at which the Court-curbing legislation was proposed, all seven cases (not including *Barenblatt* which would be an eighth) were decided by 5–4 votes with both Frankfurter and Harlan in the majority favoring the security interest in *every* case.

* * *." [129]   Insofar as judges choose to acknowledge their participation in this process, the deliberate design of social policy necessarily entails that they consider the consequences of alternative policies as they effect a balance among competing interests. In few, if any, areas of constitutional adjudication today have the Justices been quite so conscious of their role in engineering social policy, or felt so keenly about it, as in recent decisions of the Burger Court bearing upon the use of the exclusionary rule as a means for enforcing constitutional rights of defendants in criminal proceedings.

Since 1961, the exclusionary rule, which renders inadmissible at trial unconstitutionally obtained evidence, has applied to both federal and state criminal prosecutions.[130]   It is judge-made law, a sanction devised by the Court to promote from law enforcement officers respect for the Fourth Amendment's prohibition on the conduct of unreasonable searches and seizures, for the Fifth Amendment's ban on forced self-incrimination, and for the Sixth Amendment's guarantee of the right to counsel. Since the accession of the Nixon appointees, the promised product of what was ostensibly a "law and order" Presidency, the rule has fallen into increasing disfavor. A sign of the times lies in the fact that what was once referred to as "the exclusionary rule" is now called "the suppression doctrine."

Apart from those Justices who dissented from the Warren Court's decisions which extended the exclusionary rule or expanded the scope of constitutional rights to be implemented by it, the earliest call for its reconsideration came from Chief Justice Burger in a dissenting opinion in *Bivens* v. *Six Unknown Named Agents of the Federal Bureau of Narcotics.* Observing

129. An Introduction to the Philosophy of Law 47 (1922).

130. Mapp v. Ohio, 367 U.S. 643, 81 S.Ct. 1684 (1961). Prior to *Mapp*, the rule applied to exclude illegally obtained evidence from federal courts only. Before 1914, when the Supreme Court fashioned the exclusionary rule for application in federal cases in Weeks v. United States, 232 U.S. 383, 34 S.Ct. 341, the common law rule prevailed, *i. e.*, evidence was admissible no matter how it was obtained.

that the rule had been variously, but in his view inadequately, justified by "the 'sporting contest' thesis that the government must 'play the game fairly' and cannot be allowed to profit from its own illegal acts" [131] and "the theory that the relationship between the Self-Incrimination Clause of the Fifth Amendment and the Fourth Amendment requires the suppression of evidence seized in violation of the latter," [132] the Chief Justice argued that it was the "deterrent rationale" that really undergirded the rule. "Although I would hesitate to abandon it until some meaningful substitute is developed," he said, "the history of the suppression doctrine demonstrates that it is both conceptually sterile and practically ineffective in accomplishing its stated objective." [133] He continued:

> This is illustrated by the paradox that an unlawful act against a totally innocent person * * * has been left without an effective remedy, and hence the Court finds it necessary now—55 years later—to construct a remedy of its own.
>
> Some clear demonstration of the benefits and effectiveness of the exclusionary rule is required to justify it in view of the high price it extracts from society—the release of countless guilty criminals. * * * But there is no empirical evidence to support the claim that the rule actually deters illegal conduct of law enforcement officers. * * * [134]

The rule fails to deter, the Chief Justice hypothesized, for several reasons: (1) the sanction falls on the prosecutor with no direct impact on the offending police officer(s); (2) the rule falsely assumes that "law enforcement is a monolithic governmental enterprise," but the prosecutor is not an official in the police department, rarely takes part in their operations, and holds practically no disciplinary power over policemen; (3) the educative effect of the rule presumes substantial legal training by the police which they do not have, and clearly written court

---

131. 403 U.S. 388, 414, 91 S.Ct. 1999, 2013 (1971).

132. 403 U.S. at 414, 91 S.Ct. at 2014.

133. 403 U.S. at 415, 91 S.Ct. at 2014.

134. 403 U.S. at 415–416, 91 S.Ct. at 2014.

opinions that define standards of conduct when often these expectations are not precisely spelled out; and (4) the educative effect of imposing the sanction pales in the long lapse of time that frequently occurs between the time of the illegal conduct and the date on which the sanction is imposed.[135] In sum, concluded Burger, the rule "represents a mechanically inflexible response to widely varying degrees of police error and the resulting high price that society pays." [136] Instead, he suggested, "Congress should develop an administrative or quasi-judicial remedy against the government itself to afford compensation or restitution for persons whose Fourth Amendment rights have been violated." [137]

In five years, this view of the rule moved from dissent to the dominant outlook on the Court. In *Stone* v. *Powell*,[138] the Court took up the question "whether state prisoners—who have been afforded the opportunity for full and fair consideration of their reliance upon the exclusionary rule with respect to seized evidence by the state courts at trial and on direct review—may invoke their claim again on federal habeas corpus review." Because that portion of Justice Powell's opinion for the Court dealing with this issue is so clearly and concisely structured along the lines of interest balancing, it is set out at length as follows:

> The answer is to be found by weighing the utility of the exclusionary rule against the costs of extending it to collateral review of Fourth Amendment claims.
>
> The costs of applying the exclusionary rule even at trial and on direct review are well known: the focus of the trial, and the attention of the participants therein, is diverted from

---

135. 403 U.S. at 416–418, 91 S.Ct. at 2015–2016.

136. 403 U.S. at 418, 91 S.Ct. at 2016.

137. 403 U.S. at 422, 91 S.Ct. at 2017. One problem with this view, of course, is that it evidences no awareness of our experience with regulatory agencies which teaches that they tend to become the captive of the industry they are supposed to regulate. Also, it is not clear how a suit against the government is supposed to deter the individual law enforcement officer.

138. 428 U.S. 465, 96 S.Ct. 3037 (1976).

the ultimate question of guilt or innocence that should be the central concern in a criminal proceeding. Moreover, the physical evidence sought to be excluded is typically reliable and often the most probative information bearing on the guilt or innocence of the defendant. * * *

Application of the rule thus deflects the truthfinding process and often frees the guilty. The disparity in particular cases between the error committed by the police officer and the windfall afforded a guilty defendant by application of the rule is contrary to the idea of proportionality that is essential to the concept of justice. Thus, although the rule is thought to deter unlawful police activity in part through the nurturing of respect for Fourth Amendment values, if applied indiscriminately it may well have the opposite effect of generating disrespect for the law and administration of justice. These long-recognized costs of the rule persist when a criminal conviction is sought to be overturned on collateral review on the ground that a search-and-seizure claim was erroneously rejected by two or more tiers of state courts.

Evidence obtained by police officers in violation of the Fourth Amendment is excluded at trial in the hope that the frequency of future violations will decrease. Despite the absence of supportive empirical evidence, we have assumed that the immediate effect of exclusion will be to discourage law enforcement officials from violating the Fourth Amendment by removing the incentive to disregard it. More importantly, over the long term, this demonstration that our society attaches serious consequences to violation of constitutional rights is thought to encourage those who formulate law enforcement policies, and the officers who implement them, to incorporate Fourth Amendment ideals into their value system.

We adhere to the view that these considerations support the implementation of the exclusionary rule at trial and its enforcement on direct appeal of state court convictions. But the additional contribution, if any, of the consideration of search-and-seizure claims of state prisoners on collateral review is small in relation to the costs. To be sure, each case in which such claim is considered may add marginally to an awareness of the values protected by the Fourth Amendment. There is no reason to believe, however, that the overall educative effect of the exclusionary rule would be appreciably diminished if search-and-seizure claims could not be raised in federal habeas corpus review of state convictions. Nor is there reason to assume that any specific disincentive already created by the risk of exclusion of evidence at trial or the reversal of convictions on direct review would be enhanced if there were the further risk that a conviction obtained in state court and affirmed on direct review might be overturned in collateral proceedings often occurring years after the incarceration of the defendant. The view that the deterrence of Fourth Amendment violations would be furthered rests on the dubious assumption that law enforcement authorities would fear that federal habeas review might reveal flaws in a search or seizure that went undetected at trial and on appeal. Even if one rationally could assume that some additional incremental deterrent effect would be present in isolated cases, the resulting advance of the legitimate goal of furthering Fourth Amendment rights would be outweighed by the acknowledged costs to other values vital to a rational system of criminal justice.

In sum, we conclude that where the State has provided an opportunity for full and fair litigation of a Fourth Amendment claim, a state prisoner may not be granted federal habeas corpus relief on the ground that evidence obtained in an unconstitutional search or seizure was introduced at his trial. In this context the contribution of the exclusionary rule, if any, to the effectuation of the Fourth Amendment is minimal and the substantial societal costs of application of the rule persist with special force.[139]

After similarly employing the interest balancing framework in other cases, the Court announced that application of the suppression doctrine with respect to illegally seized material did not pertain to grand jury proceedings[140] or to civil proceedings instituted by the government.[141] The Court concluded that the "marginal" gain in deterrence in each case was offset by the high cost of suppressing reliable evidence, thus giving credence to Chief Justice Burger's call for the Court to make permanent its rejection of "formalistic analysis" and "apply the exclusion-

139. 428 U.S. at 489–495, 96 S.Ct. at 3049–3052.

141. United States v. Janis, 428 U.S. 433, 96 S.Ct. 3021 (1976).

140. United States v. Calandra, 414 U.S. 338, 94 S.Ct. 613 (1974).

ary rule on the basis of its benefits and costs, at least in those cases where the police conduct at issue is far from being outrageous or egregious."[142] What the Chief Justice means by eschewing "formalistic analysis" is, of course, regard for seeing these matters as involving personal constitutional rights which Justice Black held to be absolutely protected when he argued "that when the Fourth Amendment's ban against unreasonable searches and seizures is considered together with the Fifth Amendment's ban against compelled self-incrimination, a constitutional basis emerges which not only justifies but actually requires the exclusionary rule."[143] Against this light and taken together with the clear trend in the Court's balance of competing interests in Fourth Amendment cases, the import of the following statement by the Chief Justice is clear: "In its Fourth Amendment context, we have now recognized that the exclusionary rule is in no sense a *personal* constitutional right, but a judicially conceived remedial device designed to safeguard and effectuate guaranteed legal rights generally. * * * We have repeatedly emphasized that deterrence of unconstitutional or otherwise unlawful police conduct is the only valid justification for excluding reliable and probative evidence from the criminal fact-finding process."[144]

142. Brewer v. Williams, 430 U.S. 387, 427, 97 S.Ct. 1232, 1254 (1977) (dissenting opinion).

143. Mapp v. Ohio, 367 U.S. 643, 662, 81 S.Ct. 1684, 1695 (concurring opinion). This view echoes the Court's holding in Boyd v. United States, 116 U.S. 616, 6 S.Ct. 524 (1886). Not surprisingly, the Court has displayed a much diminished regard for *Boyd* recently; see Andresen v. Maryland, 427 U.S. 463, 96 S.Ct. 2737 (1976).

144. Brewer v. Williams, 430 U.S. 387, 421, 97 S.Ct. 1232, 1250 (1977) (dissenting opinion). Speaking for himself and Justices Douglas and Marshall, Justice Brennan argued that "there is no evidence that the possible deterrent effect of the rule was given any attention by the judges chiefly responsible for its formulation." United States v. Calandra, 414 U.S. 338, 356, 94 S. Ct. 613, 624 (dissenting opinion). Instead, continued Brennan, "The exclusionary rule, if not perfect, accomplished the twin goals of enabling the judiciary to avoid the taint of partnership in official lawlessness and of assuring the people—all potential victims of unlawful government conduct—that the government would not profit from

Critique

For all of its many strengths, however, the balancing of interests has a number of serious defects. Despite the ostensible sophistication in its understanding of the judicial process over that offered by absolutism, its weaknesses do not arise principally from technical or abstruse legal complications. In large measure, the flaws in interest balancing are of a kind students of political science should have little difficulty understanding. This is so because many of them derive, surprisingly enough, from a poor understanding of democracy itself, the very value on which the practice of judicial self-restraint is supposed to place such a high premium.

1. Democracy and "Undemocratic" Institutions

In a volume first published some 35 years ago, in which he advocated a theory of democratic elitism,[145] Joseph Schumpeter posed a seemingly devastating hypothetical to classical democrats:

> Let us transport ourselves into a hypothetical country, that, in a democratic way, practices the persecution of Christians, the burning of witches, and the slaughtering of Jews. We should certainly not approve of these practices on the ground that they have been decided on according to the rules of democratic procedure. But the crucial question is: would we ap-

its lawless behavior, thus minimizing the risk of seriously undermining popular trust in government." 414 U.S. at 357, 94 S.Ct. at 624.

145. In this view, government by the people is replaced by government accountable to the people. The people no longer rule directly, but retain the capacity to approve leadership through competition among political elites. This revision in democratic theory appeared to be prompted by conclusions that the masses were incapable of run-

ning government, that it was a job for professionals (politicians), and that, contrary to the traditional wisdom, it was the elites in democratic systems rather than the masses who were more committed to playing by the "rules of the game" including the maintenance of civil liberties. See Stouffer, Communism, Conformity, and Civil Liberties (1955); McClosky, *Consensus and Ideology in American Politics*, 58 Am.Pol.Sci.Rev. 361 (1964).

prove of the democratic constitution itself that produced such results in preference to a non-democratic one that would avoid them? [146]

And, given the record of mass support for totalitarian movements, especially in this century, there appears to be more than just a kernel of truth in this armchair experiment. But this hypothetical is not the dilemma that it seems because it is

> based upon a misconception of democratic procedure. His question is based on the fallacious assumption that "the persecution of Christians, the burning of witches, and the slaughtering of Jews" would be carried out "in a democratic way" and "according to the rules of democratic procedure." Clearly any one of these actions would constitute a violation of democracy even when conceived solely as a method. Religious, racial, or group persecution of any sort is in conflict with the principles of freedom of discussion and association essential to the operation of the majority rule principle. For if a minority is barred forcefully from becoming a majority, such action cannot be squared with the rules of democratic procedure. Thus Schumpeter posed a false dilemma: it is not a question of standing by one's loyalty to democracy when a minority is being brutalized; mob rule and majority tyranny are outrages against both democracy and individual liberty.[147]

My reason for starting here is simply that Professor Schumpeter and the interest balancers make the same mistake: They both identify democracy as the operation of majority rule and forget its component part, minority rights.[148] And precisely because of

146. Capitalism, Socialism and Democracy 242 (3d ed. 1950). It is, of course, possible to accept the gist of what Schumpeter has to say, i. e., that there are values that are superior to democratic procedure, without accepting his particular argument here. Indeed, this is the argument set out in Chapter 1 with respect to justifying the review power of the Court. For the reasons set out at pp. 238–244, I would contend that an argument in this form must be offered because the "minority rights" part of democratic procedure, discussed further on in this section, provides an inadequate justification.

147. Bachrach, The Theory of Democratic Elitism: A Critique 19–20 (1967).

148. This happens explicitly in Professor Commager's book yet both elements appear in the title. Ma-

this mistake, the balancers are forced into variations of the false dilemma Schumpeter poses. Almost all of the difficulties that develop with interest balancing can be traced back, in one form or another, to this inadequate definition of democracy.

The most obvious of these difficulties begins with the shallow characterization of judicial review as an "undemocratic" institution, an epithet clearly cut from the cloth of majority rule. From this, the balancers sew up a shroud which they then throw over the Court with the dual results of preparing its burial as an effective political institution and keeping the Justices who man it in the dark about the realities of the democratic process. In the first place, whether the Court is an "undemocratic" institution depends on what the Court does. Obviously, the Justices are not elected so the Court cannot be held directly accountable to a popular majority, but the Court can, if it chooses, vindicate the minority rights essential for the operation of the democratic process. Insofar as it functions in that capacity, it operates as a democratic institution; insofar as it fails to, it does not. This is simply the democratic foundation of judicial review so effectively demonstrated by Professor Rostow.[149] And secondly, as Judge Hand has convincingly shown us, once one accedes to the definition of democracy as majority rule and nothing more, and simultaneously recognizes that judges are policy-makers like other government officials, the justification for judicial review *in any form* collapses. This is so because no standard attempting to circumscribe judicial review, that is regarding it as "the shotgun behind the door" (*e. g.,* limiting intervention to cases of "clearly unconstitutional" legislation, or to cases of legislation which is "arbitrary, capricious, or unreasonable," etc.), can withstand the annihilating effect that comes with reducing all such interventions to the status of undemocratic interventions.

jority Rule and Minority Rights 55, 79–80. A more fruitful discussion of majority rule and its possible limitation is contained in the exchange between McClosky, *The Fallacy of Absolute Majority Rule*, 11 J. of Politics 637 (1949), and Kendall, *Prolegomena to Any Future Work on Majority Rule*, 12 J. of Politics 694 (1950).

149. *The Democratic Character of Judicial Review*, 66 Harv.L.Rev. 193 (1952).

Furthermore, assuming that majority rule is in itself of significant moral value such as to distinguish it from other decision-making rules,[150] it would require either a willful or astonishing ignorance of the workings of Congress to seriously contend that it measures up so superbly by the majority rule criterion as to entitle legislative action to all the deference that the restraintists think it warrants. As Professor Shapiro has demonstrated with disarming ease,[151] numerous features of Congress consistently work to impede what we might uncritically call "the popular will." While we need not elaborate their particular effects here, it should suffice to list a few of these elements: the committee system, gerrymandering, the filibuster, plurality election, the dominance of the "trustee" model of representation, and low voter turnout. Professor Shapiro rightly asks by what measure the Justices should feel obligated to defer to an institution run by a seniority system, that, for whatever other conceivable reasons it might be justified, flunks Mr. Justice Frankfurter's test of "representative[ness]" cold, and clearly "prevents the full play of the democratic process." Similar non-majoritarian imperfections haunt the selection of a President by an unrepresentative convention system and the Electoral College, and visibly mar any claim of deference by an appointed, life-tenured civil

---

150. It has been forcefully argued that any discussion of decision-making procedures at the dawn of any constitutional democracy begins from the point of unanimity rule and departures subsequently occur from it after effecting balances among the social costs which can be imposed by government, the external costs which must be endured in the absence of collective action, and the decision costs which increase as agreement among more people is required before government can act. Buchanan and Tullock, The Calculus of Consent, Chs. 6, 7 (1962). "At best, majority rule should be viewed as one among many practical expedi-

ents made necessary by the costs of securing widespread agreement on political issues when individual and group interests diverge." *ibid.*, 96; see also Ch. 17. The Constitution provides examples of several different decision-making rules depending on the perceived importance of the interest involved, ranging from the requirement of a simple majority to pass a bill to a rule of unanimity with regard to depriving any state of equal representation in the Senate.

151. Shapiro, Freedom of Speech: The Supreme Court and Judicial Review 17–25 (1966).

service. In light of this, it offends any sense of accuracy or fairness to single out the Court for indictment as an "undemocratic" institution of government.

2. A Descriptive or Prescriptive Framework?

Though it might be argued that too few court opinions set out with clarity just what interests are in conflict, those which adopt the balancing of interests framework generally accomplish that task passably well. Insofar as it provides a structure for cataloging interests and organizing court opinions, interest balancing would appear to make a worthwhile contribution. Even an approach which merely describes what interests are competing for satisfaction draws attention to the reality of choice and may help to induce awareness of the consequences of selecting one alternative resolution of the controversy over another. However, since balancers have regarded it as preferable that the interests arrayed be cast in the form of social rather than personal interests,[152] the descriptive aspect of interest balancing is not unobjectionable, as I will show later.

The critical issue, though, is whether the framework moves us beyond the descriptive stage at which interests are inventoried. Does interest balancing furnish an effective criterion to guide the judge in choosing between contending interests? The importance of this question cannot be overstated, for examination of other modes of constitutional interpretation reveals that both absolutism (pp. 111–114) and preferred freedoms (pp. 244–247) exhibit a fatal weakness which ultimately reduces each to interest balancing. In view of this, the relative success of the balancing of interests as a framework of constitutional interpretation hangs on its capacity to furnish an answer.

The criterion for choice among competing interests can be qualitative or quantitative. To aid in assessment, it might prove useful to partition them, realizing also that a balancing standard could conceivably call for some mix of the two.

152. Pound, *A Survey of Social Interests*, 3.

For reasons set forth directly below and in succeeding sections, I will demonstrate that both of these criteria remain procedurally vague and substantively vulnerable.

None of the illustrations presented in this chapter point up the use of a qualitative standard as the criterion of choice among competing interests. Though examples abound in the Court's opinions,[153] one will suffice for our purposes. Probably the best-recognized instance appears in Justice Frankfurter's opinion for the Court in *Rochin* v. *California*.[154]. In that case, the defendant swallowed two capsules to avoid having them fall into the hands of the police. After manual attempts to extract the pills failed, Rochin was taken to a hospital where police ordered his stomach pumped. The defendant regurgitated the capsules, the contents of which were subsequently identified as morphine, and a report to that effect was used to convict him. Addressing the question of whether these police procedures denied due process, Justice Frankfurter discussed at length, and in obvious response to Justice Black's stinging criticism, how the conflicting interests of law enforcement and the integrity of the defendant's person were to be weighed in light of the fundamental values of society:

> Regard for the requirements of the Due Process Clause "inescapably imposes upon this Court an exercise of judg-

153. This appears to be particularly true of, but is not by any means limited to, the reliance upon case-by-case fairness as distinguished from adopting some form of incorporating provisions of the Bill of Rights into the Due Process Clause of the Fourteenth Amendment; see Chase and Ducat, Constitutional Interpretation 913. Justice Black dates the beginning of this equation of due process with "fundamental fairness" with Twining v. New Jersey, 211 U.S. 78, 29 S.Ct. 14 (1908), A Constitutional Faith 35 (1968). For other examples, see Powell v. Alabama, 287 U.S. 45, 53 S.Ct. 55 (1932); Snyder v. Massachusetts, 291 U.S. 97, 54 S.Ct. 330 (1934); Malinski v. New York, 324 U.S. 401, 412, 65 S.Ct. 781, 787 (1945) (concurring opinion of Frankfurter, J.); Adamson v. California, 332 U.S. 46, 59, 67 S.Ct. 1672, 1679 (1947) (concurring opinion of Frankfurter, J.); Duncan v. Louisiana, 391 U.S. 145, 215, 88 S. Ct. 1444, 1460 (1968) (dissenting opinion of Harlan, J.). See also Palko v. Connecticut, 302 U.S. 319, 58 S.Ct. 149 (1937).

154. 342 U.S. 165, 72 S.Ct. 205 (1952).

ment upon the whole course of the proceedings [resulting in a conviction] in order to ascertain whether they offend those canons of decency and fairness which express the notions of justice of English-speaking peoples even toward those charged with the most heinous offenses." * * * These standards of justice are not authoritatively formulated anywhere as though they were specifics. Due process of law is a summarized constitutional guarantee of respect for those personal immunities which, as Mr. Justice Cardozo twice wrote for the Court, are "so rooted in the traditions and conscience of our people as to be ranked as fundamental", Snyder v. Commonwealth of Massachusetts, 291 U.S. 97, 105, 54 S.Ct. 330, 332, or are "implicit in the concept of ordered liberty". Palko v. State of Connecticut, 302 U.S. 319, 325, 58 S.Ct. 149, 152.

* * *

The vague contours of the Due Process Clause do not leave judges at large. We may not draw on our merely personal and private notions and disregard the limits that bind judges in their judicial function. Even though the concept of due process of law is not final and fixed, these limits are derived from considerations that are fused in the whole nature of our judicial process. * * * The Due Process Clause places upon this Court the duty of exercising a judgment, within the narrow confines of judicial power in reviewing State convictions, upon interests of society pushing in opposite directions.

Due process of law thus conceived is not to be derided as resort to a revival of "natural law." To believe that this judicial exercise of judgment could be avoided by freezing "due process of law" at some fixed stage of time or thought is to suggest that the most important aspect of constitutional adjudication is a function for inanimate machines and not for judges, for whom the independence safeguarded by Article III of the Constitution was designed and who are presumably guided by established standards of judicial behavior. Even cybernetics has not yet made that haughty claim. To practice the requisite detachment and to achieve sufficient objectivity no doubt demands of judges the habit of self-discipline and self-criticism, incertitude that one's own views are incontestable and alert tolerance toward views not shared. But these are precisely the presuppositions of our judicial process. They are precisely the qualities society has a right to expect from those entrusted with ultimate judicial power.

Restraints on our jurisdiction are self-imposed only in the sense that there is from our decisions no immediate appeal short of impeachment or constitutional amendment. But that does not make due process of law a matter of judicial caprice. The faculties of the Due Process Clause may be indefinite and vague, but the mode of their ascertainment is not self-willed. In each case "due process of law" requires an evaluation based on a disinterested inquiry pursued in the spirit of science, on a balanced order of facts exactly and fairly stated, on the detached consideration of conflicting claims, * * * on a judgment not *ad hoc* and episodic but duly mindful of reconciling the needs both of continuity and of change in a progressive society.

Applying these general considerations to the circumstances of the present case, we are compelled to conclude that the proceedings by which this conviction was obtained do more than offend some fastidious squeamishness or private sentimentalism about combatting crime too energetically. This is conduct that shocks the conscience. Illegally breaking into the privacy of the petitioner, the struggle to open his mouth and remove what was there, the forcible extraction of his stomach's contents—this course of proceeding by agents of government to obtain evidence is bound to offend even hardened sensibilities. They are methods too close to the rack and the screw to permit of constitutional differentiation.[155]

Even if we accept his characterization of the evaluation process, that the "conscience" which is "shocked" by this conduct is society's and not Mr. Justice Frankfurter's—a distinction which Justice Cardozo himself described as "shadowy and evanescent, and

---

155. 342 U.S. at 169–172, 72 S.Ct. at 208–210. Though Professor Mendelson characterizes Frankfurter as a "pragmatist," Justices Black and Frankfurter: Conflict in the Court 13, 40, 47 (1960), as compared with Black whom he describes as an "idealist," this portrayal is respectively disputed explicitly and implicitly by the writings of others who appear to regard him as an exponent for what Black so accurately calls "natural law," Jacobsohn, *Felix Frankfurter and the Ambiguities of Judicial Statesmanship*, 49 N.Y.U.L.Rev. 1 (1974) ; Stevens, *Felix Frankfurter*, in Frisch and Stevens, eds., American Political Thought: The Philosophic Dimensions of American Statesmanship 237–260 (1970).

tends to become one of words and little more" [156]—the use of such a criterion still leaves unanswered far too many embarassing questions. How are we to derive practical guidance from what are here only platitudes? For all the talk of "detachment," "objectivity," and "the spirit of science," there is the eerie feeling that the Justice has exchanged his black robe for an Ouija board or crystal ball. To talk of "the conscience of our people" is to engage in the worst sort of anthropomorphism. What we have here is not insight but blindness to the pluralism and cultural diversity within American society. And surely Justice Black scores more than debater's points when he hauls the Court up short for its use of "stretchy" and "rubberlike" words such as "fairness" and "decency." It is a lame reply to Black's attacks on such terms as invitations to limitless subjectivity and hence arbitrariness to say that any alternative will "freeze" the concept of due process forever. Finally, given the trend in balancing of making support for liberty over security the exception rather than the rule, Justice Black seems amply justified in his "even greater concern" that "the accordion-like qualities of this philosophy must inevitably imperil all the individual liberty safeguards specifically enumerated in the Bill of Rights." [157] The qualitative criterion for effecting a balance among competing interests, in sum, transforms constitutional adjudication into an excursion in intuitionism.[158]

A quantitative approach is suggested by Dean Pound's principle that competing interests be weighed so as to "[s]ecure all interests so far as possible with the least sacrifice of the totality of interests or the scheme of interests as a whole." [159] While this is hardly a model of clarity, Pound himself notes the simi-

---

156. The Nature of the Judicial Process 110. For his discussion of the judge's function in deciding cases consistent with "customary morality," see ibid., 104–111. See also note 23, supra.

157. 342 U.S. at 177, 72 S.Ct. at 212 (concurring opinion). See also his

discussion in A Constitutional Faith, Ch. 2.

158. See Rawls, A Theory of Justice § 7 (1971) [hereafter referred to as Rawls].

159. 3 Jurisprudence 334 (1959).

larity of this criterion to the pragmatist principle stated by William James, that, in Pound's words, we aim "to satisfy at all times as many demands as we can" and the Benthamite calculus by which the policy to be preferred was that advancing "the greatest good of the greatest number." [160] The evaluation of interests contemplated is clearly utilitarian. This tack, we should hasten to add, is not peculiar to Pound, but characterizes the interest balancing literature.[161] Insofar, then, as there appears to be an understandable and durable prescriptive framework, one capable of replication, the criterion for effecting a balance among interests will be the satisfaction of a greater number rather than a lesser number of claims over all. We will be looking at the application of this criterion in the next two sections.

3. Balancing Unlike Interests

It is important at this juncture to digress for the purpose of pointing up how interest balancing is *not* supposed to be conducted. Dean Pound writes:

> When it comes to weighing or valuing claims or demands with respect to other claims or demands, we must be careful to compare them on the same plane. If we put one as an individual interest and the other as a social interest we may decide the question in advance in our very way of putting it.[162]

The point is clear enough. If we apply the maximizing criterion to unlike interests, the social interest will automatically win simply because the claims of more people are to be found on that side of the scale.

Despite Dean Pound's caveat, this lapse is a familiar occurrence in opinions which undertake interest balancing. A classic example, according to Justice Black, was the *Barenblatt* case:

> But even assuming what I cannot assume, that some balancing is proper in this case, I feel that the Court after stat-

---

160. *Ibid.*

161. For example, see Braybrooke and Lindblom, Chs. 9, 10; Wasserstrom, Chs. 6, 7.

162. *A Survey of Social Interests*, 2 ; 3 Jurisprudence 328.

ing the test ignores it completely. At most it balances the right of the Government to preserve itself, against Barenblatt's right to refrain from revealing Communist affiliations. Such a balance, however, mistakes the factors to be weighed. In the first place, it completely leaves out the real interest in Barenblatt's silence, the interest of the people as a whole in being able to join organizations, advocate causes and make political "mistakes" without later being subjected to governmental penalties for having dared to think for themselves. It is this right, the right to err politically, which keeps us strong as a Nation. For no number of laws against communism can have as much effect as the personal conviction which comes from having heard its arguments and rejected them, or from having once accepted its tenets and later recognized their worthlessness. Instead, the obloquy which results from investigations such as this not only stifles "mistakes" but prevents all but the most courageous from hazarding any views which might at some later time become disfavored. This result, whose importance cannot be overestimated, is doubly crucial when it affects the universities, on which we must largely rely for the experimentation and development of new ideas essential to our country's welfare. It is these interests of society, rather than Barenblatt's own right to silence, which I think the Court should put on the balance against the demands of the Government, if any balancing process is to be tolerated. Instead they are not mentioned, while on the other side the demands of the Government are vastly overstated and called "self preservation." * * * 163

Nor is *Barenblatt* the only good example.[164]

The error seems obvious enough. But is it too obvious? Has Justice Harlan committed the error out of recklessness (which is difficult to believe for so discerning and sophisticated a scholar) or out of necessity? If we follow Justice Black's instruction and balance the interests as Pound directs, we will be weighing the interest of all of us in "self-preservation" against the interest we

163. 360 U.S. at 144, 79 S.Ct. 1102 (dissenting opinion).

164. Justice Black repeats this criticism in his dissenting opinion to

Konigsberg v. State Bar of California, 366 U.S. 36, 73–74, 81 S.Ct. 997 1019 (1961); see also In re Anastaplo, 366 U.S. 82, 81 S.Ct. 978 (1961).

all have in freedom of association. What does it mean to say we shall maximize these claims? In short, it is not clear how the application of the maximizing criterion helps us to make the choice once we have two *equal* interests to weigh.[165]

Conceivably, this difficulty can be worked out in a couple of ways. One alternative, of course, would simply be to attach weights to the various interests; the weights are only unspecified, not unspecifiable. But, in view of Pound's statement that in any scheme of social interests "first place must be given to the social interest in the general security" [166] and his regard for it as "paramount social interest" [167] this may prove to be a dubious improvement over the methodology of *Barenblatt*. A second approach lies in assessing how much of an interest is at stake as revealed by the facts of a case, and then striking a proportionate balance among partial or limited interests.[168] But this leaves us with *ad hoc* balancing, where the outcome of any case arises from a balance of particulars and generalization to other cases is either extremely difficult or not attempted. One can appreciate that the purpose in adopting an interest balancing perspective was to get out from under a preoccupation with fixed or mechanical standards that was thought to discredit absolutism. Justice Cardozo writes, "If you ask how he [the judge] is to know when one interest outweighs another, I can only answer that he must get his knowledge just as the legislator gets it, from experience and study and reflection; in brief, from life itself." [169] If this is so, has interest balancing anything to contribute as a prescriptive framework?

165. See Stone, *A Critique of Pound's Theory of Justice*, 20 Iowa L.Rev. 531, 547 (1935).

166. *A Survey of Social Interests*, 17.

167. *Ibid.*

168. Failure to accurately assess how the facts in the case at hand bounded the scope of a postulated social interest in security was a criticism of Justice Black's against interest balancing as it was employed in Konigsberg v. State Bar of California, 366 U.S. 36, 71–74, 81 S.Ct. 997, 1017–1019 (dissenting opinion).

169. The Nature of the Judicial Process 113.

4. Making "Sacrifices"

However the difficulty over maximizing interests is resolved, it is clear all interests cannot be satisfied. For all the talk of maximizing interests over all with the "least sacrifice," there remains the fact that some sacrifice there will be. Portraying the matter as one of incompletely satisfying some social interests in service of the over all betterment of the scheme of interests, however, muddies our perception of the real impact. To say that all social interests cannot be satisfied in the overall best interest of the system masks the fact that "social interests" are the demands of real people, and an acknowledgment that all of their demands cannot be met means that some people will likely have to sacrifice for the benefit of others. The question then becomes: who can justifiably be expected to bear the burden?

While it is true that Pound warned against interest balancing becoming a screen for majority—or, for that matter, minority —rule,[170] the maximization criterion, as applied to the interests of a citizenry with very unequally distributed assets and vulnerabilities, will necessarily mean that some interests, and therefore the demands of some people[171] will go unfulfilled regardless of how large the number satisfied is above the majority line. At this point, it is striking to note how the argument against interest balancing parallels the argument against the group theory of politics and pluralism.[172] All make the assumption that the gains and losses that arise from settling conflicts in interests will be spread pretty much over all the people in the society. But we know this is a fallacious assumption. More often than not, we see that those who win today do not lose tomorrow, and vice versa; those who win today generally keep on winning, and those who lose usually keep on losing. In short, social cleavages in the satisfaction of social interests repeatedly tend to fall along the same lines; they are not randomly distributed.

170. 2 Jurisprudence 386.

171. As distinguished from "some demands of *the* people."

172. See Ricci, Community Power and Democratic Theory: The Logic of Political Analysis 80–81, 188–190 (1971).

The problem presented by this exploitation of powerless, insular minorities is unlikely to be corrected in the absence of a prescriptive framework of constitutional interpretation that deliberately weights interests or otherwise qualifies their balance so as to guard against such things. A framework loose on structure is not likely to remedy the problem, particularly if the "social engineering" is done within an institution either conservative in itself (see Chapter 5) or in the hands of those far removed from the experiences of these minorities,[173] or both.

But even if the problem of permanent minorities were rectified, as by opening up the processes of political participation and increasing access to policy-making institutions, it can be argued, as John Rawls has in his volume, *A Theory of Justice*, that achieving the greatest net balance of satisfaction is unjust. I set out in the limited space here only the barest conclusions of arguments to which he devotes the entire book. In a nutshell, utilitarianism is an unacceptable basis for the creation of social policy, argues Rawls, for the following reason:

> [O]nce the principles of justice are thought of as arising from an original agreement in a situation of equality, it is an open question whether the principle of utility would be acknowledged. Offhand it hardly seems likely that persons who view themselves as equals, entitled to press their claims upon one another, would agree to a principle which may require lesser life prospects for some simply for the sake of a greater sum of advantages enjoyed by others. Since each desires to protect his interests, his capacity to advance his conception of the good, no one has a reason to acquiesce in an enduring loss for himself in order to bring about a greater net balance of satisfaction. In the absence of strong and lasting benevolent impulses, a rational man would not accept a basic structure merely because it maximized the algebraic sum of advantages irrespective of its permanent effects on his own basic rights and interests. Thus it seems that the principle of utility is incompatible with the conception of social cooperation among

173. See Schmidhauser, The Supreme Court: Its Politics, Personalities and Procedures (1960).

equals for mutual advantage. It appears to be inconsistent with the idea of reciprocity implicit in the notion of a well-ordered society. * * *[174]

In a word, the maximizing criterion is unfair because those who benefit would not willingly change places with those who sacrifice. Simply because we would not accept this lot for ourselves, there is no reason for us to expect it of others.[175]

The principles of "justice as fairness," which Professor Rawls sets out as an alternative to all forms of interest balancing, constitute a prescriptive framework. According to the first principle which focuses basically on political liberties (i. e., freedoms of speech, press, thought, association, the right to vote, eligibility to hold office, protection from arbitrary arrest, etc.), "Each person is to have an equal right to the most extensive total system of equal basic liberties compatible with a similar system of liberty for all." [176] Secondly, social and economic inequalities are to be tolerated only insofar as they work to better the condition of the most marginal (least advantaged) member of society and where they are the product of institutions open and accessible to all.[177] Furthermore, any departure from the arrangement of equal liberty is not to be balanced against, that is compensated for or justified by, greater economic or social advantages;[178] "liberty can only be restricted for the sake of liberty." [179] I have set out

174. Rawls, 14.

175. This includes distribution of advantages on the basis of virtue or moral desert. Rawls contends that "no one should be advantaged or disadvantaged by natural fortune or social circumstances in the choice of principles" because "the initial endowment of natural assets and contingencies of their growth and nurture in early life are arbitrary from a moral point of view" [that is, they are things for which the individual can claim no personal credit; they are accidental]. *ibid.*, 18, 311.

176. *Ibid.*, 302.

177. *Ibid.*, 83.

178. *Ibid.*, 61.

179. *Ibid.*, 302. Rawls continues, "a less extensive liberty must strengthen the total system of liberty shared by all;" and "a less than equal liberty must be acceptable to those with the lesser liberty" [that is, it must work to the betterment of the least advantaged].

that portion of Rawls' framework most relevant for our purposes both to show a contrast with interest balancing and because of its marked similarity to the preferred freedoms approach, discussed in the next chapter, a mode of constitutional interpretation which evolved out of a concern with the problem of permanent minorities.

5. Subordinating the Individual

The premise underlying Professor Rawls' precepts of justice is, as he put it, "men's desire to treat one another not as means only but as ends in themselves." [180] This presents a marked contrast (not as sharp, surely, as one would find in considering the function of law in a totalitarian state, but a clear contrast nonetheless) when compared with Dean Pound's exhortation that "[w]hen we are considering what claims or demands to recognize and within what limits, * * * it is important to subsume the individual interests under social interests and to weigh them as such." [181] Insofar, then, as one finds himself or herself in accord with Rawls' outlook on the moral stature of individuals in a society where government is predicated on a social contract, the violation of this premise by interest balancing constitutes an objection not merely to its prescriptive framework, if such it can be said to have, but even to its employment as a descriptive framework.

A more congenial variation on the subordinating of individual to group interests is, perhaps, Professor Shapiro's defense of judicial activism, which, in accord with his reasoning on the anomaly of regarding the Court as an "undemocratic" institution discussed earlier, contends that the Court is a representative institution because it speaks for the out-groups in society.[182] Though attribution to it of a clientele or constituency vindicates the Court's participation as a political institution and judicial activism comes to be justified as a mechanism for vindicating mi-

180. *Ibid.*, 179.

181. *A Survey of Social Interests*, 3; 3 Jurisprudence 329–330.

182. Shapiro, Freedom of Speech 34–45, 111–115; and see Ch. 4 generally.

nority rights, this functionalist line of argument, which is the backbone of the preferred freedoms approach, implies significant correlative limitations to constitutional rights, as we shall see in the next chapter (pp. 238–244).

In a world of "big business," "big labor," and "big government," where organizations of all kinds seem to be closing in around us and threaten to suffocate the individual, a defense of the Court as the defender of individuals, just because they are individuals, makes more than a little sense. It is difficult to see how the integrity and identity of the individual will be preserved in a system of law that always views his right to do something as an attribute of some social purpose, no matter how large or small the group to which he belongs.

6.   Ex Post Facto *Legislation*

In a detached, sort of antiseptic social science way, we say that judges are participants in the policy-making process. This, of course, is hardly news. But it does tend to mask things worth unmasking. In particular, what it does is cast the judicial role in terms of choosing between social interests. Probably because absolutists have always been more sensitive about casting legal questions in terms of *personal* rights and obligations, they have criticized the unfairness of the "first courts, then law" view all along for the unfairness that results when one party loses a case because the judge chooses to devise a rule the losing party could not possibly have anticipated at trial. This is particularly objectionable when it happens in criminal proceedings. When legislative bodies do it, we call it *ex post facto* lawmaking and declare it unconstitutional; when courts do it, we chalk it up to judicial policy-making.

Interest balancers have tended to develop two distinct but related avenues of response to the charge of unfairness. The first is to write it off as inevitable. Thus Morris Cohen writes, "[Another] source of opposition to the view that judges make law is found in our constitutional prohibition of *ex post facto* laws and general abhorrence of retroactive legislation, which make it very disagreeable for lawyers to admit that judges make law; for all judicial legislation is literally *ex post facto* so far as the parties before the Court are concerned." [183]   And judicial legislation is unavoidable both because of the "necessary obscurity of language" in some statutes and "because the courts have to apply a general law to a situation that could not have been foreseen by the legislature." [184]   A variation on this theme is Justice Jackson's defense of the Nuremberg Trials in the face of the charge that there existed no precedent for the convening of such a tribunal (or, more pointedly, for the indictment of several of the defendants on the heretofore unheard of count of "crimes against humanity"):

> International Law is not capable of development by the normal processes of legislation for there is no continuing international legislative authority.   Innovations and revisions in International Law are brought about by the action of governments designed to meet a change in circumstances.   It grows, as did the Common Law, through decisions reached from time to time in adapting settled principles to new situations.   The fact is that when the law evolves by the case method, as did the Common Law and as International Law must do if it is to advance at all, it advances at the expense of those who wrongly guessed the law and learned too late their error.
> *   *   * [185]

In part, Justice Jackson's unsympathetic regard for the defendants' position (however loathsome they may have been in that particular instance) partakes of a second line of justification, namely, that the social benefit of growth in the law outweighs any conceivable cost to the losing party.   In Justice Cardozo's words, concern about the cost to the loser is much ado about nothing:

> The picture of the bewildered litigant lured into a course of action by the false light of a decision, only to meet ruin when

183.   Law and the Social Order 117 (1933).

184.   *Ibid.*, 132.   (Emphasis in original deleted).

185.   2 Trial of the Major War Criminals Before the International Military Tribunal 147 (1947) ["The Blue Series"].

the light is extinguished and the decision overruled, is for the most part a figment of excited brains. The only rules there is ever any thought of changing are those that are invoked by injustice after the event to shelter and intrench itself. In the rarest instances, if ever, would conduct have been different if the rule had been known and the change foreseen. At times the change means the imposition of a bill of costs that might otherwise have been saved. That is a cheap price to pay for the uprooting of an ancient wrong. One man is made a victim to the extent of a few dollars in return for a readjustment that will save many victims in the future. * * *186

Still, what happened in *Ginzburg* v. *United States*187 seems neither inevitable nor insignificant. Ginzburg, you may remember, was convicted on charges of violating the federal obscenity statute. Though prior decisions had imposed liability depending on the obscenity of the material,188 the Court, in *Ginzburg*, chose to affirm the defendant's conviction not on the ground that he had violated the law by mailing publications obscene in themselves, but because he peddled nonobscene material in a way that pan-

186. The Growth of the Law 122. See also The Nature of the Judicial Process 143, 145, 147.

187. 383 U.S. 463, 86 S.Ct. 942 (1966).

188. The three-part test which the Court cumulated in A Book Named "John Cleland's Memoirs of a Woman of Pleasure" v. Attorney General of Massachusetts, 383 U.S. 413, 86 S.Ct. 975 (1966), from incremental announcements in Roth v. United States, 354 U.S. 476, 77 S. Ct. 1304 (1957) (appeal to prurient interest); Manual Enterprises, Inc. v. Day, 370 U.S. 478, 82 S.Ct. 1432 (1962) (patent offensiveness); Jacobellis v. Ohio, 378 U.S. 184, 84 S. Ct. 1676 (1964) (redeeming social value [with independent status as

a separate test]), focused entirely on the material itself. The approach announced in *Ginzburg*, while retaining an appraisal of the materials, harked back to the view expressed by Chief Justice Warren, concurring in *Roth*, that

It is not the book that is on trial; it is a person. The conduct of the defendant is the central issue, not the obscenity of a book or picture. The nature of the materials is, of course, relevant as an attribute of the defendant's conduct, but the materials are thus placed in context from which thy draw color and character. A wholly different result might be reached in a different setting. 354 U.S. at 495, 77 S.Ct. at 1314–1315.

dered to a "prurient interest in sex" and thus evidenced an intent to treat the materials as if they were obscene. As might be expected, this proved to be too much for Justice Black. Observing at the outset that "Ginzburg * * * is now finally and authoritatively condemned to serve five years in prison for distributing printed matter about sex which neither Ginzburg nor anyone else could possibly have known to be criminal," he continued:

> Criminal punishment by government, although universally recognized as a necessity in limited areas of conduct, is an exercise of one of government's most awesome and dangerous powers. Consequently, wise and good governments make all possible efforts to hedge this dangerous power by restricting it within easily identifiable boundaries. Experience, and wisdom flowing out of that experience, long ago led to the belief that agents of government should not be vested with power and discretion to define and punish as criminal past conduct which had not been clearly defined as a crime in advance. To this end, at least in part, written laws came into being, marking the boundaries of conduct for which public agents could thereafter impose punishment upon people. In contrast, bad governments either wrote no general rules of conduct at all, leaving that highly important task to the unbridled discretion of government agents at the moment of trial, or sometimes, history tells us, wrote their laws in an unknown tongue so that people could not understand them or else placed their written laws at such inaccessible spots that people could not read them. It seems to me that these harsh expedients used by bad governments to punish people for conduct not previously clearly marked as criminal are being used here to put Mr. Ginzburg in prison for five years.[189]

Black was not alone in this view. Among the four dissenters was Harlan, Jr., who, professing astonishment at the "judicial improvisation" that led the Court "in effect to write a new statute," wrote, "This curious result is reached through the elaboration of a theory of obscenity entirely unrelated to the language,

189. 383 U.S. at 477, 86 S.Ct. at 950–951. See also Fuller, The Morality of Law (1964).

purposes, or history of the federal statute now being applied, and certainly different from the test used by the trial court to convict the defendants." [190]

Hopefully, decisions like *Ginzburg* are rare occurrences. It would, of course, be inaccurate and unfair to argue that miscarriages of justice on the scale of that in the *Ginzburg* case occur every time interest balancing is employed. It would not be inaccurate or unfair to say that interest balancing increases the risk.

190.   383 U.S. at 494–495, 86 S.Ct. at 954.

Chapter 4

The Preferred Freedoms Approach

If there was some single point at which all of the objections to interest balancing coalesced, it was around the problem of permanent minorities. Whether in the Court's own weighing of competing interests or in its chronic acquiescence in that job when done by the legislature, interest balancing had failed to distinguish between social interests in decisions about the content of public policy and social interests in the procedures by which those policy decisions were made. The failure to make this distinction was the point at which the shallow definition of democracy fused with interest balancing's exploitive potential. Its regard for all social interests as pretty much equal and interchangeable and its ready application of the maximizing criterion resulted in what critics saw as the exploitation of vulnerable minorities by a persistent majoritarianism. In a society where, presumably, men and women were thought to control their own fate, where the distribution of public goods was supposed to bear some relation to one's effective political participation, but where the resources to participate were unequally distributed, the balancing of interests came to be viewed by some as a variation on that perverse arrangement of social interests, espoused by Thrasymachus, in which justice was defined as "the interest of the stronger."[1] In short, interest balancing had itself been weighed and found wanting. From the seeds of this dissatisfaction sprouted a third mode of constitutional interpretation which I shall refer to as the "preferred freedoms" approach.

A Preface to Preferred Freedoms: The Higher Plane of Economic Liberties Before 1937

If attacks on judicial activism have generally pictured the Court as a vehicle for minority rule, there is certainly plenty of

---

1. Plato, The Republic 46 (Jowett trans. 1944).

evidence in the half century of Court decisions prior to 1937 to support the charge. When the preference for freedom first came to the Court, it came in that era, and that preference was for economic freedom. The effect of this was to convert the Court into a bastion of special privilege for the well-to-do, to make it the protector of the propertied classes and large business corporations. Populated with railroad and corporation lawyers, the Court manipulated constitutional doctrines to unhorse legislative attempts at the regulation of business enterprise both on the national and state levels.[2] While there is no need to retell the complete narrative here, it may be useful to recount at least part of it since opponents of judicial activism tend to rely on analogies between the Court's posture in that era and contemporary advocacy of preferred freedoms for the purpose of discrediting the latter.[3]

Though the Court chronically intervened in economic policy-making to strike a balance between the right of the states to regulate business enterprise and the proportion of the business

2. See Twiss, Lawyers and the Constitution: How Laissez Faire Came to the Supreme Court (1942); Corwin, Liberty Against Government, Ch. 4 (1948); Pritchett, The American Constitution, Ch. 31 (2d ed. 1968); Kelly and Harbison, The American Constitution, Chs. 19–21, 26–27 (4th ed. 1970); Miller, The Supreme Court and American Capitalism (1968). See also Hofstadter, Social Darwinism in American Thought, Chs. 2, 3 (Rev. ed. 1955).

3. For example, Justice Black decried, as a reversion to "natural law" thinking rather like that of the pre-1937 Court, Warren Court decisions which generated new "fundamental" liberties such as the right to privacy, or recognized "suspect classes" other than racial minorities; see Griswold v. Connecticut 381 U.S. 479, 522–524, 85 S.Ct. 1678, 1702–1703 (1965) (dissenting opinion); Harper v. Virginia State Board of Elections, 383 U. S. 663, 675–678, 86 S.Ct. 1079, 1086–1088 (1966) (dissenting opinion). And Justice Rehnquist has written that the liberty of contract and the right to privacy "are 'sisters under the skin.' ". *Is an Expanded Right to Privacy Consistent With Fair and Effective Law Enforcement? Or, Privacy, You've Come a Long Way, Baby*, 23 Kan. L.Rev. 1, 6 (1974). See also Weber v. Aetna Casualty & Surety Co., 406 U.S. 164, 177, 92 S.Ct. 1400, 1407 (1972) (dissenting opinion of Rehnquist, J.); Roe v. Wade, 410 U.S. 113, 174, 93 S.Ct. 705, 737 (1973) (dissenting opinion of Rehnquist, J.).

"affected with a public interest," [4] to oversee the "fairness" of rate structures for public utilities and other regulated industries,[5] and, less occasionally, to beat back such "radical" ventures as the progressive income tax,[6] perhaps the best-remembered blows struck by the Court, in its advancement of *laissez faire* capitalism,[7] were the successive knock-out punches it administered to regulatory legislation by employing the doctrines of dual federalism and liberty of contract. The impact of dual federalism, discussed earlier (pp. 57–64), was, of course, to strip the national government of all regulatory power over the means of production (manufacturing, mining, and agriculture) and to relegate their control to the states. Following up with the liberty of contract, it then killed off much of that regulatory legislation at the state level and took with it some additional federal laws as well. A brief discussion of the liberty of contract may prove useful because the style of its employment bears some similarity to the preferred freedoms approach.

Liberty of contract was a judicial invention from the Due Process Clauses of the Fifth and Fourteenth Amendments, both of which prohibit the national and state governments respectively from "depriv[ing] any person of life, liberty, or property, without due process of law * * *." From this ostensible procedural guarantee that government would not resort to unusual or irregular means of regulation, the Court manufactured a substantive right, the "liberty of contract," which provided that,

4. See, *e. g.*, Munn v. Illinois, 94 U. S. 113, 24 L.Ed. 77 (1877); Wolff Packing Co. v. Court of Industrial Relations, 262 U.S. 522, 43 S.Ct. 630 (1923); Tyson Bros. v. Banton, 273 U.S. 418, 47 S.Ct. 426 (1927). *Cf.* Nebbia v. New York, 291 U.S. 502, 54 S.Ct. 505 (1934).

5. See, *e. g.*, Chicago, Milwaukee, St. Paul R. R. Co. v. Minnesota, 134 U.S. 418, 10 S.Ct. 462 (1890); Smyth v. Ames, 169 U.S. 466, 18 S. Ct. 418 (1898); Missouri ex rel.

Southwestern Bell Telephone Co. v. Public Service Com'n, 262 U.S. 276, 43 S.Ct. 544 (1923); St. Louis & O'Fallon Ry. v. United States, 279 U.S. 461, 49 S.Ct. 384 (1929).

6. Pollock v. Farmers' Loan & Trust Co., 158 U.S. 601, 15 S.Ct. 912 (1895).

7. See note 2, *supra*. See also Commons, Legal Foundations of Capitalism (1924).

even if executed with procedural correctness, economic regulation had to be specially justified; hence, the preference for freedom. The Court paved the way for its use with a ruling in 1886 that a corporation was a "person" within the meaning of the Fourteenth Amendment.[8] This was followed the next year with the warning that not all legislation supported by the invocation of the "police power" would pass. The Court, said Harlan, Sr., would not be "misled by mere pretenses." If the exercise of the state police power, said Justice Harlan, "has no real or substantial relation to those objects [for which the legislation was enacted], or is a palpable invasion of rights secured by the fundamental law, it is the duty of the courts to so adjudge * * *." [9] Within a decade, the Court had invalidated its first piece of legislation on the ground it infringed the liberty of contract. By its ruling in that case, *Allgeyer* v. *Louisiana*,[10] the Court struck down a state statute attempting to regulate out-of-state insurance companies doing business in the state. An economic liberty used to preserve the right of consumers to be defrauded by the predatory practices of unscrupulous insurance companies, however, soon became the vehicle by which to enforce "equal" bargaining rights between employees and employers.

By the turn of the century, sympathetic legislatures sought to modify the enormous disparity in bargaining power between the individual employee and the giant corporation. The use of the state police power either to encourage workers to band together and, through unionization, achieve real parity in bargaining strength with a corporate employer, or to set outside limits on the provisions of labor contracts with respect to wages, hours, and working conditions which management might offer, received a generally hostile reception from the Court. Relying on the liberty of contract, which it purported to find in the Due Process Clauses, the Court struck down federal and state legislation which outlawed "yellow dog" clauses (promises by laborers not

8. Santa Clara County v. Southern Pacific Railroad Co., 118 U.S. 394, 6 S.Ct. 1132 (1886).

9. Mugler v. Kansas, 123 U.S. 623, 661, 8 S.Ct. 273, 297 (1887).

10. 165 U.S. 578, 17 S.Ct. 427 (1897).

to join, or, if a member, to withdraw from, a union) in employment contracts,[11] and set minimum wages.[12] The Court was somewhat less rigid, though still exacting, when it scrutinized maximum hours laws. It found redeeming merit and the requisite relation to protecting health in a Utah statute limiting the workday to eight hours for employees in the mining and smelting industry,[13] in one Oregon statute limiting the workday for women to 10 hours,[14] and in another Oregon law extending this maximum hours limitation to all mill and factory workers,[15] but it found health and welfare arguments insufficient to sustain New York's maximum hours legislation covering bakers.[16]

The theme to the Court's decisions applying the liberty of contract was, perhaps, most clearly echoed in *Wolff Packing Co.* v. *Court of Industrial Relations.* Striking down a Kansas statute which established an industrial relations court with authority to settle labor-management disputes in the state's essential industries. Chief Justice Taft intoned: "Freedom is the general rule, and restraint the exception. The legislative authority to abridge can be justified only by exceptional circumstances." [17]

The Court's infatuation with liberty of contract died with the opening shot of the Constitutional Revolution of 1937. In *West Coast Hotel Co.* v. *Parrish,* a decision upholding the constitutionality of a Washington minimum wage law, Chief Justice Hughes, speaking for the Court, exclaimed:

> What is this freedom? The Constitution does not speak of freedom of contract. It speaks of liberty and prohibits the

11. Adair v. United States, 208 U.S. 161, 28 S.Ct. 277 (1908); Coppage v. Kansas, 236 U.S. 1, 35 S.Ct. 240 (1915).

12. Adkins v. Children's Hospital, 261 U.S. 525, 43 S.Ct. 394 (1923); Morehead v. New York ex rel. Tipaldo, 298 U.S. 587, 56 S.Ct. 918 (1936).

13. Holden v. Hardy, 169 U.S. 366, 18 S.Ct. 383 (1898).

14. Muller v. Oregon, 208 U.S. 412, 28 S.Ct. 324 (1908).

15. Bunting v. Oregon, 243 U.S. 426, 37 S.Ct. 435 (1917).

16. Lochner v. New York, 198 U.S. 45, 25 S.Ct. 539 (1905).

17. 262 U.S. 522, 534, 43 S.Ct. 630, 632 (1923).

deprivation of liberty without due process of law. In prohibiting that deprivation, the Constitution does not recognize an absolute and uncontrollable liberty. Liberty in each of its phases has its history and connotation. But the liberty safeguarded is liberty in a social organization which requires the protection of law against evils which menace the health, safety, morals, and welfare of the people. Liberty under the Constitution is thus necessarily subject to the restraints of due process, and regulation which is reasonable in relation to its subject and is adopted in the interests of the community is due process.[18]

Though the story of the Constitutional Revolution, which began with the *West Coast Hotel Co.* case, could largely be told in a single volume of the *United States Reports*—volume 301, to be exact—the complete dimensions of the change were not clear until after Justice Rutledge had taken his seat in 1943. With the exception of Justice Roberts, all of the Justices then sitting had been appointed by FDR. Yet this transition had bequeathed three significant trends that were to fracture the cohesion of the Roosevelt appointees. First, it ended the activism of the Court in the area of economic regulation and transferred its interest to the domain of civil liberties. Second, it rekindled the debate over activism and self-restraint among the new liberal Justices, virtually all of whom had been openly critical of the vigor of the old Court. Finally, it signaled the acceptance of the balancing of interests approach to adjudication over the old legal method of "mechanical jurisprudence." No longer did the Court seem bent on presenting the image that judges were merely the instrument through which the law spoke neutrally and impartially, and where syllogistic reasoning and literal interpretation were viewed as the life of the law. Instead, the new Justices avowed a legal method which showed a more sophisticated awareness of the political implications in the value choices they made. They saw themselves as decision-makers who deliberately weigh the conflicting claims of competing interests in the society in the light of some broad policy goals.

18.   300 U.S. 379, 391, 57 S.Ct. 578,
581–582 (1937).

Constitutional Rights and the Democratic Enterprise

A third mode of constitutional interpretation, the preferred freedoms approach, sought to distinguish use of a stiffer standard in assessing infringements of civil rights and liberties from the reasonableness test applied to legislation involving economic regulation. In this way, several of the Justices sought to explain supplanting not merely self-restraint for activism, but one kind of activism for another. Though a number of cases [19] had talked in one way or another of more closely scrutinizing abridgments of civil liberties before its clearest enunciation in *Thomas v. Collins* (pp. 213–219) in 1945, the strongest suggestion for a justification prior to that comprised the famous footnote 4 of Justice Stone's opinion for the Court in *United States v. Carolene* Products Co. Stone wrote:

> There may be narrower scope for operation of the presumption of constitutionality when legislation appears on its face to be within a specific prohibition of the Constitution, such as those of the first ten Amendments, which are deemed equally specific when held to be embraced within the Fourteenth. * * *
>
> It is unnecessary to consider now whether legislation which restricts those political processes which can ordinarily be expected to bring about repeal of undesirable legislation, is to be subjected to more exacting judicial scrutiny under the general prohibitions of the Fourteenth Amendment than are most other types of legislation. * * *
>
> Nor need we enquire whether similar considerations enter into the review of statutes directed at particular religious, * * * or national, * * * or racial minorities * * * whether prejudice against discrete and insular minorities may be a special condition, which tends seriously to curtail the operation of those political processes ordinarily to be relied upon to protect minorities, and which may call for a correspondingly more searching judicial inquiry. * * * [20]

19. They are enumerated together with relevant excerpts in Justice Frankfurter's concurring opinion in Kovacs v. Cooper, 336 U.S. 77, 90–94, 69 S.Ct. 448, 455–457 (1949).

20. 304 U.S. 144, 152–153, 58 S.Ct. 778, 783–784 (1938).

Thus the argument for preferred freedoms, in short, appeared to be tied to the defense of minority rights, squarely addressing the problem of permanent minorities, and implicitly justified as strengthening the democratic process.

The justification offered for the use of the double standard was the assertion that there were some liberties which were so fundamental to the democratic order that their preservation merited special consideration. After all, who could imagine a democracy existing without freedom of speech, or thought, or association, or of the press? Yet democracy, it was argued, could survive without the ownership of private property.[21] Because they were essential to all that was basic to democratic government, these freedoms were placed in a "preferred position." The usual presumption of constitutionality and the test of mere "reasonableness," used to settle challenges to economic regulation, were thought insufficient to protect these basic liberties from devastating abridgment.

Though this mode of constitutional interpretation came to be called by many different names,[22] the conclusion that a given liberty was fundamental to the democratic process had the same effect. As with the regard for economic liberty in a bygone day, it evoked the assumption that freedom was the rule and restraint the exception, and so called into play a standard of more intense scrutiny for regulatory legislation. For the sake of clarity, it may prove helpful to see the standard as a three-part test, although its employment by the Justices was rarely so neatly segmented, often times was incomplete, and occasionally was un-

---

21. An intriguing question is whether other civil liberties, for example the guarantee against unreasonable searches and seizures, are better protected when predicated on property rights. For a discussion of two Fourth Amendment doctrines, the *Gouled* rule and the physical trespass concept, in this light, see Dionisopoulos and Ducat, The Right to Privacy: Essays and Cases 15–19 (1976).

22. Aside from being referred to as the preferred freedoms approach, it has been called the preferred position, strict scrutiny, the compelling interest test, the double standard, and the new equal protection, among others.

dertaken with the use of slightly different words. The standard may be sketched as follows:

1. Where legislation abridges a preferred freedom on its face,[23] the usual presumption of constitutionality is reversed; that is, legislation directly infringing a fundamental freedom is assumed to be unconstitutional until the government demonstrates otherwise.

2. The government must show that exercise of a fundamental freedom presents a clear and imminent danger;[24] or, in other words, the state must establish that the legislation advances a "compelling interest."

3. The legislation must be narrowly drawn so as to present a precise response to the problem, and must not impair basic liberties by its overbreadth; that means, the regulatory policy at issue must constitute the least restrictive alternative.

23. It is worth emphasizing that the infringement must be direct, not peripheral. A good illustration of the lack of facial abridgment is provided by the statute at issue in United States v. O'Brien, 391 U.S. 367, 88 S.Ct. 1673 (1968). In that case, the defendant, who was protesting the Vietnam war, was convicted under a federal law which made it a criminal offense to burn a draft card. Distinguishing other cases, Chief Justice Warren, speaking for the Court, pointed out, "The statute attacked in the instant case has no such inevitable unconstitutional effect, since the destruction of Selective Service certificates is in no respect inevitably or necessarily expressive." 391 U.S. at 385, 88 S.Ct. at 1683. The Court went on to uphold the law on grounds of administrative convenience.

24. The preferred freedoms approach originated with the attempt by the more liberal Justices to shore up Holmes' "clear and present danger" test against the onslaught of interest balancing. See Shapiro, Freedom of Speech: The Supreme Court and Judicial Review, Chs. 2, 4 (1966). Reference to "clear and present danger," therefore, marks earlier formulations of this standard; contemporary use overwhelmingly favors the "compelling interest" phraseology. Occasionally, however, recent applications have returned to the original phrasing, as, for example, when dealing with due process issues in involuntary civil commitment where the "dangerousness" of a possible mental patient is of particular relevance; see, e. g., Lessard v. Schmidt, 349 F.Supp. 1078 (E.D.Wis.1972); Lynch v. Baxley, 386 F.Supp. 378 (M.D.Ala.1974).

It is at once apparent that problems posed by the conflict of the exercise of governmental power and the assertion of civil liberties were not to be resolved by somehow merely maximizing claims. At least if this was maximizing, it was maximizing in a much more sophisticated sense than interest balancing had spelled out. If some rights, like those contained in the First Amendment, were in a preferred position, it stood to reason that everyone in the society was entitled to those rights before claims to secondary rights [25]—say, the right to dispose of your property as you saw fit—could be validated. Thus, in a conflict between those persons in society who were attempting to have their basic rights vindicated as against a larger number of their fellow citizens who were seeking to have lesser rights extended, the former claims must prevail over the latter, notwithstanding the fact that the number of individuals in the first group might be considerably less than the number of persons in the second.

Relying on this method of constitutional interpretation, liberal Justices on the Court sought to guarantee equal basic rights to those who lived on the periphery of the society—the poor, radicals, religious dissenters, blacks, Spanish-speaking people, city dwellers, juveniles, people accused of crime, and so on. In sum, as with other constitutional approaches already described, the preferred freedoms concept was premised on an answer to the question about the Court's unique capacity to do justice. Here justice was embodied in the mediation of the harshness and potential exploitation of majority rule; it was embodied in a concern for guaranteeing substantive equality in the allocation of rights and responsibilities in the society. Using this framework of constitutional interpretation during much of the 1940s and 1960s, and continuing though at a slowed pace through the 1970s,[26] the Court acted to integrate what had heretofore been

25. This function is performed in Rawls' concept of justice as fairness by the lexical ordering of the two principles of justice; see Chapter 3, p. 186. For his discussion of the priority principle, see Rawls, A Theory of Justice §§ 39, 82 (1971) [hereafter referred to as Rawls].

26. Among the articles which have focused in one way or another on

out-groups into the political system and to extend to those individuals who had been discriminated against, fuller protection and participation in society.

Rights deemed "fundamental" were not always found in the text of the Bill of Rights, nor were all of the provisions of the first ten amendments protective of basic liberties. The upshot of this was that preferred freedoms advocates often picked and chose from among the guarantees of the Bill of Rights [27] and then added to these other essential liberties [28] before the complete universe of preferred freedoms could be described. The conclusion that a right was "fundamental" had a dual impact.

the preferred freedoms approach or on the Court's application of it are: Mason, *The Core of Free Government, 1938–40: Mr. Justice Stone and "Preferred Freedoms,"* 65 Yale L.J. 597 (1956); McKay, *The Preference for Freedom,* 34 N. Y.U.L.Rev. 1182 (1959); Hyman and Newhouse, *Standards for Preferred Freedoms: Beyond the First,* 60 Nw.U.L.Rev. 1 (1965); Reinstein, *The Welfare Cases: Fundamental Rights, the Poor, and the Burden of Proof in Constitutional Litigation,* 44 Temple L.Q. 1 (1970); Gunther, *Foreword: In Search of Evolving Doctrine on a Changing Court: A Model for a Newer Equal Protection,* 86 Harv. L.Rev. 1 (1972); Tribe, *Toward a Model of Roles in the Due Process of Life and Law,* 87 Harv.L.Rev. 1 (1973); Note, *The Less Restrictive Alternative in Constitutional Adjudication: An Analysis, a Justification, and Some Criteria,* 27 Vanderbilt L.Rev. 972 (1974); Christie, *A Model of Judicial Review of Legislation,* 48 So.Cal.L.Rev. 1306 (1975); Linde, *Due Process of Lawmaking,* 55 Neb.L.Rev. 197 (1975).

27. This, however, was not a practice new, by any means, with the preferred freedoms approach. The inclusion of only "fundamental" rights was explicitly adopted by the Court at the turn of the century responding to the question "Does the Constitution follow the flag?" in the Insular Cases. See Downes v. Bidwell, 182 U.S. 244, 282–283, 21 S.Ct. 770, 785 (1901); Hawaii v. Mankichi, 190 U.S. 197, 217–218, 23 S.Ct. 787, 791 (1903). See also Dorr v. United States, 195 U.S. 138, 24 S.Ct. 808 (1904). Another example of the practice is the dawn of "selective incorporation" with Justice Cardozo's opinion for the Court in Palko v. Connecticut, 302 U.S. 319, 58 S.Ct. 149 (1937).

28. For example, the right to travel, Shapiro v. Thompson, 394 U.S. 618, 89 S.Ct. 1322 (1969); the right to vote, Reynolds v. Sims, 377 U.S. 533, 84 S.Ct. 1362 (1964); the right to privacy, Griswold v. Connecticut, 381 U.S. 479, 85 S.Ct. 1678 (1965); and the right to marry, Loving v. Virginia, 388 U.S. 1, 87 S.Ct. 1817 (1967).

It not only brought about the application of the strict scrutiny standard, it also identified a given liberty as a prime candidate for incorporation into the Due Process Clause of the Fourteenth Amendment and thus as a limitation against state action.

Furthermore, as the footnote in the *Carolene Products* case foretold, the strict scrutiny standard had relevance beyond the analysis of legislation alleged to infringe a preferred freedom. This framework of constitutional adjudication also came to be applied to asserted denials of equal protection where the categories created by the legislation amounted to "suspect classes," that is "discrete and insular minorities." While, of course, virtually all legislation discriminates in one way or another in allocating rights and resources to various groups, the focus here was on the creation of legal categories along certain lines that were held to constitute *invidious* or impermissible discrimination. Surely the most traditionally-recognized of these "suspect classes" was race; [29] another was alienage.[30] It was characteristic of the exponents of preferred freedoms not only to stand fast on the application of strict scrutiny to legislation which ran along these lines, but to reach out and identify other classes or categories as "suspect" in law.[31]

To sum up, then: The preferred freedoms approach constituted a two-tiered framework of constitutional adjudication. The

29. See The Slaughterhouse Cases, 83 U.S. (16 Wall.) 36, 21 L.Ed. 394 (1873); Strauder v. West Virginia, 100 U.S. 303, 25 L.Ed. 664 (1880); and especially: Hirabayashi v. United States, 320 U.S. 81, 63 S.Ct. 1375 (1943); Bolling v. Sharpe, 347 U.S. 497, 74 S.Ct. 693 (1954); McLaughlin v. Florida, 379 U.S. 184, 85 S.Ct. 283 (1964); Loving v. Virginia, 388 U.S. 1, 87 S.Ct. 1817 (1967).

30. See Yick Wo v. Hopkins, 118 U. S. 356, 6 S.Ct. 1064 (1886); and especially: Truax v. Raich, 239 U.S. 33, 36 S.Ct. 7 (1915); Oyama v. California, 332 U.S. 633, 68 S.Ct. 269 (1948); Takahashi v. Fish & Game Com'n, 334 U.S. 410, 68 S.Ct. 1138 (1948); Graham v. Richardson, 403 U.S. 365, 91 S.Ct. 1848 (1971); Sugarman v. Dougall, 413 U.S. 634, 93 S.Ct. 2842 (1973); in re Griffiths, 413 U.S. 717, 93 S.Ct. 2851 (1973).

31. For example, sex, illegitimacy, and indigency; see the discussion, *infra*, pp. 222–234.

lower tier was comprised of secondary freedoms (including economic liberties) and non-suspect discriminations. In the constitutional evaluation of legislation bearing upon these, interest balancing was retained; that is, statutes of this sort were tested by employing the rule of reasonableness with the usual presumption of constitutionality, the burden being placed on anyone who attacked the legislation to show that it was arbitrary, capricious, or irrational. In the upper tier, or preferred position, were fundamental liberties and suspect classes. Legislation concerning them was subjected to higher-powered analysis, balancing with a bias, so to say. The application of judicial review in this manner revealed a deep commitment by Justices William O. Douglas, Earl Warren, William Brennan, Thurgood Marshall, Abe Fortas, Arthur Goldberg, Wiley Rutledge, and Frank Murphy to the belief that vindication of basic liberties for peripheral groups in the society took precedence over the extension of additional rights to society's larger in-groups. In short, because of its unique capacity to do this kind of justice, the Court was actively obliged to use its power of judicial review to temper the policies of the "silent majority."

Beyond Preferred Freedoms: Justice Marshall's View of Constitutional Interpretation

In view of what other schools of constitutional interpretation have had to say about judicial activism and given the fact that the Court today is dominated by Justices oriented to interest balancing, it is puzzling, perhaps, to find that the most vocal contemporary critic of preferred freedoms is Justice Marshall. If somewhat surprising, this occurrence is not inexplicable. While the Burger Court has not discarded strict scrutiny, it has curtailed its use. With the exception of the right to privacy,[32] the present Court has displayed a tendency to define basic liberties as guarantees specifically mentioned in or immediately

---

32. See Griswold v. Connecticut, 381   v. Wade, 410 U.S. 113, 93 S.Ct. 705
     U.S. 479, 85 S.Ct. 1678 (1965); Roe   (1973).

inferable from, the Bill of Rights,[33] in accord with only the first paragraph of footnote 4 in *Carolene Products,* and this has generally meant First Amendment freedoms. The Burger Court has also restricted the recognition of any "suspect classes" beyond race and alienage.[34] The impact of these developments, of course, has been to increase the number of interests relegated to the bottom tier, and is, therefore, perfectly in keeping with an expanded use of interest balancing. Understandably, Justice Marshall's dissatisfaction with preferred freedoms derives in part from the extent to which the framework shelters something less than a total commitment by the Court to come to the aid of society's underdogs. But his criticisms go beyond this, and, oddly enough, at one point, bear a close resemblance to some observations made years earlier by Justice Frankfurter.

A comprehensive statement of Justice Marshall's position emerges from a trilogy of dissents which he penned in equal protection cases over a six-year period.[35] Splicing together excerpts from these opinions, it is possible to reconstruct four lines of argument: (1) that the Burger Court's notion of what interests are to be found in the upper tier is both too limited and at

33. Said Justice Powell, speaking for the Court, in San Antonio Independent School Dist. v. Rodriguez, 411 U.S. 1, 33–34, 93 S.Ct. 1278, 1297 (1974):

It is not the province of this Court to create substantive constitutional rights in the name of guaranteeing equal protection of the laws. Thus, the key to discovering whether education is "fundamental" is not to be found in comparisons of the relative societal significance of education as opposed to subsistence or housing. Nor is it to be found by weighing whether education is as important as the right to travel. Rather, the answer lies in assessing whether there is a right to education explic-

itly or implicitly guaranteed by the Constitution. * * *

34. See the discussion, *infra,* pp. 222–234.

35. Dandridge v. Williams, 397 U.S. 471, 508, 90 S.Ct. 1153, 1173 (1970); San Antonio Independent School Dist., 411 U.S. 1, 70, 93 S.Ct. 1278, 1315 (1973); Massachusetts Board of Retirement v. Murgia, 427 U.S. 307, 317, 96 S.Ct. 2562, 2568 (1976). See also Yarbrough, *The Burger Court and Unspecified Rights: On Protecting Fundamental "Rights" or "Interests" Through a Flexible Conception of Equal Protection,* a paper delivered at the 1977 annual meeting of the Midwest Political Science Ass'n.

odds with the reality of past Court decisions; (2) that there are serious defects associated with the two-tier approach even if it were hospitably employed; (3) that the gulf between the Court's rhetoric about applying the two-tier framework and the actuality of a variable approach should not continue to exist; and (4) that a more flexible alternative, a sliding scale of interests, is to be preferred to the two-tier model.

As a beginning, Marshall attacks the Court's narrow conception of basic liberties. It will not do, he argues, to assert that only rights appearing in the text of the amendments can be certified as fundamental freedoms. The *Reports* are riddled with decisions in which strict scrutiny has been applied to liberties which are nowhere to be found in the Constitution, such as the right to travel, the right to procreate, the right to vote in state elections, and the right to an appeal in a criminal case.[36] Nor will it do to say that the identification of fundamental rights beyond the text of the Constitution "necessarily degenerate[s] into an unprincipled, subjective, 'picking and choosing' between various interests * * *." Marshall continues:

> Although not all fundamental interests are constitutionally guaranteed, the determination of which interests are fundamental should be firmly rooted in the text of the Constitution. The task in every case should be to determine the extent to which constitutionally guaranteed rights are dependent on interests not mentioned in the Constitution. As the nexus between the specific constitutional guarantee and the nonconstitutional interest draws closer, the nonconstitutional interest becomes more fundamental and the degree of judicial scrutiny applied when the interest is infringed on a discriminatory basis must be adjusted accordingly. Thus, it cannot be denied that interests such as procreation, the exercise of the state franchise, and access to criminal appellate processes are not fully guaranteed to the citizen by our Constitution. But these interests have nonetheless been afforded special judicial consideration in the face of discrimination because they are, to some extent, interrelated with constitutional guaran-

36. San Antonio Independent School Dist. v. Rodriguez, 411 U.S. 1, 98–102, 93 S.Ct. 1278, 1330–1332 (1973) (dissenting opinion).

Ducat Const.Interpre. MTB—8

tees. Procreation is now understood to be important because of its interaction with the established constitutional right of privacy. The exercise of the state franchise is closely tied to basic civil and political rights inherent in the First Amendment. And access to criminal appellate processes enhances the integrity of the range of rights implicit in the Fourteenth Amendment guarantee of due process of law. Only if we closely protect the related interests from state discrimination do we ultimately ensure the integrity of the constitutional guarantee itself. This is the real lesson that must be taken from our previous decisions involving interests deemed to be fundamental.[37]

Likewise, limiting "suspect classes" to only racial classifications flys in the face of what is common knowledge, that there are other powerless, "discrete and insular minorities," victimized by traditional prejudice, for example, the poor,[38] women (though not, of course, a minority, but still an identifiable class),[39] illegitimate children,[40] and the aged.[41] Such a limited definition of "suspect class," Marshall argues, is mere pretense since the Court in past cases examined legislation bearing upon other recognizable "minorities" in a fashion clearly out of keeping with the usual deference that attaches to the reasonableness standard.[42]

Even if the Court were to opt for a more expansive definition of "fundamental" rights and "suspect classes," the preferred freedoms approach carries additional difficulties. As Justice Frankfurter maintained from the start, the approach tends to

37. 411 U.S. at 102–103, 93 S.Ct. at 1332–1333.

38. James v. Valtierra, 402 U.S. 137, 143, 91 S.Ct. 1331, 1334 (1971) (dissenting opinion of Marshall, J.).

39. See Frontiero v. Richardson, 411 U.S. 677, 93 S.Ct. 1764 (1973).

40. San Antonio Independent School Dist. v. Rodriguez, 411 U.S. 1, 108–109, 93 S.Ct. 1278, 1335 (1973). See also note 90, *infra*.

41. Massachusetts Board of Retirement v. Murgia, 427 U.S. 307, 323–324, 96 S.Ct. 2562, 2571–2572 (1971).

42. San Antonio Independent School Dist. v. Rodriguez, 411 U.S. 1, 105–110, 93 S.Ct. 1278, 1334–1336 (1973); Massachusetts Board of Retirement v. Murgia, 427 U.S. 307, 320–321, 96 S.Ct. 2562, 2570 (1976).

invite knee-jerk or mechanical reactions to legislation in place of considered judgment.[43]   Though it is difficult to see why this *must* be a feature of employing the two-tier model, still, as Justice Marshall notes, invariably legislation alleged to infringe an upper-tier interest never survives scrutiny while statutes assessed in terms of their reasonableness are almost always upheld.   Thus the critical determination in constitutional adjudication, so far as the preferred freedoms framework is concerned, consists of how the interests are initially pigeonholed, not the specifics of the legislation.[44]   A defect which is inherent in the two-tier model, however, is the compressing of all interests to form a dichotomy with the effect that the standard of constitutional adjudication fails to take into account the variation in importance among interests within the class of "fundamental" rights or the differential vulnerability of groups labeled "suspect classes."   In Marshall's view, the unfortunate impact of this oversight becomes most apparent when we focus our attention on the especially diverse interests lumped together in the lower tier, for example, legislation regulating business enterprise and statutes affecting the welfare rights of the poor, all to be tested by the same constitutional standard of reasonableness.[45]

The fiction of employing the two-tier framework should not, in his view, be permitted to continue.   For Marshall, this is no dry, technical matter:

> [T]here are problems with deciding cases based on factors not encompassed by the applicable standards.   First, the approach is rudderless, affording no notice to interested parties of the standards governing particular cases and giving no firm guidance to judges who, as a consequence, must assess the constitutionality of legislation before them on an *ad hoc* basis.   Second, and not unrelatedly, the approach is unpredicta-

---

43. Kovacs v. Cooper, 336 U.S. 77, 96, 69 S.Ct. 448, 458 (1949) (concurring opinion).

44. Massachusetts Board of Retirement v. Murgia, 427 U.S. 307, 319, 96 S.Ct. 2562, 2569–2570.

45. Dandridge v. Williams, 397 U.S. 471, 520, 90 S.Ct. 1153, 1179; Massachusetts Board of Retirement v. Murgia, 427 U.S. 307, 321–323, 96 S. Ct. 2562, 2570–2571.

ble and requires holding this Court to standards it has never publicly adopted. Thus, the approach presents the danger that, as I suggest has happened here, relevant factors will be misapplied or ignored. * * * [46]

In place of the preferred freedoms approach, Justice Marshall urges the Court to openly acknowledge the sliding scale of constitutional analysis he says it has been covertly employing and proportion the degree of scrutiny to the importance of the interests at issue. In his words:

A principled reading of what this Court has done reveals that it has applied a spectrum of standards in reviewing discrimination allegedly violative of the Equal Protection Clause. This spectrum clearly comprehends variations in the degree of care with which the Court will scrutinize particular classifications, depending, I believe, on the constitutional and societal importance of the interest adversely affected and the recognized invidiousness of the basis upon which the particular classification is drawn. I find in fact that many of the Court's recent decisions embody the very sort of reasoned approach to equal protection analysis for which I previously argued—that is, an approach in which "concentration [is] placed upon the character of the classification in question, the relative importance to individuals in the class discriminated against of the governmental benefits that they do not receive, and the asserted state interests in support of the classification." Dandridge v. Williams, *supra*, 397 U.S., at 520–521, 90 S.Ct., at 1180 (dissenting opinion).[47]

This approach does not rule out the possibility that some rights would be regarded as so vital they would almost always be sustained. As he explained in a footnote three years later:

Some classifications are so invidious that they should be struck down automatically absent the most compelling state interest, and by suggesting the limitations of strict scrutiny analysis I do not mean to imply otherwise. The analysis should be accomplished, however, not by stratified notions of "suspect" classes and "fundamental" rights, but by individu-

46. Massachusetts Board of Retirement v. Murgia, 427 U.S. 307, 321, 96 S.Ct. 2562, 2570.

47. San Antonio Independent School Dist. v. Rodriguez, 411 U.S. 1, 98–99, 93 S.Ct. 1278, 1330 (1973).

alized assessments of the particular classes and rights involved in each case. Of course, the traditional suspect classes and fundamental rights would still rank at the top of the list of protected categories, so that in cases involving those categories analysis would be functionally equivalent to strict scrutiny. Thus, the advantages of the approach I favor do not appear in such cases, but rather emerge in those dealing with traditionally less protected classes and rights. * * *[48]

Thus the real effect of this proposed revision in the Court's approach, as Marshall concedes, is not to force reevaluation of upper-tier interests, but to vindicate more of those presently consigned to the bottom tier.

The activist drift of Marshall's proposal is readily apparent. And the justification is not materially different from that once offered for preferred freedoms. Says Marshall:

> In summary, it seems to me inescapably clear that this Court has consistently adjusted the care with which it will review state discrimination in light of the constitutional significance of the interests affected and the invidiousness of the particular classification. In the context of economic interests, we find that discriminatory state action is almost always sustained, for such interests are generally far removed from constitutional guarantees. Moreover, "[t]he extremes to which the Court has gone in dreaming up rational bases for state regulation in that area may in many instances be ascribed to a healthy revulsion from the Court's earlier excesses in using the Constitution to protect interests that have more than enough power to protect themselves in the legislative halls." Dandridge v. Williams, 397 U.S., at 520, 90 S.Ct., at 1179 (dissenting opinion). But the situation differs markedly when discrimination against important individual interests with constitutional implications and against particularly disadvantaged or powerless classes is involved. The majority suggests, however, that a variable standard of review would give this Court the appearance of a "super-legislature." * * * I cannot agree. Such an approach seems to me a part of the guarantees of our Constitution and of the historic

48. Massachusetts Board of Retirement v. Murgia, 427 U.S. 307, 319, note 1, 96 S.Ct. 2562, 2569.

experiences with oppression of and discrimination against discrete, powerless minorities which underlie that document. In truth, the Court itself will be open to the criticism raised by the majority so long as it continues on its present course of effectively selecting in private which cases will be afforded special consideration without acknowledging the true basis of its action.[49]

To be sure, the charge Marshall feels obliged to answer here is hardly new; interest balancers previously rebuffed preferred freedoms, too, for transforming the Court into a "super-legislature."[50] It is a criticism that always accompanies the active use of judicial review. Whether there is merit to the charge, as always, depends upon one's assumptions about what constitutes the Court's "proper" role in the political system. The ambiguity in Justice Marshall's approach to constitutional interpretation, however, may occasion the objection that Professor Rawls' articulation of a concept of justice (pp. 185–186) is preferable because it is clearer.

Illustrations

Consistent with my intention of providing a wide variety of illustrations for each of the modes of constitutional interpretation, I have chosen the following examples of preferred freedoms analysis to show the framework as it has been employed to invalidate legislation which: (1) infringed a First Amendment right; (2) distributed a fundamental freedom unequally; (3) allocated rights or privileges along lines thought to constitute "suspect classes"; and (4) deprived lower economic groups of an equal share of the resources constituting a basic governmental function. These illustrations involve a dissection of one or two

49. San Antonio Independent School Dist. v. Rodriguez, 411 U.S. 1, 109–110, 93 S.Ct. 1278, 1335–1336 (1973).

50. See especially Justice John Harlan, Jr.'s dissenting opinion in Shapiro v. Thompson, 394 U.S. 618, 655, 89 S.Ct. 1322, 1342 (1969); see also his dissenting opinions in Reynolds v. Sims, 377 U.S. 533, 589, 84 S.Ct. 1362, 1395 (1964); Carrington v. Rash, 380 U.S. 89, 97, 85 S.Ct. 775, 780 (1965); Harper v. Virginia State Board of Elections, 383 U.S. 663, 680, 86 S.Ct. 1079, 1089 (1966).

opinions for each type of example. Since examples of the application of this framework abound, any number of other cases conceivably might have been chosen, a matter that is repeatedly underscored in the footnotes which acknowledge other illustrations. Once again, it is worth emphasizing that the purpose of these examples is not to give a history of a particular issue or doctrine in constitutional law, but to present multidimensional illustrations of this mode of constitutional interpretation.

1. The Infringement of Free Speech: Thomas v. Collins

Since its emergence as a third mode of constitutional interpretation, preferred freedoms analysis has marked numerous Court opinions dealing with First Amendment rights—freedoms of speech,[51] assembly,[52] association,[53] press,[54] and religion [55]—with

---

1. See, e. g., Speiser v. Randall, 357 U.S. 513, 78 S.Ct. 1332 (1958); N. A. A. C. P. v. Button, 371 U.S. 415, 83 S.Ct. 328 (1963); Tinker v. Des Moines Independent Community School Dist., 393 U.S. 503, 89 S.Ct. 733 (1969); Street v. New York, 394 U.S. 576, 89 S.Ct. 1354 (1969); Cohen v. California, 403 U.S. 15, 91 S.Ct. 1780 (1971); Coates v. Cincinnati, 402 U.S. 611, 91 S.Ct. 1686 (1971); Gooding v. Wilson, 405 U.S. 518, 92 S.Ct. 1103 (1972); Buckley v. Valeo, 424 U.S. 1, 96 S.Ct. 512 (1976).

52. See, e. g., Terminiello v. Chicago, 337 U.S. 1, 69 S.Ct. 894 (1949); Edwards v. South Carolina, 372 U. S. 229, 83 S.Ct. 680 (1963); Cox v. Louisiana, 379 U.S. 536, 85 S.Ct. 453 (1965); Cox v. Louisiana, 379 U.S. 559, 85 S.Ct. 476 (1965); Brown v. Louisiana, 383 U.S. 131, 143, 86 S.Ct. 719, 724 (1966) (concurring opinion of Brennan, J.); Amalgamated Food Employees Union v. Logan Valley Plaza, 391 U.S. 308, 88 S.Ct. 1601 (1968); Police Dept. of City of Chicago v. Mosley, 408 U.S. 92, 92 S.Ct. 2286 (1972); Grayned v. City of Rockford, 408 U.S. 104, 92 S.Ct. 2294 (1972).

53. See, e. g., N. A. A. C. P. v. Alabama ex rel. Patterson, 357 U.S. 449, 78 S.Ct. 1163 (1958); Bates v. City of Little Rock, 361 U.S. 516, 80 S.Ct. 412 (1960); Shelton v. Tucker, 364 U.S. 479, 81 S.Ct. 247 (1960); Gibson v. Florida Legislative Investigation Comm., 372 U.S. 539, 83 S.Ct. 889 (1963); Baggett v. Bullitt, 377 U.S. 360, 84 S.Ct. 1316 (1964); Aptheker v. Secretary of State, 378 U.S. 500, 84 S.Ct. 1659 (1964); DeGregory v. Attorney General of New Hampshire, 383 U. S. 825, 86 S.Ct. 1148 (1966); Elfbrandt v. Russell, 384 U.S. 11, 86 S.Ct. 1238 (1966); Keyishian v. Board of Regents, 385 U.S. 589, 87 S.Ct. 675 (1967); United States v.

54. See note 54 on page 214.

55. See note 55 on page 214.

Other guarantees contained in the Bill of Rights,[56] and with additional liberties recognized as fundamental.[57] While any of these

Robel, 389 U.S. 258, 88 S.Ct. 419 (1967); Kusper v. Pontikes, 414 U. S. 51, 94 S.Ct. 303 (1973).

54. See, e. g., Bantam Books v. Sullivan, 372 U.S. 58, 83 S.Ct. 631 (1963); New York Times Co. v. Sullivan, 376 U.S. 254, 84 S.Ct. 710 (1965); Freedman v. Maryland, 380 U.S. 51, 85 S.Ct. 734 (1965); Lamont v. Postmaster General, 381 U.S. 301, 85 S.Ct. 1493 (1965); New York Times Co. v. United States, 403 U.S. 713, 91 S.Ct. 2140 (1971); Branzburg v. Hayes, 408 U.S. 665, 725, 92 S.Ct. 2646, 2671 (1972) (dissenting opinion of Stewart, J.).

55. See, e. g., Sherbert v. Verner, 374 U.S. 398, 83 S.Ct. 1790 (1963).

56. Somewhat analogous to the preferred freedoms approach in part has been the shifting of the burden of proof to the government to show that an individual in police custody has knowingly and voluntarily waived his rights prior to a criminal interrogation and that incriminating statements he made were not coerced. Miranda v. Arizona, 384 U.S. 436, 86 S.Ct. 1602 (1966). A comparable burden is placed on the government when the Court chooses to accentuate the importance of the Warrant Clause in interpreting the Fourth Amendment; in that event, we might say that "reasonableness" attaches to test the opportunity of the police to procure a warrant (subject to certain highly-limited and well-defined exceptions) rather than to the over all assessment of police search and

seizure conduct. See Chimel v. California, 395 U.S. 752, 89 S.Ct. 2034 (1969); Coolidge v. New Hampshire, 403 U.S. 443, 91 S.Ct. 2022 (1971); Cardwell v. Lewis, 417 U.S. 583, 596, 94 S.Ct. 2464, 2472 (1974) (dissenting opinion of Stewart, J.); Cady v. Dombrowski, 413 U.S. 433, 450, 93 S.Ct. 2523, 2532 (1973) (dissenting opinion of Brennan, J.).

A more comprehensive and straightforward application of the preferred freedoms approach is exemplified in the Massachusetts Supreme Judicial Court's consideration of the constitutionality of the death penalty in terms of the commonwealth's constitution. Both in framing the issue for argument and in its subsequent disposition, the court postulated the existence of a fundamental right to life, focused on whether the government could advance a compelling interest for its restriction, and inquired whether capital punishment constituted the least restrictive alternative. See Commonwealth v. O'Neal, 367 Mass. 440, 327 N.E.2d 662 (1975); —— Mass. ——, 339 N.E.2d 676 (1975).

57. For example, the right to travel: Aptheker v. Secretary of State, 378 U.S. 500, 84 S.Ct. 1659 (1964); Shapiro v. Thompson, 394 U.S. 618, 89 S.Ct. 1322 (1969); the right to privacy: Griswold v. Connecticut, 381 U.S. 479, 85 S.Ct. 1678 (1965); Roe v. Wade, 410 U.S. 113, 93 S.Ct. 705 (1973); the right to procreate: Skinner v. Oklahoma ex rel. Wil-

would prove suitable as illustrations, the Court's opinion in *Thomas* v. *Collins* [58] represents the earliest complete, and thus, the classic articulation of the preferred freedoms approach. Coming to us as it does from an earlier era in the Court's history, when preferred freedoms was most readily associated with the attempt to shore up the "clear and present danger" test against efforts at interest balancing in free speech cases, its phrasing of the approach to constitutional interpretation adds a certain depth to this series of illustrations.

At issue in that case was a Texas statute which required all labor organizers to register with the Texas Secretary of State and receive a permit before engaging in that activity. Thomas, a union leader, came to the state to address a mass meeting of workers sponsored by a union in its effort to organize oil workers. Anticipating noncompliance with the law, the state Attorney General sought and received a restraining order forbidding Thomas to address the labor rally. After being served with a copy of the order, Thomas determined to defy it because, he concluded, it abridged his right to free speech. At the conclusion of his address to the mass meeting, he openly solicited new union members. He was subsequently arrested, adjudged to be in contempt, and sentenced to three days in jail and a $100 fine. On appeal, the Supreme Court found that the statute "as * * * applied in this case imposed previous restraint upon appellant's rights of free speech and free assembly" [59] and reversed the judgment.

Speaking for a bare majority on the Court, Justice Rutledge, noting that the case presented the problem of where "the individual's freedom ends and the State's power begins," observed that, with regard to so delicate a choice on that border, "the

liamson, 316 U.S. 535, 62 S.Ct. 1110 (1942); the right to marry, Loving v. Virginia, 388 U.S. 1, 87 S.Ct. 1817 (1967). See also notes 67 and 68, *infra*, for preferred freedoms analyses of statutes bearing respectively upon the right to vote and the right to have one's vote count equally.

58.   323 U.S. 516, 65 S.Ct. 315 (1945).

59.   323 U.S. at 518, 65 S.Ct. at 317.

60.   323 U.S. at 529, 65 S.Ct. at 322.

usual presumption supporting legislation is balanced by the preferred place given in our scheme to the great, the indispensable democratic freedoms secured by the First Amendment." [60] Justice Rutledge continued:

> For these reasons any attempt to restrict those liberties must be justified by clear public interest, threatened not doubtfully or remotely, but by clear and present danger. The rational connection between the remedy provided and the evil to be curbed, which in other contexts might support legislation against attack on due process grounds, will not suffice. These rights rest on firmer foundation. Accordingly, whatever occasion would restrain orderly discussion and persuasion, at appropriate time and place, must have clear support in public danger, actual or impending. Only the gravest abuses, endangering paramount interests, give occasion for permissible limitation. It is therefore in our tradition to allow the widest room for discussion, the narrowest range for its restriction, particularly when this right is exercised in conjunction with peaceable assembly. It was not by accident or coincidence that the rights to freedom in speech and press were coupled in a single guaranty with the rights of the people peaceably to assemble and to petition for redress of grievances. All these, though not identical, are inseparable. They are cognate rights * * *.[61]

Cases such as this, said the Court, could not be decided either merely by pointing out, on the one hand, that the statute aimed at economic regulation or that Thomas was a paid speaker, or, on the other hand, simply by asserting that freedom of speech was involved or that the interests of workingmen were at stake. Justice Rutledge explained:

> These comparisons are at once too simple, too general, and too inaccurate to be determinative. Where the line shall be placed in a particular application rests, not on such generalities, but on the concrete clash of particular interests and the community's relative evaluation both of them and of how the one will be affected by the specific restriction, the other by its absence. * * *[62]

61. 323 U.S. at 530, 65 S.Ct. at 322–323.

62. 323 U.S. at 531, 65 S.Ct. at 323.

While this was a "judgment in the first instance * * * for the legislative body," the intrusion upon First Amendment freedoms could be sustained "only if grave and impending public danger requires this." [63]

Conceding that the regulation of organized labor was rightly within government's power of "protecting the public interest," the Court nonetheless observed that freedoms of speech and assembly were clearly implicated in public discussion of the advantages and disadvantages of unions. Quoting an earlier decision, the Court concluded, " 'Free discussion concerning the conditions in industry and the causes of labor disputes appears to us indispensable to the effective and intelligent use of the processes of popular government to shape the destiny of modern industrial society.' " [64]   Said the Justices, the Texas court "did not give sufficient weight" to the implication of First Amendment values "particularly by its failure to take account of the blanketing effect of the prohibition's present application upon public discussion and also of the clear and present danger test in these circumstances." [65]

Reconstructing events, the Court found that Thomas had not asked for or accepted funds for the union, nor had he taken applications for membership. Rather, he had publicly proclaimed the advantages of unionism and endeavored to persuade workingmen to join the local. Thomas' appearance was but a part of a general debate and drive for unionization which was clearly protected by the First Amendment. Given that Thomas was there only to speak, the Court held that the statute, which "forbids any language which conveys, or reasonably could be found to convey, the meaning of invitation" to join a union, was too sweeping and overbroad. Said the Court:

> That there was restriction upon Thomas' right to speak
> and the rights of the workers to hear what he had to say,

63. 323 U.S. at 531–532, 65 S.Ct. at
323.

U.S. 88, 103, 60 S.Ct. 736, 744
(1940).

64. 323 U.S. at 532, 65 S.Ct. at 323,
quoting Thornhill v. Alabama, 310

65. 323 U.S. at 532, 65 S.Ct. at 324.

there can be no doubt. The threat of the restraining order, backed by the power of contempt and of arrest for crime, hung over every word. A speaker in such circumstances could avoid the words "solicit," "invite," "join." It would be impossible to avoid the idea. * * * General words create different and often particular impressions on different minds. No speaker, however careful, can convey exactly his meaning, or the same meaning, to the different members of an audience. * * *

* * * No speaker, in such circumstances, safely could assume that anything he might say upon the general subject would not be understood by some as an invitation. In short, the supposedly clear-cut distinction between discussion, laudation, general advocacy, and solicitation puts the speaker in these circumstances wholly at the mercy of the varied understanding of his hearers and consequently of whatever inference may be drawn as to his intent and meaning.

Such a distinction offers no security for free discussion. In these conditions it blankets with uncertainty whatever may be said. It compels the speaker to hedge and trim. He must take care in every word to create no impression that he means, in advocating unionism's most central principle, namely, that workingmen should unite for collective bargaining, to urge those present to do so. The vice is not merely that invitation, in the circumstances shown here, is speech. It is also that its prohibition forbids or restrains discussion which is not or may not be invitation. The sharp line cannot be drawn surely or securely. The effort to observe it could not be free speech, free press, or free assembly, in any sense of free advocacy of principle or cause. The restriction's effect, as applied, in a very practical sense was to prohibit Thomas not only to solicit members and memberships, but also to speak in advocacy of the cause of trade unionism in Texas, without having first procured the card. Thomas knew this and faced the alternatives it presented. When served with the order he had three choices: (1) To stand on his right and speak freely; (2) to quit, refusing entirely to speak; (3) to trim, and even thus to risk the penalty. He chose the first alternative. We think he was within his rights in doing so.[66]

66. 323 U.S. at 534–536, 65 S.Ct. at
    324–325.

Finally, concluded the Court, the meeting was entirely peaceful, the statements made were neither illegal in themselves or showed any tendency to incite a riot, and the state had produced no reason, therefore, to substantiate its limitation on speech soliciting union membership.

2. *Sharing Equally in the Right to Vote: The* Kramer *Case*

Fundamental freedoms are also abridged when they are unequally shared. Long ago reasoning that the right to vote constituted a basic liberty, the Court has repeatedly employed the preferred freedoms approach in equal protection cases to vindicate both the equal opportunity to vote [67] and the right to have that vote count equally.[68] An unusually clear example of the former is the Court's opinion in *Kramer* v. *Union Free School District No. 15.*[69]

At issue in *Kramer* was the validity of a section of New York's Education Law which provided that, in certain school districts, residents otherwise qualified to vote in national and state elections could vote in school district elections only if they either owned or leased taxable real property within the district

67. See Carrington v. Rash, 380 U.S. 89, 85 S.Ct. 775 (1965); Harper v. Virginia State Board of Elections, 383 U.S. 663, 86 S.Ct. 1079 (1966); Cipriano v. City of Houma, 395 U. S. 701, 89 S.Ct. 1897 (1969); Phoenix v. Kolodziejski, 399 U.S. 204, 90 S.Ct. 1990 (1970); Dunn v. Blumstein, 405 U.S. 330, 92 S.Ct. 995 (1972). Cases focusing on restrictive access to the ballot by candidates have also employed strict scrutiny; see Williams v. Rhodes, 393 U.S. 23, 89 S.Ct. 5 (1968); Bullock v. Carter, 405 U.S. 134, 92 S.Ct. 849 (1972); Lubin v. Panish, 415 U.S. 709, 94 S.Ct. 1315 (1974).

68. In the reapportionment cases of the late 1960s, the high point for the application of strict scrutiny to legislative districting, the preferred freedoms approach was employed somewhat in reverse. The Court began by examining the variance from one man-one vote in the population of districts (the least restrictive alternative) and placed the burden on the state to justify any deviation from precise mathematical equality in terms of a compellin, state interest. See Reynolds v. Sims, 377 U.S. 533, 84 S. Ct. 1362 (1964); Swann v. Adams, 385 U.S. 440, 87 S.Ct. 569 (1967); Kirkpatrick v. Preisler, 394 U.S. 526, 89 S.Ct. 1225 (1969).

69. 395 U.S. 621, 89 S.Ct. 1886 (1969).

or were parents or guardians of children enrolled in the local public schools. The statute was attacked as a violation of the Fourteenth Amendment's Equal Protection Clause.

The Court, speaking through Chief Justice Warren, began by acknowledging that because the franchise " 'is preservative of other basic civil and political rights,' " "we must give the statute a close and exacting examination." [70] Since "statutes distributing the franchise constitute the foundation of our representative society," the Court reasoned that "any unjustified discrimination" as to who may participate "undermines the legitimacy of representative government." [71] "Accordingly," observed Chief Justice Warren,

> when we are reviewing statutes which deny some residents the right to vote, the general presumption of constitutionality afforded state statutes and the traditional approval given state classifications if the Court can conceive of a "rational basis" for the distinctions made are not applicable. * * *
> The presumption of constitutionality and the approval given "rational" classifications in other types of enactments are based on an assumption that the institutions of state government are structured so as to represent fairly all the people. However, when the challenge to the statute is in effect a challenge of this basic assumption, the assumption can no longer serve as the basis for presuming constitutionality. And, the assumption is no less under attack because the legislature which decides who may participate at the various levels of political choice is fairly elected. Legislation which delegates decision making to bodies elected by only a portion of those eligible to vote for the legislature can cause unfair representation. Such legislation can exclude a minority of voters from any voice in the decisions just as effectively as if the decisions were made by legislators the minority had no voice in selecting.[72]

In this instance, the Court noted that the only justification offered by the state "for the exclusion of seemingly interested and

70. 395 U.S. at 626, 89 S.Ct. at 1889, in part quoting Reynolds v. Sims, 377 U.S. 533, 562, 84 S.Ct. 1362, 1381 (1964).

71. *Ibid.*

72. 395 U.S. at 627–628, 89 S.Ct. at 1890.

informed residents" [73] was that the statute enfranchised those " 'whom the State could understandably deem to be the most intimately interested in actions taken by the school board.' " [74] Furthermore, the state argued that " 'the task of * * * balancing the interest of the community in the maintenance of orderly school district elections against the interest of any individual in voting in such elections should clearly remain with the Legislature.' " [75]   However, the Chief Justice pointed out, "the issue is not whether the legislative judgments are rational," but, since "[a] more exacting standard obtains," whether the statutory provisions "do in fact sufficiently further a compelling state interest to justify denying the franchise to appellant and members of his class." [76]   And, said the Court, "close scrutiny of the * * * classifications [contained in the statute] demonstrates that they do not accomplish this purpose with sufficient precision * * *." The Chief Justice continued:

> Whether classifications allegedly limiting the franchise to those resident citizens "primarily interested" deny those ex-

73. As the Court described the excluded class, 395 U.S. at 630, 89 S. Ct. at 1891:

> Besides appellant and others who similarly live in their parents' homes, the statute also disenfranchises the following persons (unless they are parents or guardians of children enrolled in the district public school): senior citizens and others living with children or relatives; clergy, military personnel, and others who live on tax-exempt property; boarders and lodgers; parents who neither own nor lease qualifying property and whose children are too young to attend school; parents who neither own nor lease qualifying property and whose children attend private schools.

At the time *Kramer* was decided, however, the Court had yet to hold that the franchise could be curtailed or weighted in special function district elections. See Salyer Land Co. v. Tulare Lake Basin Water Storage Dist., 410 U.S. 719, 93 S.Ct. 1224 (1973); Associated Enterprises, Inc. v. Toltec Watershed Improvement Dist., 410 U.S. 743, 93 S.Ct. 1237 (1973).

74. 395 U.S. at 633, 89 S.Ct. at 1892, quoting argument of the appellees.

75. *Ibid.* It is worth noting that, in phrasing the controversy in these terms, the government has committed the classic blunder, discussed earlier (pp. 181–183), of balancing unlike interests.

76. 395 U.S. at 633, 89 S.Ct. at 1892–1893.

cluded equal protection of the laws depends, *inter alia*, on whether all those excluded are in fact substantially less interested or affected than those the statute includes. In other words, the classifications must be tailored so that the exclusion of appellant and members of his class is necessary to achieve the articulated state goal. Section 2012 does not meet the exacting standard of precision we require of statutes which selectively distribute the franchise. The classifications in § 2012 permit inclusion of many persons who have, at best, a remote and indirect interest, in school affairs and, on the other hand, exclude others who have a distinct and direct interest in the school meeting decisions.[77]

The limitations on voting imposed by that section of New York's Education Law at issue, concluded the Court, "are not sufficiently tailored to those 'primarily interested' in school affairs to justify the denial of the franchise" [78] to residents otherwise qualified to vote.

3. "Suspect Classes" and Strict Scrutiny: Classifications Based on Gender and Illegitimacy

If a majority of the present Court have never subscribed to the proposition that women and illegitimate children constitute "suspect classes," and thus summon forth the "strict scrutiny" standard, clearly enough agree with Justice Marshall that "[i]t is far too late in the day to contend that the Fourteenth Amendment prohibits only racial discrimination." [79] Together with a number of cases involving legal classifications cutting against

---

77. 395 U.S. at 632, 89 S.Ct. at 1892. As the Court explained in an accompanying footnote:

   For example, appellant resides with his parents in the school district, pays state and federal taxes and is interested in and affected by school board decisions; however, he has no vote. On the other hand, an uninterested unemployed young man who pays no state or federal taxes, but who rents an apartment in the district, can participate in the election.

78. 395 U.S. at 633, 89 S.Ct. at 1893.

79. James v. Valtierra, 402 U.S. 137, 145, 91 S.Ct. 1331, 1335 (1971) (dissenting opinion). *Cf.* Weber v. Aetna Casualty & Surety Co., 406 U.S. 164, 177, 92 S.Ct. 1400, 1407 (dissenting opinion of Rehnquist, J.).

the indigent,[80] the Court's decisions in several equal protection cases concerning classifications drawn along the lines of gender and illegitimacy account for pretty much all of what deviation exists from Justice Marshall's observation that when "legislation * * * drop[s] into the bottom tier, and * * * [is] measured by the mere rationality test * * * that test * * * leaves little doubt about the outcome; the challenged legislation is always upheld." [81] In contrast to the majority's ambivalence, there has been no doubt in the minds of preferred freedoms advocates that legislation which singles out either women or illegitimate children presents a "suspect" classification.

The closest women have come to recognition as a "suspect class" in the Court's equal protection jurisprudence [82] is an explicit statement in Justice Brennan's *plurality* opinion in *Frontiero* v. *Richardson* that "classifications based upon sex, like classifications based upon race, alienage, or national origin, are inherently suspect, and must therefore be subjected to strict judicial scrutiny." [83] This conclusion derived from the following findings:

[O]ur statute books gradually became laden with gross, stereotyped distinctions between the sexes and, indeed, throughout much of the 19th century the position of women in our society was, in many respects, comparable to that of blacks under the pre-Civil War slave codes. Neither slaves nor women could hold office, serve on juries, or bring suit in their own names, and married women traditionally were denied the legal capacity to hold or convey property or to serve as legal guardians of their own children. * * * And although blacks were guaranteed the right to vote in 1870,

80. See notes 106–108, *infra*; see also Bullock v. Carter, 405 U.S. 134, 92 S.Ct. 849 (1972); Lubin v. Panish, 415 U.S. 709, 94 S.Ct. 1315 (1974).

81. Massachusetts Board of Retirement v. Murgia, 427 U.S. 307, 319, 96 S.Ct. 2562, 2570 (dissenting opinion).

82. See Chase and Ducat, 1977 Supplement to Constitutional Interpretation, Ch. 10e.

83. 411 U.S. 677, 682, 93 S.Ct. 1764, 1768 (1973).

women were denied even that right—which is itself "preservative of other basic civil and political rights"—until adoption of the Nineteenth Amendment half a century later.

It is true, of course, that the position of women in America has improved markedly in recent decades. Nevertheless, it can hardly be doubted that, in part because of the high visibility of the sex characteristic, women still face pervasive, although at times more subtle, discrimination in our educational institutions, in the job market and, perhaps most conspicuously, in the political arena. * * *

[S]ince sex, like race and national origin, is an immutable characteristic determined solely by the accident of birth, the imposition of special disabilities upon the members of a particular sex because of their sex would seem to violate "the basic concept of our system that legal burdens should bear some relationship to individual responsibility * * *." Weber v. Aetna Casualty & Surety Co., 406 U.S. 164, 175, 92 S.Ct. 1400, 1407 (1972). And what differentiates sex from such nonsuspect statuses as intelligence or physical disability, and aligns it with the recognized suspect criteria, is that the sex characteristic frequently bears no relation to ability to perform or contribute to society. As a result, statutory distinctions between the sexes often have the effect of invidiously relegating the entire class of females to inferior legal status without regard to the actual capabilities of its individual members.[84]

In that case, applying strict scrutiny to federal statutes which provided that married servicemen automatically qualified to receive increased quarters allowances and medical and dental benefits for their wives but that female personnel in the armed forces could not receive these fringe benefits unless their husbands were in fact dependent on them for over one-half their support, the Court held the statutory scheme unconstitutional. The government proffered as its sole justification, "administrative convenience"; that is, because wives in our society are usually dependent on their husbands but rarely is the reverse true, it would be cheaper and more expeditious to presume the

84. 411 U.S. at 685–687, 93 S.Ct. at 1769–1770.

dependency of wives upon husbands and place the burden on the wives to establish spousal dependency in the reverse cases. Addressing the government's contention, Justice Brennan wrote:

> The Government offers no concrete evidence, however, tending to support its view that such differential treatment in fact saves the Government any money. In order to satisfy the demands of strict judicial scrutiny, the Government must demonstrate, for example, that it is actually cheaper to grant increased benefits with respect to *all* male members, than it is to determine which male members are in fact entitled to such benefits and to grant increased benefits only to those members whose wives actually meet the dependency requirement. Here, however, there is substantial evidence that, if put to the test, many of the wives of male members would fail to qualify for benefits. And in light of the fact that the dependency determination with respect to the husbands of female members is presently made solely on the basis of affidavits rather than through the more costly hearing process, the Government's explanation of the statutory scheme is, to say the least, questionable.
>
> In any case, our prior decisions make clear that, although efficacious administration of governmental programs is not without some importance, "the Constitution recognizes higher values than speed and efficiency." * * * And when we enter the realm of "strict judicial scrutiny," there can be no doubt that "administrative convenience" is not a shibboleth, the mere recitation of which dictates constitutionality. * * * On the contrary, any statutory scheme which draws a sharp line between the sexes, *solely* for the purpose of achieving administrative convenience, necessarily commands "dissimilar treatment for men and women who are * * * similarly situated," and therefore involves the "very kind of arbitrary legislative choice forbidden by the [Constitution] * * *." Reed v. Reed, 404 U.S., at 77, 76, 92 S.Ct., at 254. We therefore conclude that, by according differential treatment to male and female members of the uniformed services for the sole purpose of achieving administrative convenience, the challenged statutes violate the Due Process Clause of the Fifth Amendment insofar as they require a female member to prove the dependency of her husband.[85]

85. 411 U.S. at 689–691, 93 S.Ct. at
1771–1772.

In a concurring opinion, Justice Powell rejected the plurality's characterization of sex as a "suspect" classification as unnecessary and presumptuous in view of the pending ratification of the Equal Rights Amendment.

In other decisions focusing on gender-based distinctions, those Justices we think of as comprising the more liberal wing of the Court have reiterated the characterization of sex as a "suspect" classification from dissent.[86] In cases other than *Frontiero,* gender-based legislation has either been explicitly evaluated in terms of the means-to-ends reasonableness test [87] or by analogizing the fact situation at hand to *Frontiero* but stopping short of adopting the "suspect class" designation.[88] A recent and suggestive exception (along the lines proposed by Justice Marshall as an escape from the rigid two-tier model) appears in Justice Brennan's opinion for the Court, striking down an Oklahoma statute which established a lower minimum drinking age for women than men, in which seven members of the Court subscribed to the principle that "classifications by gender must serve *important* governmental objectives and must be *substantially* related to achievement of those objectives." [89]

86. See Kahn v. Shevin, 416 U.S. 351, 357, 94 S.Ct. 1734, 1738 (1974) (dissenting opinion of Brennan, J.); Geduldig v. Aiello, 417 U.S. 484, 497, 94 S.Ct. 2485, 2492 (1974) (dissenting opinion of Brennan, J.); Schlesinger v. Ballard, 419 U.S. 498, 511, 95 S.Ct. 572, 579 (1975) (dissenting opinion of Brennan, J.).

87. See *Kahn* and *Schlesinger, ibid.*; see also Stanton v. Stanton, 421 U.S. 7, 95 S.Ct. 1373 (1975).

88. See Weinberger v. Wiesenfeld, 420 U.S. 636, 95 S.Ct. 1225 (1975); Califano v. Goldfarb, 430 U.S. 199, 97 S.Ct. 1021 (1977).

89. Craig v. Boren, 429 U.S. 190, 197, 97 S.Ct. 451, 457 (1976) [Em-phasis supplied as suggested by Justice Rehnquist's dissent]; see also Califano v. Webster, 430 U.S. 313, 97 S.Ct. 1192 (1977). In Justice Rehnquist's view "[t]he only redeeming feature of the Court's opinion" was "that it apparently signals a retreat by those who joined the plurality opinion in *Frontiero* v. *Richardson* * * * from their view that sex is a 'suspect' classification for purposes of equal protection analysis." 429 U.S. at 217, 97 S.Ct. at 467. If true, it is also worth noting that the Court's position here was hardly a victory for the traditional approach to equal protection espoused by Rehnquist, since six Justices joined Brennan's opinion of the

Unlike their explicit acknowledgment of women as constituting a "suspect class," the Court's advocates of strict scrutiny have not, in so many words, tendered the same characterization of illegitimate children. Yet, if one looks to actions rather than words, the message comes through with unmistakable clarity: the core supporters of judicial activism on the Burger Court— Justices Douglas, Brennan, and Marshall—have never voted to sustain legislation which distinguished between legitimate and illegitimate children in the distribution of rights or benefits, whatever the rubric of constitutional adjudication employed.[90] While it may be that they concluded such statutory line-drawing was irrational *per se*, it is interesting to note that when any of these Justices joined an opinion of the Court written by someone else, the opinion failed to reach the "suspect class" issue.[91]

Though the majority viewpoint on the Court recognizes that "the legal status of illegitimacy, however defined, is, like race or national origin, a characteristic determined by causes not within the control of the illegitimate individual, and * * * bears no relation to the individual's ability to participate in and contrib-

Court (three of them filing separate concurring opinions). Said Justice Powell, "While I would not endorse th[e] characterization [of this decision as a 'middle-tier' approach] and would not welcome a further subdividing of equal protection analysis, candor compels the recognition that the relatively deferential 'rational basis' standard of review normally applied takes on a sharper focus when we address a gender-based classification." 429 U.S. at 211, note, 97 S.Ct. at 464 (concurring opinion).

90. See Levy v. Louisiana, 391 U.S. 68, 88 S.Ct. 1509 (1968); Glona v. American Guarantee & Liability Insurance Co., 391 U.S. 73, 88 S.Ct. 1515 (1968); Labine v. Vincent, 401 U.S. 532, 91 S.Ct. 1017 (1971); Weber v. Aetna Casualty & Surety Co., 406 U.S. 164, 92 S.Ct. 1400 (1972); Gomez v. Perez, 409 U.S. 535, 93 S.Ct. 872 (1973); New Jersey Welfare Rights Organization v. Cahill, 411 U.S. 619, 93 S.Ct. 1700 (1973); Jimenez v. Weinberger, 417 U.S. 628, 94 S.Ct. 2496 (1974); Mathews v. Lucas, 427 U.S. 495, 96 S. Ct. 2755 (1976); Norton v. Mathews, 427 U.S. 524, 96 S.Ct. 2771 (1976); Trimble v. Gordon, 430 U. S. 762, 97 S.Ct. 1459 (1977).

91. See *Weber, Gomez, New Jersey Welfare Rights Organization*, and especially *Jimenez, ibid.*; but *cf. Trimble*.

ute to society," [92] still it holds that illegitimacy need not be elevated to a "suspect" classification. This conclusion of the majority's appears to rest on several arguments: (1) that all classifications in law resting upon illegitimacy are not untenable, and the truly arbitrary uses of the distinction can be effectively dealt with by "less demanding standards"; (2) that "illegitimacy does not carry an obvious badge, as race or sex do"; and (3) that "discrimination against illegitimates has never approached the severity or pervasiveness of the historic legal and political discrimination against women and Negroes." [93]   As a result, "discrimination between individuals on the basis of their legitimacy does not 'command extraordinary protection from the majoritarian political process.' " [94]   The trend in the Court's decisions, therefore, has been to evaluate discrimination against illegitimates by examining whether a given statute presents an "insurmountable barrier" to equal treatment [95] and whether there is a significant countervailing social interest at stake.[96]

Whether it be in restrictions placed upon illegitimates to bring a wrongful death action, or to inherit property, or to claim social security benefits, the more liberal elements on the Court have consistently emphasized the lack of personal fault and, hence, the essential arbitrariness of singling out illegitimates for less than equal treatment.   A typical view is this excerpt from Justice Brennan's dissent in *Labine* v. *Vincent,* a decision up-

92. Mathews v. Lucas, 427 U.S. 495, 505, 96 S.Ct. 2755, 2762.

93. 427 U.S. at 505–506, 96 S.Ct. at 2762.

94. 427 U.S. at 506, 96 S.Ct. at 2762, in part quoting San Antonio Independent School Dist. v. Rodriguez, 411 U.S. 1, 28, 93 S.Ct. 1278, 1294.

95. That is, whether there is anything that bars treatment equal with legitimate children provided the father subsequently marries the mother or otherwise acknowledges the illegitimate child.   Labine v. Vincent, 401 U.S. 532, 91 S. Ct. 1017.

96. Such as preventing spurious claims to estates, stabilizing land titles, and promptly determining the inheritance of property.   See Weber v. Aetna Casualty & Surety Co., 406 U.S. 164, 92 S.Ct. 1400, commenting on the importance of the interests asserted by the state in *Labine.*

holding the constitutionality of Louisiana's statutes which disadvantage illegitimate children as against legitimate offspring and collateral claimants in the inheritance of an estate where the father died without leaving a will:

> The Court nowhere mentions the central reality of this case: Louisiana punishes illegitimate children for the misdeeds of their parents. * * * It is certainly unusual in this country for a person to be legally disadvantaged on the basis of factors over which he never had any control. * * * The state court below explicitly upheld the statute on the ground that the punishment of the child might encourage the parents to marry. If that is the State's objective, it can obviously be attained far more directly by focusing on the parents whose actions the State seeks to influence. Given the importance and nature of the decision to marry, * * * I think that disinheriting the illegitimate child must be held to "bear no intelligible proper relation to the consequences that are made to flow" from the State's classification. * * *
>
> In my judgment, only a moral prejudice, prevalent in 1825 when the Louisiana statutes under consideration were adopted, can support Louisiana's discrimination against illegitimate children. Since I can find no rational basis to justify the distinction Louisiana creates between an acknowledged illegitimate child and a legitimate one, that discrimination is clearly invidious. * * * 97

Whether the allies of strict scrutiny have chosen to label illegitimates a "suspect class" is academic, for the most part, since their consistent regard for the principle of personal faultlessness has served the same purpose.

4. Funding Public Education With the Local Property Tax

A common feature in the funding of public education throughout the country has been reliance upon the levy of a local property tax within each school district. The proceeds are invariably supplemented by state grants distributed in accordance with a formula usually guaranteeing each district a certain basic min-

---

97. 401 U.S. 532, 557–558, 91 S.Ct. 1017, 1030–1031 (1971).

imum revenue. Taken together with other supplemental aid, the various state monies, however, do not come close to offsetting the disparity in tax bases among the school districts of a given state. As a result, since the money any district has available is critically influenced by the size of its tax base, districts with less taxable resources generate less of a per capita student expenditure on education and are forced to tax at a higher rate than wealthier districts. In numerous federal and state cases, plaintiff parents residing in the poorer school districts have attacked the constitutionality of this financing scheme, alleging it deprives their children of equal protection. The gist of their contention has been that varying the quality of education with the wealth of the district in which a child happens to live infringes a fundamental right to equal educational opportunity.

Though the United States Supreme Court rejected this constitutional challenge in *San Antonio Independent School District* v. *Rodriguez*,[98] holding that wealth is not a "suspect" classification, that education is not a fundamental right, and thus that deference is due the federal principle allowing the states and local communities to have the final say on the means by which public education shall be funded, there is still merit in examining the allegations in preferred freedoms terms as an example of an approach to constitutional interpretation. This, I hasten to add, is not a sterile exercise, since it provides a good illustration of how preferred freedoms conceives "suspect classes" and postulates fundamental rights which are not spelled out in the text of the Constitution; and because, whatever the fate of this equal protection challenge has been in terms of the federal Constitution, parallel preferred freedoms analysis has been employed as a matter of state constitutional interpretation to sustain the attack on local property tax financing. The focus of this illustration is the opinion of the California Supreme Court in *Serrano* v. *Priest,* which originally held that state's version of the school financing program to be in violation of both the federal and state

98. 411 U.S. 1, 93 S.Ct. 1278 (1973).

constitutions,[99] a judgment that was subsequently revised in the face of *Rodriguez* to rest solely on the interpretation of certain provisions of the California constitution analogous to the Equal Protection Clause.[100]   In substance but not, of course, in style, the points elaborated by Justice Sullivan, speaking for the court in *Serrano,* anticipated many of the arguments voiced by Justice Marshall dissenting in *Rodriguez.*

We need not detail here the California Supreme Court's conclusion that wide disparities existed in the revenue available to the state's school districts.   Suffice it to say that the differences were not *de minimis,* and that the state grants were "inadequate to offset the inequalities inherent in a financing system based on widely varying local tax bases." [101]   Indeed, since half of the state aid was "distributed on a uniform per pupil basis to all districts, irrespective of a district's wealth," the court concluded that the state's basic aid "actually widens the gap between rich and poor districts." [102]   In sketching out the preferred freedoms analysis embodied in the court's opinion, that proceeded from this empirical finding, it might be helpful to observe the divisions within Justice Sullivan's opinion, focusing respectively on wealth as a "suspect" classification, on education as a fundamental interest, and on the failure of the state, in the court's view, to produce a compelling interest in support of its funding system.

With respect to wealth as a "suspect" classification, the court began by observing that "[i]n recent years, the United States Supreme Court has demonstrated a marked antipathy toward legislative classifications which discriminate on the basis of certain 'suspect' personal characteristics.   One factor which has repeatedly come under the close scrutiny of the high court is

---

99. 5 Cal.3d 584, 96 Cal.Rptr. 601, 487 P.2d 1241 (1971).

100. 18 Cal.3d 728, 135 Cal.Rptr. 345, 557 P.2d 929 (1976).

101. 5 Cal.3d at 594, 96 Cal.Rptr. at 608, 487 P.2d at 1248.

102. 5 Cal.3d at 594–595, 96 Cal. Rptr. at 608, 487 P.2d at 1248.

wealth." [103]   The court then went on to quote from the Supreme Court's opinion in *Harper* v. *Virginia State Board of Elections:* " 'Lines drawn on the basis of wealth or property, like those of race [citations], are traditionally disfavored.' " [104]   In that case, the court pointed out, the Supreme Court characterized the wealth classification implicit in Virginia's poll tax as " 'introduc[ing] a capricious or irrelevant factor' " into the measure of a voter's eligibility, and elsewhere indicated that " 'a careful examination on our part is especially warranted where lines are drawn on the basis of wealth * * * [a] factor which would independently render a classification highly suspect and thereby demand a more exacting judicial scrutiny.' " [105]   The California court then cited, among other cases, Supreme Court decisions that struck down an Illinois statute which furnished indigents a free copy of the trial record for perfecting an appeal in a criminal proceeding only in capital cases,[106] a California law which provided counsel free of charge to indigents seeking to appeal a criminal conviction only after a state court found there to be

---

103. 5 Cal.3d at 597, 96 Cal.Rptr. at 610, 487 P.2d at 1250. But Justice Powell, speaking for the Court, has said, "In a sense, every denial of welfare to an indigent creates a wealth classification as compared to nonindigents who are able to pay for the desired goods or services. But this Court has never held that financial need alone identifies a suspect class for purposes of equal protection analysis." Maher v. Roe, 432 U.S. 464, 471, 97 S.Ct. 2376, 2381 (1977). And, speaking for the Court in another case, he observed:

The individuals, or groups of individuals, who constituted the class discriminated against in our prior cases shared two distinguishing characteristics: because of their impecunity they were completely unable to pay for some desired benefit, and as a consequence, they sustained an absolute deprivation of a meaningful opportunity to enjoy that benefit. * * *

San Antonio Independent School Dist. v. Rodriguez, 411 U.S. 1, 20, 93 S.Ct. 1278, 1290. Justice Powell perhaps also should have added that, more often than not, a "fundamental" right was involved.

104. *Ibid.*, quoting 383 U.S. 663, 668, 86 S.Ct. 1079, 1082.

105. *Ibid.*, respectively quoting *Harper, ibid.*, and McDonald v. Board of Election Commissioners of Chicago, 394 U.S. 802, 807, 89 S.Ct. 1404, 1407–1408 (1969).

106. Griffin v. Illinois, 351 U.S. 12, 76 S.Ct. 585 (1956).

merit in an appeal,[107] and legislation which provided that indigents convicted of an offense "work off" in prison any fine they could not pay.[108] The California court found the proposition "irrefutable" that "the school financing system classifies on the basis of wealth." [109] While the classification at issue in *Serrano* revolved around district rather than personal wealth, the court held:

> We think that discrimination on the basis of district wealth is equally invalid. The commercial and industrial property which augments a district's tax base is distributed unevenly throughout the state. To allot more educational dollars to the children of one district than to those of another merely because of the fortuitous presence of such property is to make the quality of a child's education dependent upon the location of private commercial and industrial establishments. Surely, this is to rely on the most irrelevant of factors as the basis for educational financing.[110]

The court also rejected the notion that, since the classification was *de facto* rather than *de jure,* the property tax financing system could stand. Justice Sullivan explained: "First, none of the wealth classifications previously invalidated by the United States Supreme Court or this court has been the product of purposeful discrimination. Instead, these prior decisions have involved 'unintentional' classifications whose impact simply fell more heavily on the poor." [111] And secondly, concluded the court, "[W]e find the case [at hand] unusual in the extent to which governmental action *is* the cause of the wealth classifications" because "[t]he school funding scheme is mandated in every detail" by the state constitution and statutes, because zoning ordinances and land use controls "which promote economic exclusivity" are promulgated by government, and because "[g]overnmental action drew

107. Douglas v. California, 372 U.S. 353, 83 S.Ct. 814 (1963).

108. Williams v. Illinois, 399 U.S. 235, 90 S.Ct. 2018 (1970); Tate v. Short, 401 U.S. 395, 91 S.Ct. 668 (1971).

109. 5 Cal.3d at 598, 96 Cal.Rptr. at 610, 487 P.2d at 1250.

110. 5 Cal.3d at 601, 96 Cal.Rptr. at 612–613, 487 P.2d at 1252–1253.

111. 5 Cal.3d at 602, 96 Cal.Rptr. at 613, 487 P.2d at 1253.

the school district boundary lines, thus determining how much local wealth each district would contain." [112] Noting that, up until then, "wealth classifications have been invalidated only in conjunction with a limited number of fundamental interests," [113] the California court, without the benefit of "direct authority," went on to conclude that, like the rights of defendants in criminal prosecutions and like the right to vote, education constituted a fundamental interest. The court found two significant aspects to the "indispensable role which education plays in the modern industrial state": [114] as "a major determinant of an individual's chances for economic and social success in our competitive society" and as "a unique influence on a child's development as a citizen and his participation in political and community life." [115] The California court found "[t]he classic expression" of "[t]he fundamental importance of education" in the following excerpt, quoted by Justice Sullivan, from the Supreme Court's landmark desegregation decision:

> "Today, education is perhaps the most important function of state and local governments. Compulsory school attendance laws and the great expenditures for education both demonstrate our recognition of the importance of education to our democratic society. It is required in the performance of our most basic public responsibilities, even service in the armed forces. It is the very foundation of good citizenship. Today it is a principal instrument in awakening the child to cultural values, in preparing him for later professional training, and in helping him to adjust normally to his environment. In these days, it is doubtful that any child may reasonably be expected to succeed in life if he is denied the opportunity of an education. Such an opportunity, where the state has undertaken to provide it, is a right which must be made available to all on equal terms." [116]

112. 5 Cal.3d at 603, 96 Cal.Rptr. at 614, 487 P.2d at 1254.

113. 5 Cal.3d at 604, 96 Cal.Rptr. at 615, 487 P.2d at 1255.

114. 5 Cal.3d at 605, 96 Cal.Rptr. at 615, 487 P.2d at 1255.

115. 5 Cal.3d at 605, 96 Cal.Rptr. at 615-616, 487 P.2d at 1255-1256.

116. 5 Cal.3d at 605-606, 96 Cal. Rptr. at 616-617, 487 P.2d at 1256-1257, in part quoting Brown v. Board of Education, 347 U.S. 483, 493, 74 S.Ct. 686, 691 (1954).

Analogizing education to voting in importance as "crucial to participation in, and the functioning of, a democracy," the court added, "At a minimum, education makes more meaningful the casting of a ballot. More significantly, it is likely to provide the understanding of, and the interest in, public issues which are the spur to involvement in other civic and political activities." [117] Summing up, Justice Sullivan wrote:

> We are convinced that the distinctive and priceless function of education in our society warrants, indeed compels, our treating it as a "fundamental interest."
>
> First, education is essential in maintaining what several commentators have termed "free enterprise democracy"—that is, preserving an individual's opportunity to compete successfully in the economic marketplace, despite a disadvantaged background. Accordingly, the public schools of this state are the bright hope for entry of the poor and oppressed into the mainstream of American society.
>
> Second, education is universally relevant. * * *
>
> Third, public education continues over a lengthy period of life—between 10 and 13 years. Few other government services have such sustained, intensive contact with the recipient.
>
> Fourth, education is unmatched in the extent to which it molds the personality of the youth of society. While police and fire protection, garbage collection and street lights are essentially neutral in their effect on the individual psyche, public education actively attempts to shape a child's personal development in a manner chosen not by the child or his parents but by the state. * * *
>
> Finally, education is so important that the state has made it compulsory—not only in the requirement of attendance but also by assignment to a particular district and school. Although a child of wealthy parents has the opportunity to attend a private school, this freedom is seldom available to the indigent. * * * [118]

Reaching "the final step in the application of the 'strict scrutiny' equal protection standard," the court focused on "whether

---

117. 5 Cal.3d at 607–608, 96 Cal. Rptr. at 618, 487 P.2d at 1258.

118. 5 Cal.3d at 608–610, 96 Cal. Rptr. at 618–619, 487 P.2d at 1258–1259.

the California school financing system, as presently structured, is necessary to achieve a compelling state interest." [119]   As to the first of the justifications tendered by the state, "the granting to local districts of effective decision-making over the administration of their schools," the court said, "[E]ven assuming arguendo that local administrative control may be a compelling state interest, the present financial system cannot be considered necessary to furthering this interest." Continued Justice Sullivan, "No matter how the state decides to finance its system of public education, it can still leave th[e] decision-making power [over whom to hire, how to schedule course offerings, etc.] in the hands of local districts." [120]   And, as for the second justification asserted by the state, "that of allowing a local district to choose how much it wishes to spend on the education of its children," Justice Sullivan retorted, "such fiscal freewill is a cruel illusion for the poor school districts." [121]   He continued:

> In summary, so long as the assessed valuation within a district's boundaries is a major determinant of how much it can spend for its schools, only a district with a large tax base will be truly able to decide how much it really cares about education. The poor district cannot freely choose to tax itself into an excellence which its tax rolls cannot provide. Far from being necessary to promote local fiscal choice, the present financing system actually deprives the less wealthy districts of that option.[122]

The court also rejected as "unreasoned apprehensions" the contention of the defendant government officials that if the Equal Protection Clause were read to command that education be made available to all on an equal basis, the same principle must be deemed to apply to all tax-supported public services, and that

---

119. 5 Cal.3d at 610, 96 Cal.Rptr. at
619–620, 487 P.2d at 1259–1260.

120. 5 Cal.3d at 610, 96 Cal.Rptr. at
620, 487 P.2d at 1260.

121. 5 Cal.3d at 611, 96 Cal.Rptr. at
620, 487 P.2d at 1260.

122. *Ibid.*

such a requirement would spell the destruction of local government.[123] Concluded the court:

> The California public school financing system, as presented to us by plaintiffs' complaint supplemented by matters judicially noticed, since it deals intimately with education, obviously touches upon a fundamental interest. For the reasons we have explained in detail, this system conditions the full entitlement to such interest on wealth, classifies its recipients on the basis of their collective affluence and makes the quality of a child's education depend upon the resources of his school district and ultimately upon the pocketbook of his parents. We find that such financing system as presently constituted is not necessary to the attainment of any compelling state interest. Since it does not withstand the requisite "strict scrutiny," it denies to the plaintiffs and others similarly situated the equal protection of the laws. * * * [124]

Critique

However true it may be that the Court's experience with preferred freedoms confirms the accuracy of Justice Marshall's observations, it is at least equally clear that his criticisms do not go far enough in probing the inadequacies of this mode of constitutional interpretation. As with the alternative adjudicative frameworks, its deficiencies amount to more than merely technical problems of application; the weaknesses often go to the very assumptions upon which the approach has been built. The discussion which follows focuses on the problems of the framework in dealing with civil liberties. Obviously, where interests have been relegated to the bottom tier, so that regulation of them is to be assessed in terms of reasonableness, the deficiencies of in-

123. 5 Cal.3d at 613-614, 96 Cal. Rptr. at 622, 487 P.2d at 1262. Justices bent on striking down congressional exercise of the commerce and taxing powers to regulate the means of production before 1937 otherwise imagined a similar parade of horribles with respect to the federal system. See Hammer v. Dagenhart, 247 U.S. 251, 277, 38 S.Ct. 529, 533 (1918); United States v. Butler, 297 U.S. 1, 77, 56 S.Ct. 312, 324 (1936).

124. 5 Cal.3d at 614-615, 96 Cal. Rptr. at 623, 487 P.2d at 1263.

terest balancing, which were discussed in the preceding chapter, also apply.

1. Inadequate Justification

As repeatedly noted, preferred freedoms obtain their status, and this mode of constitutional interpretation derives its justification, from immediate association with the maintenance of the democratic process. Because certain freedoms make it possible for democracy to work—for minorities to become majorities—they are acclaimed "fundamental." But this rationale proves troublesome because it spawns at least three separate difficulties, all with a common cause of complaint: a justification for constitutional interpretation which is simply too narrow.

First, it should be readily apparent that not all of the liberties, within and without the Bill of Rights, which the Court has accorded "fundamental" status, bear a relation to the conduct of democracy, much less are crucial to its maintenance. Consider, for example, the right to travel, the right to privacy, the right to marry, the right to procreate, the right against compelled self-incrimination, the right against unreasonable searches and seizures, the right to counsel, and so on. I am not disputing that these are valuable rights; I think they are. But they are not central, if relevant at all, to the conduct of the democratic process; they are simply not supportable on that basis. Indeed, probably very few of the rights judged important enough to incorporate into the Fourteenth Amendment, which is surely one litmus of fundamentality, could survive this very limited criterion. At best, the democratic enterprise rubric would seem to support only First Amendment rights,[125] and perhaps not even all of them.[126] To begin with, then, the justification for pre-

125. Plus, perhaps, the right to vote and the right to an education.

126. Conceivably, the right to free exercise of one's religious belief could present a problem in terms of this justification. While it is surely apparent that religion is not essential to maintain a democracy, one could reason that societies in the past had been torn apart by religious persecution and this guarantee, together with the Establishment Clause, was intended to remove this traditional factionalism from the political process.

ferred freedoms, without some modification, is inadequate to support the rights already named fundamental.

Secondly, this rationale puts the cart before the horse. It supposes that democracy is an end and the exercise of human rights are so many means to that end. This surely misconceives the arrangement. Democracy is not an end in itself, but a means to the end of human happiness. It is a political method which exists for our use, not the other way around. That several well-intentioned liberal Justices have displayed considerable confusion about a truth so simple as this, is, I think, a powerful indication of the mesmerizing and potentially destructive effect of seeing all interests as social interests without understanding that such a scheme necessarily subordinates the individual to the collectivity.

And third, an inevitable byproduct of this social function rationale is its translation into constitutional standards. A good example is provided by the Court's first obscenity decision. Speaking for the Court, Justice Brennan, interestingly enough, announced, without even so much as a nod in the direction of the relationship between viewing pornographic materials and the commission of sex offenses, that

> [I]t is apparent that the unconditional phrasing of the First Amendment was not intended to protect every utterance.
> *   *   *
>
> The protection given speech and press was fashioned to assure unfettered interchange of ideas for the bringing about of political and social changes desired by the people. *   *   *
>
> All ideas having even the slightest redeeming social importance—unorthodox ideas, controversial ideas, even ideas hateful to the prevailing climate of opinion—have the full protection of the guaranties, unless excludable because they encroach upon the limited area of more important interests. But implicit in the history of the First Amendment is the rejection of obscenity as utterly without redeeming social importance. *   *   * [127]

127. Roth v. United States, 354 U.S. 476, 483–484, 77 S.Ct. 1304, 1308–1309 (1957).

The concept of redeeming social value was subsequently elevated to a position as one of the components of the Court's tripartite test for obscenity.[128] Nor was this focus on social utility as a constitutional standard peculiar to obscenity; Court decisions on the use of "fighting words" [129] and on libel [130] were cut from the same cloth. Perhaps the most effective rejoinder to this line of argument was delivered by Justice Douglas when, dissenting from an obscenity decision nearly a decade later, he wrote:

> Some of the tracts for which these publishers go to prison concern normal sex, some homosexuality, some the masochistic yearning that is probably present in everyone and dominant in some. Masochism is a desire to be punished or subdued. In the broad frame of reference the desire may be expressed in the longing to be whipped and lashed, bound and gagged, and cruelly treated. Why is it unlawful to cater to the needs of this group? They are, to be sure, somewhat offbeat, nonconformist, and odd. But we are not in the realm of criminal conduct, only ideas and tastes. Some like Chopin, others like "rock and roll." Some are "normal," some are masochistic, some deviant in other respects, such as the homosexual. Another group also represented here translates mundane articles into sexual symbols. This group, like those embracing masochism, are anathema to the so-called stable majority. But why is freedom of the press and expression denied them? Are they to be barred from communicating in symbolisms important to them? When the Court today speaks of "social value," does it mean a "value" to the majority? Why is not a minority "value" cognizable? The masochistic group is one; the deviant group is another. Is it not important that members of those groups communicate with each other? Why is communication by the "written word" forbidden? If we were wise enough, we might know that communication may have greater therapeutical value than any sermon that those of the "normal" community can ever offer. But if the communication is of value to the ma-

---

128. Jacobellis v. Ohio, 378 U.S. 184, 84 S.Ct. 1676 (1964); A Book Named "John Cleland's Memoirs of a Woman of Pleasure" v. Attorney General of Massachusetts, 383 U.S. 413, 86 S.Ct. 975 (1966).

129. Chaplinsky v. New Hampshire, 315 U.S. 568, 62 S.Ct. 766 (1942).

130. Beauharnais v. Illinois, 343 U. S. 250, 72 S.Ct. 725 (1952).

sochistic community or to others of the deviant community, how can it be said to be "utterly without redeeming social importance"? "Redeeming" to whom? "Importance" to whom?[131]

The social function defense of First Amendment freedoms is probably best set forth in a monograph by Alexander Meiklejohn.[132] Drawing implicitly on a model of Athenian democracy where the discussion of public issues presumably proceeded with the rationality and dispassion of a Socratic dialogue, an environment that contrasts sharply with his image of the rough-and-tumble conflict of ideas that attends Holmes' free market democracy, Meiklejohn begins from the premise that freedom of speech is essential to self-government. But since it is the collective democratic venture that provides the justification for free speech, its exercise is not contingent upon the desire of the speaker, but the need of the community. Free speech is a social interest, not a personal right; it exists because we need to hear all sides of an issue, not because someone wants to speak. Freedom of speech, then, is simply the correlative of the obligation to hear. It is this kind of speech, public speech, which is protected by the First Amendment. And, since it is imperative that we hear all of the relevant information and arguments bearing on a social issue, that right is absolute. By contrast, speech which does not bear on public issues, private speech, is guaranteed by the Fifth Amendment which provides that that liberty, like life and property, may be regulated in accordance with due process of law.

It is at once apparent that what distinguishes "public" from "private" speech, and thus entitles the former to absolute protection, is that political speech has redeeming social value. What is, perhaps, not readily apparent is that this constitutes a content-oriented test of free speech. As such, it stands in sharp contrast to Holmes' "clear and present danger" test which fo-

131. Ginzburg v. United States, 383 U.S. 463, 489, 86 S.Ct. 942, 973 (1966).

132. Free Speech and Its Relation to Self-Government (1948); reprinted in Political Freedom 8–89 (1960).

cused on the effects of speech. No matter how emphatically one proclaims that "public" speech is absolute, it still remains that only by examining the content of speech can one assay whether it is "public speech." Thus, in Meiklejohn's paradigm, it is inescapable that one's right to speak depends upon what one has to say (rather than upon the disruptive effect a speech may provoke). In fact, the potential for government's intrusion is far greater here than with any ideologically-neutral effects test, for if Holmes is right that censorship is born out of a firm belief by those in power that what they think is right—in Holmes' words, "If you have no doubt of your premises or your power and want a certain result with all your heart" [133]—how is it possible to assess the requisite social relevance of speech so as to determine if it is public speech without prejudging the merit of its contribution, or, in a word, its truth? And, since the quality of redeeming social value is hardly self-evident, Justice Douglas' criticisms apply with equal force here.

Indeed, if one were surprised earlier, in our examination of Justice Black's First Amendment views, to find that speech could at once be both absolute and yet narrower in scope than we might be led to believe at first glance, surely that is even truer here, since, unlike Black, Meiklejohn has further constricted the domain of absolutely-protected speech to contain only "political" speech. Thus it is that the narrow justification of freedom of expression as essential to the democratic process ends up yielding a correspondingly narrow conception of protected expression.

Furthermore, it is by no means clear that "public" and "private" speech can be segregated as neatly as Meiklejohn might wish. And, interestingly enough, the best examples for demonstrating the vagaries of this approach are the very areas in which the Court has, at one time or another, trotted out the concept of redeeming social value. A couple of examples will

133. Abrams v. United States, 250 U.S. 616, 630, 40 S.Ct. 17, 22 (1919) (dissenting opinion).

suffice: Suppose we are confronted with a play, as indeed we were with several in the 1960s, which protests the ugliness and brutality of war by employing unprintable language, complete nudity, and gratuitous violence in an attempt to shock the audience into an appreciation of the horror of it all? Or suppose we have a newspaper article which contains spicy revelations about the love life of a public official or the president of one of the largest corporations? Where is the bright line that divides public and private speech in these cases and countless others like them? Indeed, it was precisely the genuine difficulty of this task that characterized the string of libel and "false light" cases in which the Court was asked successively to expand the concept of "fair comment" by the press to public officials, public figures, and to private citizens caught up in matters of public interest.[134] The Court's experience in the area of libel alone attests to the complexity of the undertaking.

In sum, then, reliance solely upon the maintenance of the democratic enterprise as the rationale for preferred freedoms is too dangerous, too narrow, and too simplistic. Though it is a justification long advanced by well-intentioned libertarians, it is an approach that would seem more at home in a totalitarian state where, in order to justify its sufferance by the government, a book, a picture, a play, or a ballet, has to have some little social moral to tell. It is possible to salvage the concept of preferred freedoms, but not unless one is prepared to acknowledge that democracy is simply a political method and to recognize that individuals are ends in themselves and not means only. Preferred freedoms can then reflect that body of liberties which

---

134. See New York Times v. Sullivan, 376 U.S. 254, 84 S.Ct. 710 (1964); Rosenblatt v. Baer, 383 U. S. 75, 86 S.Ct. 669 (1966); Time, Inc. v. Hill, 385 U.S. 374, 87 S.Ct. 534 (1967); Curtis Publishing Co. v. Butts and Associated Press v. Walker, 388 U.S. 130, 87 S.Ct. 1975 (1967); Rosenbloom v. Metromedia, Inc., 403 U.S. 29, 91 S.Ct. 1811 (1971); Gertz v. Robert Welch, Inc., 418 U.S. 323, 94 S.Ct. 2997 (1974); Cantrell v. Forest City Publishing Co., 419 U.S. 245, 95 S. Ct. 465 (1974); Time, Inc. v. Firestone, 424 U.S. 448, 96 S.Ct. 958 (1976).

sustain the identity of the individual.[135] First Amendment freedoms, like other fundamental freedoms within and without the text of the Constitution, serve many functions, but among them must be the enhancement of individual integrity.[136]

2. When Preferred Freedoms Collide

As an outgrowth of the "clear and present danger" test, the preferred freedoms doctrine was conceived in the tension between individual liberty and public safety. Its component parts clearly show that the approach was intended for application in controversies where the individual and the government, as the principal antagonists, represented adverse interests. But when two preferred freedoms collide, the framework provides no guidance for the resolution of the conflict.[137] In cases where two ba-

135. See Bay, The Structure of Freedom (1958); and see Roe v. Wade, 410 U.S. 113, 209, 93 S.Ct. 705, 756 (1973) (concurring opinion of Douglas, J.).

136. See, e. g., Emerson, Toward a General Theory of the First Amendment, 72 Yale L.J. 877 (1963); reprinted as a book (1966).

137. It may be that Rawls' principle of focusing on the impact on the most disadvantaged member of society (p. 186) presents a way to break this deadlock. However, it is not clear how an assessment of such effects would take place within the narrow confines of the judicial process. Confronting a somewhat similar undertaking, Justice Jackson, in rejecting the "clear and present danger" test as a useful constitutional standard for reviewing the conviction of several Communist Party leaders under the Smith Act on charges of conspiring to advocate the overthrow of the government by force and violence, wrote:

If we must decide that this Act and its application are constitutional only if we are convinced that petitioner's conduct creates a "clear and present danger" of violent overthrow, we must appraise impounderables, including international and national phenomena which baffle the best informed foreign offices and our most experienced politicians. We would have to foresee and predict the effectiveness of Communist propaganda, opportunities for infiltration, whether, and when, a time will come that they consider propitious for action, and whether and how fast our existing government will deteriorate. And we would have to speculate as to whether an approaching Communist coup would not be anticipated by a nationalistic fascist movement. No doctrine can be sound whose application requires us to make a prophecy of

sic liberties confront one another, interest balancing becomes inevitable. More often than not, the basis for decision in these instances remains undisclosed, and the preference for one fundamental liberty over the other appears to rest simply on assertion.

This is particularly true of the conflict between freedom of the press and the right to privacy which characterizes the Court's decisions on libel. A good example of this genre, though not a libel case, is *Time, Inc.* v. *Hill*.[138] In that case, the plaintiff brought suit under a New York statute for invasion of privacy after a story appearing in *Life* magazine reported that a new play portrayed the much-publicized experience of the Hill family whose members had been held captive at home by three escaped convicts. Though members of the Hill family were not mistreated, the play, which presented a fictionalized account of a family held captive under similar circumstances, contained violence. Furthermore, the story was supplemented by photographs of scenes from the play taken in the former Hill family home. The Court made no mention whatever of any fundamental right to privacy in its decision to reverse a $30,000 award for compensatory damages and remand the case. Instead, the Court's opinion focused on extending to "matters of public interest" the *New York Times* rule (with respect to the collection of damages by public officials for defamatory falsehoods relating to their conduct in office) that the plaintiff be required to show that the statement was made either with the knowledge it was false or with reckless disregard for the truth. Said Justice Fortas dissenting:

> I do not believe that the First Amendment precludes effective protection of the right of privacy—or, for that matter, an effective law of libel. I do not believe that we must or should,

that sort in the guise of a legal decision. The judicial process simply is not adequate to a trial of such far-flung issues. The answers given would reflect our own political predilections and nothing more.

Dennis v. United States, 341 U.S. 494, 570, 71 S.Ct. 857, 898 (1951) (concurring opinion).

138.   385   U.S.   374,   87   S.Ct.   534 (1967).

in deference to those whose views are absolute as to the scope of the First Amendment, be ingenious to strike down all state action, however circumspect, which penalizes the use of words as instruments of aggression and personal assault. There are great and important values in our society, none of which is greater than those reflected in the First Amendment, but which are also fundamental and entitled to this Court's careful respect and protection. * * *

* * *

The Court today does not repeat the ringing words of so many of its members on so many occasions in exaltation of the right of privacy. * * * In my opinion, the jury instructions, although they were not a textbook model, satisfied this standard.

* * * The English language is not so esoteric as to permit serious consequences to turn upon a supposed difference between the instructions to the jury and this Court's formulation. Nor is the First Amendment in such delicate health that it requires or permits this kind of surgery, the net effect of which is not only an individual injustice, but an encouragement to recklessness and careless readiness to ride roughshod over the interests of others.

The courts may not and must not permit either public or private action that censors or inhibits the press. But part of this responsibility is to preserve values and procedures which assure the ordinary citizen that the press is not above the reach of the law—that its special prerogatives, granted because of its special and vital functions, are reasonably equated with its needs in the performance of these functions. For this Court totally to immunize the press—whether forthrightly or by subtle indirection—in areas far beyond the needs of news, comment on public persons and events, discussion of public issues and the like would be no service to freedom of the press, but an invitation to public hostility to that freedom. This Court cannot and should not refuse to permit under state law the private citizen who is aggrieved by the type of assault which we have here and which is not within the specially protected core of the First Amendment to recover compensatory damages for recklessly inflicted invasion of his rights.[139]

139. 385 U.S. at 412–420, 87 S.Ct. at 554–559.

Insofar as we are presented with the collision of two preferred freedoms, a prospect not likely to be reduced given the predisposition of judicial activists for generating additional fundamental liberties outside the text of the Constitution, the deadlock encountered by the preferred freedoms framework is identical to that faced by absolutism. If interest balancing is to be avoided, it will require further prioritizing of basic rights, something which the preferred freedoms approach presently fails to provide.[140]

3. The Problem of Subjectivity

Justice Marshall is surely right to concede that "the process of determining which interests are fundamental is a difficult one." [141] He has argued that the attribution of fundamentality to rights or interests need not proceed subjectively or arbitrarily and that the degree of scrutiny should be adjusted by determining the proximity of the interest to specifically-guaranteed constitutional rights (pp. 207–208). This explanation, however, is far from the point of being helpfully clear. Part of the problem why subjectivity appears to present such a problem for strict scrutiny may be simply that fundamentality is not an absolute but a relational quality. "Fundamental" to what? Without an understanding of what the rights or interests are fundamental to, the difficulty of identifying specially-protected rights is indeed "insurmountable." To borrow a phrase from Justice Marshall, "the approach is rudderless." If one replies by saying that the rights so called at present are fundamental to the democratic enterprise, the difficulty, as we have already determined, is two-fold: first, that justification is too narrow to be defensible; and second, the rights currently in that category exceed the justification. And the Court has yet to overtly acknowledge the ascription of rights as

---

140. An illustration somewhat along these lines is provided by Justice Douglas' concurring opinion in Roe v. Wade, 410 U.S. 113, 209, 93 S.Ct. 705, 756.

141. San Antonio Independent School Dist. v. Rodriguez, 411 U.S. 1, 102, 93 S.Ct. 1278, 1332 (1973) (dissenting opinion).

fundamental to the integrity of the individual. If and when it does, it remains to be seen whether, relying upon that criterion, protected interests can be determined with any meaningful guidance. But the prospects are not good, since the broader the goal to be attained, the less likely it will be that one can specify with any sense of precision the means for arriving at it. In the long run, the objectivity with which one identifies fundamental rights is not likely to be appreciably greater than with those qualities of fairness, decency, and "conduct that shocks the conscience" indigenous to interest balancing.

4. Judicial Vulnerability

While we need not reiterate here all of the perils of judicial activism that potentially accompany exercise of the review power on the scale preferred freedoms entails, still a few thoughts are in order. The first of these is simply that, try hard as we might to shrug off the likelihood as remote, the dangers of provoking a costly reaction from Congress, or from an ebbing of the Court's prestige, are real. This does not call for disuse of the review power, or even adopting the regimen of interest balancing, but it does counsel some prudence and sensitivity as to how much the market will bear at any one time. For example, it was no mere coincidence that twice in his last twenty years on the bench, Justice Douglas was the object of impeachment efforts, the second of which was plenty serious.[142] And congressional dissatisfaction with many Warren Court decisions played no small role in the nonappointment of Abe Fortas as Chief Justice in 1968.[143] Add to this the buffeting the Court took in the presidential campaign of the same year,[144] and the fact that continued criticism of the Court became sufficiently strident that so

142. See 1970 Cong.Quart.Wkly.Rep. 2786–2789; and see 1953 Cong. Quart.Almanac 311.

143. See Shogan, A Question of Judgment: The Fortas Case and the Struggle for the Supreme Court (1972).

144. See Chase and Ducat, *The Warren Court and the Second Constitutional Revolution,* in Corwin's The Constitution and What It Means Today 258–260 (13th ed. 1973); see also White, The Making of the President 1968, 34, 189, 346 (1969).

unlikely a defender of the Warren Court as Attorney General John Mitchell was moved to speak out for temperance, moderation, and respect,[145] and the message comes through loud and clear. And whatever may be said of the rightness of the Warren Court rulings on criminal procedure or racial discrimination, or the Burger Court's abortion decision, the fact is that these decisions have not enhanced the Court's prestige. The Court today is not more popular, but less popular, for its activism. This is not to say that the Court should console itself with weathervane jurisprudence or that it should never have made those decisions, but only that there may be a limit at any one time as to what the Court's prestige will sustain; and the Court cannot afford, if it seeks to remain even a modestly effective political institution, to proceed in blissful disregard of its base of support.

In this regard, it would be a serious mistake for the Court to assume, as Professor Shapiro appears to,[146] that, by wielding the preferred freedoms approach, the Court can hope to generate an effective power base from which to withstand congressional sanctions, for any clientele the Court might acquire in this manner would, by definition, be composed of powerless minorities and thus possess insufficient clout to turn the tide.[147] If the key to the Court's effectiveness is its role as legitimizing agent, it must sustain a relatively broad base of public support. This entails gauging the resentment of those who are prone to see the Court as an instrument of minority rule. It is more than a bit doubtful, to take an example from the docket for this Term, that the assumption of a high-profile representational role in behalf of society's disadvantaged would significantly advance the

---

145. New York Times, May 2, 1970, p. 1.

146. Freedom of Speech 34–39, 111–115.

147. The prospect of putting together a sizable coalition of the underrepresented is also likely to be much less than might be imagined at first, since, as noted before, social cleavages tend to reinforce one another. Consequently, individuals delineated as one minority are likely to substantially overlap other minorities so that adding up the groups is probably going to yield only very modest fractional increments.

Court's effectiveness in resolving the *Bakke* case, embodying as that controversy does many of the worst fears, jealousies, and anxieties that separate the "insular minorities" and society's more numerous and thus more powerful groups.[148]

Doubtless Professor Bickel accurately characterized the Warren Court when, quoting Namier, he said of it that it " 'imagine[d] the past and remember[ed] the future.' "[149] Those Justices, who lent their strength to the dominant tones of equality and liberty reflected in the Court's activism of the 1960s, banked on the fact that, in the years ahead, the results those decisions achieved would be rightly regarded as true to the promise of American life and the reasoning by which they got there would pale into insignificance. So the Warren Court frequently colored the past to justify its vision of the future. Taking a leaf from Chief Justice Marshall, the Justices pinned their hopes on the path of history which was well marked by themes of the broadening base of popular participation in government and the wider distribution of social benefits. But progress can rarely be seen as a perfectly straight line; it takes place only in the context of pendulum-like swings in social movements. Whether the Court zigged when it should have zagged in the late 'sixties may be a product of the time lag that affects the staffing of that institution in such a pronounced way. At any rate, it is not nearly so important as understanding that a rigid attachment to activism jeopardizes the Court as an institution. Conceding, as I would, the Court's unusual capacity to help in bettering the conditions of the underrepresented, in the first instance this prospect depends on its ability to remain afloat.

5. *The Coexistence of Liberty and Order*

Since it was the purpose of the preferred freedoms doctrine to balance with a bias favorable to liberty in assessing intrusions by government on the exercise of basic rights, it was to be ex-

---

148. See Greenfield, *How to Resolve the Bakke Case*, Newsweek, Oct. 27, 1977, p. 128.

149. The Supreme Court and the Idea of Progress 13 (1970).

pected that substantially fewer statutes would withstand strict scrutiny than would pass muster under the lenient test of reasonableness. This much is understandable. But some cause for concern is surely prompted by Justice Marshall's observation that, once an interest is elevated to the upper tier, a statute which seeks to impose limitations on such a basic right is *always* struck down. Applications of the preferred freedoms test which yield such preordained results are only one indication of a belief seemingly that liberty ought automatically to prevail over public order.

The fiber of the preferred freedoms test doubtless reflects a healthy revulsion against the repeated inability of proponents of interest balancing on the Court to protect civil liberties in times of crisis, such as the Red Hunt of the late 'teens and early 'twenties and the Cold War hysteria of the 'fifties. But at least a couple applications of the test appear to go beyond merely the presumption against the legitimacy of governmental regulation unless the facts demonstrate otherwise. In the course of reaching a conclusion that a given statute was either overbroad in itself or so construed as to be overbroad (and therefore unconstitutional or unconstitutionally applied), the Court, on occasion, has substituted its own speculation about the possible basis for conviction under the law in the face of facts that clearly seem to show the defendant's conduct constituted more than simply the expression of political views.

A case in point is *Terminiello* v. *Chicago*.[150] In that decision, the Court reversed the defendant's conviction for "breach of the peace." After pointing out that, in his charge to the jury, the trial judge had defined those words "to include speech which 'stirs the public to anger, invites dispute, brings about a condition of unrest, or creates a disturbance * * *,' " Justice Douglas went on to emphasize the importance of free speech to the democratic process in making government responsive, effect-

150.   337 U.S. 1, 69 S.Ct. 894 (1949).

ing peaceful change, and promoting diversity of ideas and programs, and observed:

> Accordingly a function of free speech under our system of government is to invite dispute. It may indeed best serve its high purpose when it induces a condition of unrest, creates dissatisfaction with conditions as they are, or even stirs people to anger. Speech is often provocative and challenging. It may strike at prejudices and preconceptions and have profound unsettling effects as it presses for acceptance of an idea. That is why freedom of speech, though not absolute * * * is nevertheless protected against censorship or punishment, unless shown likely to produce a clear and present danger of a serious substantive evil that rises far above public inconvenience, annoyance, or unrest. * * * There is no room under our Constitution for a more restrictive view. For the alternative would lead to standardization of ideas either by legislatures, courts, or dominant political or community groups.[151]

Since the Court found the trial judge's construction of the ordinance far too broad such that "[a] conviction resting on any of those grounds may not stand," and, since "[f]or all anyone knows [Terminiello] was convicted under the parts of the ordinance (as construed) which, for example, make it an offense merely to invite dispute or to bring about a condition of unrest,"[152] the Court reversed the conviction. Yet, as the lengthly recitation of facts in Justice Jackson's dissenting opinion makes clear, "the local trial court that tried Terminiello * * * was dealing with a riot and with a speech that provoked a hostile mob and incited a friendly one, and threatened violence between the two."[153] As the undisputed facts show, Terminiello spoke in an auditorium filled with about 800 people, most of them sympathizers, while a hostile crowd of about double that size milled about outside. In vigorous and often vicious terms, Terminello attacked several prominent figures in the Roosevelt administration as Communists, called people of a left-wing political out-

151. 337 U.S. at 4–5, 69 S.Ct. at 896.   153. 337 U.S. at 13, 69 S.Ct. at 900.

152. 337 U.S. at 5–6, 69 S.Ct. at 896.

look "scum," and vilified several religious and racial minorities. Despite police efforts to cordon off the area, there were disturbances in the crowd, there was much pushing and shoving, rocks and bricks were thrown, some 28 windows were broken, stink bombs were set off, and there was evidence that individuals outside kept breaking into the meeting hall.

Another example is the Court's decision in *Street* v. *New York*,[154] which reversed a conviction under a state statute that made it a misdemeanor to "publicly mutilate, deface, defile, or defy, trample upon, or cast contempt upon either by words or act" an American flag. The defendant, who was black, became upset when he heard over an afternoon radio broadcast that James Meredith, a figure in the civil rights movement, had been shot by a sniper. He proceeded to burn a flag on a streetcorner near his apartment. As a police officer neared the scene, where a small crowd had gathered, the officer heard Street say "We don't need no damn flag." After inquiring whether Street had set the flag on fire, and receiving a straightforward admission, the officer arrested Street. The Court concluded that the state could not constitutionally punish anyone for publicly defying or casting contempt verbally on the flag. And since it could not be ascertained from the record whether the judge, who rendered judgment in a bench trial, rested the conviction in whole or in part on the defendant's words rather than his conduct, the Court reversed the judgment on grounds that conviction would be unconstitutional where it rested "*solely* on his words" or "upon *both* his words and his act." Dissenting "because the Court * * * has declined to meet and resolve the basic question presented in this case," namely, "whether the deliberate act of burning an American flag in public as a 'protest' may be punished as a crime"[155] (and subsequently answering that question in the affirmative), Chief Justice Warren said:

> But the Court specifically refuses to decide this issue. Instead, it searches microscopically for the opportunity to de-

154. 394 U.S. 576, 89 S.Ct. 1354   155. 394 U.S. at 595, 89 S.Ct. at
(1969).   1367.

cide the case on [a] peripheral * * * ground, holding that it is impossible to determine the basis for appellant's conviction. In my opinion a reading of the short trial record leaves no doubt that appellant was convicted solely for burning the American flag.

* * *

I am in complete agreement with the general rule that this Court should not treat broad constitutional questions when narrow ones will suffice to dispose of the litigation. However, where only the broad question is presented, it is our task and our responsibility to confront that question squarely and resolve it. * * *[156]

Taken together, the foreordained outcome of strict scrutiny and the Court's speculative overreaching in these cases leave the distinct impression that preferred freedoms advocates see liberty and order as mutually exclusive interests—that, in the words of Justice Jackson describing the majority in *Terminiello*, "The Court seems to regard these as enemies of each other and to be of the view that one must forego order to achieve liberty."[157] This is not only a foolish view, it is a dangerous one; for it is impossible to have any civil liberties at all without some minimum of public order. Justice Jackson's dissent in *Terminiello* was written less than three years after he had returned from his assignment as chief American prosecutor at the Nuremberg Trials. With obvious allusion to the ineffectiveness of the Weimar Republic in sustaining that minimum public order which makes democracy possible, Justice Jackson insightfully concluded:

Hitler summed up the strategy of the mass demonstration as used by both fascism and communism: "We should not work in secret conventicles but in mighty mass demonstrations, and it is not by dagger and poison or pistol that the road can be cleared for the movement but *by the conquest of the streets*. We must teach the Marxists that the future *master of the streets* is National Socialism, just as it will some day be the master of the state." [Emphasis supplied.]

156. 394 U.S. at 595–596, 604, 89 S. Ct. at 1367, 1372.

157. 337 U.S. at 14, 69 S.Ct. at 900 (dissenting opinion).

* * * from *"Mein Kampf."* First laughed at as an extravagant figure of speech, the battle for the streets became a tragic reality when an organized *Sturmabterlung* began to give practical effect to its slogan that "possession of the streets is the key to power in the state." * * *

The present obstacle to mastery of the streets by either radical or reactionary mob movements is not the opposing minority. It is the authority of local governments which represent the free choice of democratic and law-abiding elements, of all shades of opinion but who, whatever their differences, submit them to free elections which register the results of their free discussion. The fascist and communist groups, on the contrary, resort to these terror tactics to confuse, bully and discredit those freely chosen governments. Violent and noisy shows of strength discourage participation of moderates in discussions so fraught with violence and real discussion dries up and disappears. And people lose faith in the democratic process when they see public authority flouted and impotent and begin to think the time has come when they must choose sides in a false and terrible dilemma such as was posed as being at hand by the call for the Terminiello meeting: "Christian Nationalism or World Communism— Which?"

This drive by totalitarian groups to undermine the prestige and effectiveness of local democratic governments is advanced whenever either of them can win from this Court a ruling which paralyzes the power of these officials. This is such a case. The group of which Terminiello is a part claims that his behavior, because it involved a speech, is above the reach of local authorities.

If the mild action those authorities have taken is forbidden, it is plain that hereafter there is nothing effective left that they can do. If they can do nothing as to him, they are equally powerless as to rival totalitarian groups. Terminiello's victory today certainly fulfills the most extravagant hopes of both right and left totalitarian groups, who want nothing so much as to paralyze and discredit the only democratic authority that can curb them in their battle for the streets.

* * *

However, * * * wholesome principles [of "clear and present danger" and proscribing the use of "fighting words"] are abandoned today and in their place is substituted a dogma of absolute freedom for irresponsible and provocative utterance which almost completely sterilizes the power of local authorities to keep the peace as against this kind of tactics.

* * *

This Court has gone far toward accepting the doctrine that civil liberty means the removal of all restraints from these crowds and that all local attempts to maintain order are impairments of the liberty of the citizen. The choice is not between order and liberty. It is between liberty with order and anarchy without either. There is danger that, if the Court does not temper its doctrinaire logic with a little practical wisdom, it will convert the constitutional Bill of Rights into a suicide pact.[158]

158. 337 U.S. at 24–25, 28, 37, 69 S.
    Ct. at 904–905, 906, 911.

Chapter 5
The Court as a Conservative Institution

At this stage, it might be tempting to tritely conclude that the possibilities of the Court as a reformist institution depend upon those Justices who comprise it. And so, of course, they do, in part. Substantially more interesting than this, however, is to ask whether there exist any objective limitations inhering in the institution which inhibit the chances; if so, what they are; and what conceivably their impact might be in marking out a role for the Court in the political system. Or, putting the matter more directly, is there a case to be made by those favoring social change—that is, by liberals and radicals—for the resolution of the major issues of the day in other than a judicial forum?

Conservatism and the Judicial Process

A logical place to begin is with a survey of those features that bias the judicial process in the direction of conservatism. While I am not unaware that use of the terms "liberal" and "conservative" has been variously attacked as notoriously imprecise and no longer even relevant to the description of contemporary politics,[1] the terms are useful enough for my purposes here. Suffice it to say that the discussion below employs the term "conservative" in two senses, following somewhat the form of Rossiter.[2] In its first sense, I use the term *conservative* to mean simply that a given practice or doctrine tends to minimize or retard social change. And, in its second sense, I use the term *Conservative* to signify that a given practice or doctrine tends to benefit the propertied classes and to disadvantage those without wealth. Because maintenance of the *status quo* is invariably in

---

1. See Lowi, The End of Liberalism, Ch. 3 (1969); Bell, The End of Ideology 393–407 (Rev. ed. 1962).

2. Conservatism in America, Ch. 1 (2d ed. 1962).

the interest of those presently advantaged by the system, use of the terms, though, tends to be mutually reinforcing.

Surely one such aspect of adjudication which readily comes to mind is the deeply ingrained predisposition to view and resolve current disputes as extensions of previous ones. Reliance upon precedent is probably the most obvious conservative influence at work in the judicial process. To the extent that the justification offered for any judicial decision consists of analogies whose persuasiveness turns on the goodness of fit between present and past fact patterns, applying the clearest precedent in any given case will necessarily minimize innovation and, therefore, the potential for change. The prospect for substantially altering the existing state of affairs appears only when judges overrule a precedent,[3] when they write on a clean slate,[4] and when, exalting the spirit of the law above its form, they apply an existing principle of law in an unforeseeable new context.[5] But these are not everyday occurrences.

Implicit both in the treatment of like cases alike, which is the animating principle behind reliance on precedent, and in regard for neutral principles as the stuff of which adequate legal justifications are made is the definition of justice as formal or procedural equality. But this is a Conservative notion of justice because it looks only to the superficial equality of legal parties in the application of rules and principles without any attention to the disparity in wealth or power which may separate them. One of the best examples of this, of course, was the Court's rec-

3. For example, see West Coast Hotel Co. v. Parrish, 300 U.S. 379, 57 S.Ct. 578 (1937); United States v. Darby, 312 U.S. 100, 61 S.Ct. 451 (1941); Brown v. Board of Education, 347 U.S. 483, 74 S.Ct. 686 (1954); Malloy v. Hogan, 378 U.S. 1, 84 S.Ct. 1489 (1964).

4. For example, see Marbury v. Madison, 5 U.S. (1 Cr.) 137, 2 L.Ed. 60 (1803); Fletcher v. Peck, 10 U.

S. (6 Cr.) 87, 3 L.Ed. 162 (1810); McCulloch v. Maryland, 17 U.S. (4 Wheat.) 316, 4 L.Ed. 579 (1819); Gibbons v. Ogden, 22 U.S. (9 Wheat.) 1, 6 L.Ed. 23 (1824).

5. For example, see Olmstead v. United States, 277 U.S. 438, 471–485, 48 S.Ct. 564, 570–575 (1928) (dissenting opinion of Brandeis, J.); and see Katz v. United States, 389 U.S. 347, 88 S.Ct. 507 (1967).

ognition of both individuals and corporations as "persons" within the meaning of the Fourteenth Amendment and its decisions vindicating the liberty of contract in employer-employee negotiations, willfully blind to the vast discrepancy in bargaining power between the two. It was this sense in which legal equality treats unequals equally which provoked Anatole France to caustically remark on "the majestic equality of the laws, which forbid rich and poor alike to sleep under bridges, to beg in the streets, and to steal their bread." [6]

The conservatism of the judicial process is reinforced by adhering to the precept that cases should be decided on the narrowest possible ground. If incrementalism in judicial decision-making provides for some movement in the law, as against that associated with a static approach of fixed rules, still the practice of deciding no more than one has to decide brakes the pace of social change.

As important as these limitations on the manner by which the merits of disputes are revolved is the Court's store of instruments for nondecision. Rulings that constrict the meaning of such requisites as case and controversy,[7] standing,[8] and

---

6. Le Lys Rouge [The Red Lily], Ch. 7 (n. d., orig. pub. 1894).

7. That is, whether the interests opposed in a given controversy are sufficiently adverse and concrete, thereby eliminating hypothetical and abstract, moot, and collusive claims, and precluding the rendering of advisory opinions. See Bator, Mishkin, Shapiro, and Wechsler, Hart and Wechsler's The Federal Courts and the Federal System 102–149 (2d ed. 1973) [hereafter referred to as Hart and Wechsler].

8. That is, whether the parties named in a suit are proper parties to bring legal action either because their interests have been damaged or because their legal rights have been abridged. See Shapiro, The Supreme Court and Administrative Agencies 121–125 (1968); Hart and Wechsler 150–214. Also see Scott, *Standing in the Supreme Court—A Functional Analysis*, 86 Harv.L. Rev. 645 (1973); Sedler, *Standing, Justiciability and All That: A Behavioral Analysis*, 25 Vanderbilt L.Rev. 479 (1972); Monaghan, *Constitutional Adjudication: The Who and When*, 82 Yale L.J. 1363 (1973); Orren, *Standing to Sue: Interest Group Conflict in the Federal Courts*, 70 Am.Pol.Sci.Rev. 723 (1976).

ripeness,[9] are critical because they govern access to the judicial process. Insofar as Court decisions accentuate requirements that a plaintiff sustain immediate and tangible injury, such rulings lean in a conservative direction simply because they postpone the opportunities for intervention by the judiciary and, hence, favor the *status quo*. But constrictive interpretations of these doctrines are also deeply Conservative because their effect is to demand that those possessing much less in the way of resources put proportionately more on the line just to get to court. For those without wealth and position, the price of admission to the judicial process often becomes the wager of one's job,[10] or a jail term,[11] if, in fact, access to the courts is not entirely precluded because the injury cannot be personalized.[12] And, lest it be overlooked, there are clearly both conservative and Conservative overtones in relitigating a matter to the point where, and if, the merits of the case are finally reached. Looking at the other side of the coin, it should be said that the case and controversy, standing, and ripeness requirements cannot be reduced beyond a certain point without threatening the very integrity of adjudication itself. Earlier intervention by the courts, which is the product of loosening these requirements, invites the judicial process to take up less solid and more hypothetical cases where the contours of a dispute may be pretty fuzzy, in turn leaving the Court to difficult and hazardous problems of proof and evidence and heightening the risk of far-reaching and unwise rul-

9. That is, whether the issues have sufficiently crystalized so as to permit the court to reach the merits of a controversy. See Shapiro, The Supreme Court and Administrative Agencies 116–121; Hart and Wechsler 133–149.

10. See United Public Workers v. Mitchell, 330 U.S. 75, 67 S.Ct. 556 (1947); International Longshoremen's & Warehousemen's Union v. Boyd, 347 U.S. 222, 74 S.Ct. 447 (1954).

11. For example, *cf.* Griswold v. Connecticut, 381 U.S. 479, 85 S.Ct. 1678 (1965), with Tileston v. Ullman, 318 U.S. 44, 63 S.Ct. 493 (1943), and Poe v. Ullman, 367 U.S. 497, 81 S.Ct. 1752 (1961).

12. For example, see Warth v. Seldin, 422 U.S. 490, 95 S.Ct. 2197 (1975); United States v. Richardson, 418 U.S. 166, 94 S.Ct. 2940 (1974); Schlesinger v. Reservists Committee to Stop the War, 418 U.S. 208, 94 S.Ct. 2925 (1974).

ings which must later be seriously modified or entirely retracted because they went too far on the basis of too little knowledge.

To these features can be added a series of various other elements which also impede the judicial process as a ready instrument of social change and benefit those better off: the sophistication of recognizing when legal rights may be violated in the first place, the traditional domination of the bench by individuals of upper and upper middle class backgrounds, the impediments to class action suits,[13] the expense of litigation, and the slowness with which the process moves.

I do not pretend this to be anything approaching a complete inventory. There are many other features of the judicial process that can also be tagged as conservative, either with a big or a little "c," or both. But even this brief canvass of those aspects most likely to come to mind for even a casual student of the Court goes a long way toward making the point that the judicial process is far from being as neutral in political impact as the scales of blind justice reassure it is in the formal and abstract legal sense. There is, then, more than a little cause for concern among those seeking to speed social change—those who want us to move in something other than low gear—to suspect that the judicial process may prove less than the optimum vehicle for reform.

The "Political Questions" Doctrine and the Limits of Adjudication

A more subtle but equally revealing vantage point on the relation between the judicial process and the pace of social change is suggested by the doctrines woven about the Court's historical shunning of "political questions." The attempts to define what it is about these issues that makes them questions which the Court will not address have been endless.[14] One view focuses on

13. For example, see Eisen v. Carlisle & Jacquelin, 417 U.S. 156, 94 S. Ct. 2140 (1974); and see Note, *Developments in the Law—Class Actions*, 89 Harv.L.Rev. 1319 (1976).

14. The general approaches are reviewed in Professor Scharpf's article, see note 17, *infra*. See also Henkin, *Is There a "Political Question" Doctrine?* 85 Yale L.J. 597

the substance of such questions and argues that the subject matter of certain disputes is determinative. The resolution of some matters, it is argued, has been withheld from the province of the judiciary and explicitly delegated by the Constitution to other branches of government. Another school of thought contends that justiciable questions are distinguished from "political" ones because of the form in which they are cast. Some matters, it is said, are not resolvable by the Court because they are not presented in a form to which the Court can apply a standard of adjudication. And finally, there are, of course, the prudential theories of the "political question." According to this interpretation, the Court avoids passing on certain issues out of respect to their political delicacy for the government as a whole, or, in terms of the narrower "hot potato" thesis, it evades matters which are too controversial or where, were the Court to render judgment, its ruling would very likely not be enforced or respected.[15] These three principal stances on the "political question" doctrine are respectively reflected in definitions one, two, and three through six, in the following paragraph from Justice Brennan's opinion for the Court in *Baker* v. *Carr*:

> It is apparent that several formulations which vary slightly according to the settings in which the questions arise may describe a political question, although each has one or more elements which identify it as essentially a function of the separation of powers. Prominent on the surface of any case held to involve a political question is found a textually demonstrable constitutional commitment of the issue to a coordinate political department; or a lack of judicially discoverable and manageable standards for resolving it; or the impossibility of deciding without an initial policy determination of a kind clearly for nonjudicial discretion; or the impossibility of a court's undertaking independent resolution without expressing lack of the respect due coordinate branches of government; or an unusual need for unquestioning adherence to

(1976); Rosenblum, *Justiciability and Justice: Elements of Restraint and Indifference*, 15 Cath.U.L.Rev. 141 (1966); Hart and Wechsler 214–241.

15. See Strum, The Supreme Court and "Political Questions": A Study in Judicial Evasion (1974).

a political decision already made; or the potentiality of embarrassment from multifarious pronouncements by various departments on one question.[16]

Of all these, the second notion of what it means to call something a "political question" is particularly relevant for our purposes here. It suggests a functional approach to defining what is excluded from the Court's consideration—that the form in which questions are cast plus certain inherent limitations on the functioning of the judicial process are critical to determining whether the Court not only will, but *can*, render a judgment in a given controversy.[17]

The notion of a functional approach to understanding "political questions" demands, in turn, a definition of what it is that we mean by the judicial process; for only if we know the essentials of that process can we determine what kinds of questions enable it to function. A particularly incisive contribution in this respect is Professor Fuller's clarification of the concept of adjudication. In his words:

> [T]he fundamental characteristic of adjudication * * * lies in the particular form of participation it accords to the affected party. That participation consists in the institutionally protected opportunity to present proofs and arguments for a decision in his favor. This is, in effect, nothing more than an unfamiliar formulation of a very familiar conception, that of giving the affected party "his day in court." The formulation I am offering has the advantage, I believe, of clarifying what is necessary to make the party's day in court meaningful. For one thing, he must have some conception of the issues toward which his proofs and arguments are to be directed, if his opportunity to present proofs and arguments is to be meaningful. * * * *[18]

16. 369 U.S. 186, 217, 82 S.Ct. 691, 710 (1962).

17. See Scharpf, *Judicial Review and the Political Question: A Functional Analysis*, 75 Yale L.J. 517 (1966).

18. Fuller, *Adjudication and the Rule of Law*, 54 Proc.Am.Soc.Int.L. 1, 2 (1960) [hereafter referred to as Fuller]. Reprinted from the Proceedings of the American Society of International Law with permission.

While this formulation stresses the importance of the adversary process, clearly, effective participation in adjudication presupposes agreement as much as it does difference between the parties. It presupposes common recognition of a fixed standard to which the parties can pitch their proofs and arguments if participation is to have a chance of affecting the decision and thus be meaningful. But where does such a standard come from? The answer is that such standards are the stuff of which precedents are made, those principled decisions of which Professor Wechsler spoke. As in the story of the blind men who touch the elephant at different points and who report to us different ideas about its shape, Fuller and Wechsler have simply described adjudication by touching it at different spots. It is, in fact, the connection between the two that makes adjudication a process. Fuller has described adjudication in terms of inputs, while Wechsler focuses on the outputs. The link between them is a feed-back loop by which past principled decisions furnish the settled standards to which future litigants pitch their proofs and arguments in cases yet to come. If adjudication is seen as a process, it also serves to explain why arguments between some people who say "First law, then courts" and others who contend "First courts, then law" have a chicken-and-egg quality. Such arguments are futile. These debaters have simply stopped adjudication at one point; they have offered us a snapshot of something that, to be seen accurately, really requires a motion picture.

With this understanding of what it is that gives adjudication its distinctiveness, we can consider what Professor Fuller means when he asserts that "adjudication is a process of decision badly suited to the solution of polycentric problems." [19] A polycentric problem is one that has many centers; that is, it is a problem the parts of which are interconnected so that decision with respect to any one component of the problem has immediate impli-

See also Fuller, *Collective Bargaining and the Arbitrator*, 1963 Wis.L. Rev. 3. *Cf.* Chayes, *The Role of the Judge in Public Law Litigation*, 89 Harv.L.Rev. 1281 (1976).

19. *Ibid.*, 3.

cations for the decision of every other part of the problem. Fuller provides the following helpful illustration of such a problem:

> What is a polycentric problem? Fortunately I am in a position to borrow a recent illustration from the newspapers. Some months ago a wealthy lady by the name of Timken died in New York leaving a valuable, but somewhat miscellaneous, collection of paintings to the Metropolitan Museum and the National Gallery "in equal shares," her will indicating no particular apportionment. When the will was probated the judge remarked something to the effect that the parties seemed to be confronted with a real problem. The attorney for one of the museums spoke up and said, "We are good friends. We will work it out somehow or other." What makes this problem of effecting an equal division of the paintings a polycentric task? It lies in the fact that the disposition of any single painting has implications for the proper disposition of every other painting. If it gets the Renoir, the Gallery may be less eager for the Cezanne, but all the more eager for the Bellows, et cetera. If the proper apportionment were set for argument, there would be no clear issue to which either side could direct its proofs and contentions. Any judge assigned to hear such an argument would be tempted to assume the rôle of mediator, or to adopt the classical solution: Let the older brother (here the Metropolitan) divide the estate into what he regards as equal shares, let the younger brother (the National Gallery) take his pick.[20]

What is critical here is the *form* of the problem. Indeed, as the following compendium of examples by Fuller shows, there are many problems, quite different in substance, which share this common attribute of polycentricity:

> Let me now give a series of illustrations of polycentric problems, some of which have been assigned, with poor success, to adjudicative treatment, some of which have been proposed for adjudicative treatment, and some of which are so obviously unsuited for adjudicative decision that no one has

<hr>

20. *Ibid.* Reprinted from the Proceedings of the American Society of International Law with permission.

dreamed of subjecting them to it: setting prices and wages within a managed economy to produce a proper flow of goods; redrawing the boundaries of election districts to make them correspond to shifts in population; assigning the players of a football team to their respective positions; designing a system of throughways into a metropolitan area; allocating scarce funds for projects of scientific research; allocating air routes among our various cities; drawing an international boundary across terrain that is complicated in terms of geography, natural resources, and ethnology; allocating radio and television channels to make balanced programs as accessible to the population as possible.[21]

These problems are ill-suited to adjudication because the judicial process deals most effectively with severable, rather than intertwined, issues. In these examples, "[t]here is and can be no single solution or issue toward which the affected party may direct his proofs and arguments. The mode of participation in the decision accorded to him, that is the opportunity to present proofs and arguments for a decision in his favor, therefore loses most of its meaning. * * * [T]he deciding agency must direct its mind toward considerations much more important than those contained in the fragmentary presentation open to any single party." [22] Polycentric problems, as Fuller is quick to point out, are not insoluble, but are simply better suited to other methods of disposition, preferably to methods which allow simultaneous attack on all aspects of the problem, such as bargaining or managerial authority.

I think we may say that polycentric problems and "political questions" are one and the same thing, at least "political questions" in the sense of issues which defy resolution by judicially-manageable standards. At this point, we might quit discussion of the "political question" doctrine, content that we have defined part of that realm of issues which the Court has chosen not to confront. But this would be a serious error, for it would assume

21. *Ibid.*, 3–4. Reprinted from the Proceedings of the American Society of International Law with permission.

22. *Ibid.*, 4.

a finality of decision which we know is not true of the Court and the political process.

All legal questions, justiciable and nonjusticiable alike, are political questions; that is, they all call upon the Court to allocate a limited pot of rights and resources. If it is so, as we are forever fond of requoting de Tocqueville that "[t]here is hardly a political question in the United States which does not sooner or later turn into a judicial one," [23] and, taking a leaf from Fuller, that "the polycentricity of any given problem is a matter of degree," [24] then a truly interesting possibility emerges. It is simply this: that "political questions" can be and, indeed, are transformed into justiciable ones. The Court's own experience on the reapportionment question—to take only one issue—bears this out. What was once rejected as a "political question" when litigated under the Guarantee Clause, a decade and a half later became a justiciable issue when litigated as a violation of equal protection.

What is interesting about this transformation process is its likely impact on the scope of social change. Because a polycentric problem demands simultaneous attention to many issues, its resolution should logically be expected to produce large-scale change. Justiciable questions, on the other hand, are severable; and *seriatim* treatment of them can be expected to deflate the over all scope of social change since simultaneous resolution of the issues is replaced with incrementalism. Because the process of transformation not only blows out of a polycentric problem a greater potential for change and slows consideration of its component issues as well, the reduction of "political" to justiciable questions reveals a further conservative bias in the judicial process. Since one of the great truths about modern society, as compared with life in a simpler era, is a growing interdependence among people and material developments, the prognosis for a lessening of this transformation process is not encouraging.[25]

23. Democracy in America 270 (Mayer, ed. 1969).

24. Fuller, 5.

25. Looking back on the Turner thesis, it may be tempting to speculate whether another effect of the frontier in American history was

This outlook should reinforce a genuine reluctance on the part of those favorably disposed to increase the pace of social change to continue to rely on adjudication as a desirable method for redressing political grievances.

The Progressive Case for Judicial Self-Restraint

If the Scottish poet, Robert Burns, was right when he wrote that the greatest gift to be given would be the capacity "[t]o see oursels as others see us," [26] we can learn much from foreign observers of American democracy. Alexis de Tocqueville was probably the most incisive of these social commentators. Felix Frankfurter, who became a naturalized American citizen, stands in that tradition. And the last paragraph of his dissent in the flag salute case constitutes a particularly apt starting point in fleshing out a progressive case for the practice of judicial self-restraint:

> Of course patriotism cannot be enforced by the flag salute. But neither can the liberal spirit be enforced by judicial invalidation of illiberal legislation. Our constant preoccupation with the constitutionality of legislation rather than with its wisdom tends to preoccupation of the American mind with a false value. The tendency of focusing attention on constitutionality is to make constitutionality synonymous with wisdom, to regard a law as all right if it is constitutional. Such an attitude is a great enemy of liberalism. Particularly in legislation affecting freedom of thought and freedom of speech much which should offend a free-spirited society is constitutional. Reliance for the most precious interests of civilization, therefore, must be found outside of their vindica-

to temporarily reduce or put off the impact—or our perception of the full impact—of polycentric questions on American society. Turner's thesis about the prime significance of the frontier in shaping American history, together with various critiques and defenses of his theory, is presented in Taylor, ed., The Turner Thesis: Concerning the Role of the Frontier in American History (3d ed. 1972); Billington, ed., The Frontier Thesis: Valid Interpretation of American History? (1966).

26. "To a Louse," 1 The Poems and Songs of Robert Burns 194 (Kinsley, ed. 1968).

tion in courts of law. Only a persistent positive translation of the faith of a free society into the convictions and habits and actions of a community is the ultimate reliance against unabated temptations to fetter the human spirit.[27]

This view is reinforced by and elaborated in the first four paragraphs of his dissent in *Baker* v. *Carr*, a decision in which the Court held, among other things, that the plaintiffs challenging the malapportionment of state legislative districts under the Equal Protection Clause presented a justiciable issue (though the Court refrained from indicating at that time what it subsequently spelled out as the only permissible constitutional standard for legislative districting, namely, one man-one vote):

> The Court today reverses a uniform course of decision established by a dozen cases, including one by which the very claim now sustained was unanimously rejected only five years ago. The impressive body of rulings thus cast aside reflected the equally uniform course of our political history regarding the relationship between population and legislative representation—a wholly different matter from denial of the franchise to individuals because of race, color, religion or sex. Such a massive repudiation of the experience of our whole past in asserting destructively novel judicial power demands a detailed analysis of the role of this Court in our constitutional scheme. Disregard of inherent limits in the effective exercise of the Court's "judicial Power" not only presages the futility of judicial intervention in the essentially political conflict of forces by which the relation between population and representation has time out of mind been and now is determined. It may well impair the Court's position as the ultimate organ of "the supreme Law of the Land" in that vast range of legal problems, often strongly entangled in popular feeling, on which this Court must pronounce. The Court's authority—possessed of neither the purse nor the sword—ultimately rests on sustained public confidence in its moral sanction. Such feeling must be nourished by the Court's complete detachment, in fact and in appearance, from politi-

---

27. West Virginia State Board of Education, 319 U.S. 624, 670–671, 63 S.Ct. 1178, 1200 (1943).

cal entanglements and by abstention from injecting itself into the clash of political forces in political settlements.

A hypothetical claim resting on abstract assumptions is now for the first time made the basis for affording illusory relief for a particular evil even though it foreshadows deeper and more pervasive difficulties in consequence. The claim is hypothetical and the assumptions are abstract because the Court does not vouchsafe the lower courts—state and federal —guidelines for formulating specific, definite, wholly unprecedented remedies for the inevitable litigations that today's umbrageous disposition is bound to stimulate in connection with politically motivated reapportionments in so many States. In such a setting, to promulgate jurisdiction in the abstract is meaningless. It is as devoid of reality as "a brooding omnipresence in the sky," for it conveys no intimation what relief, if any, a District Court is capable of affording that would not invite legislatures to play ducks and drakes with the judiciary. For this Court to direct the District Court to enforce a claim to which the Court has over the years consistently found itself required to deny legal enforcement and at the same time to find it necessary to withhold any guidance to the lower court how to enforce this turnabout, new legal claim, manifests an odd—indeed an esoteric —conception of judicial propriety. One of the Court's supporting opinions, as elucidated by commentary, unwittingly affords a disheartening preview of the mathematical quagmire (apart from divers judicially inappropriate and elusive determinants) into which this Court today catapults the lower courts of the country without so much as adumbrating the basis for a legal calculus as a means of extrication. Even assuming the indispensable intellectual disinterestedness on the part of judges in such matters, they do not have accepted legal standards or criteria or even reliable analogies to draw upon for making judicial judgments. To charge courts with the task of accommodating the incommensurable factors of policy that underlie these mathematical puzzles is to attribute, however flatteringly, omnicompetence to judges. The Framers of the Constitution persistently rejected a proposal that embodied this assumption and Thomas Jefferson never entertained it.

Recent legislation, creating a district appropriately described as "an atrocity of ingenuity," is not unique. Considering the gross inequality among legislative electoral units within almost every State, the Court naturally shrinks from asserting that in districting at least substantial equality is a constitutional requirement enforceable by courts. Room continues to be allowed for weighting. This of course implies that geography, economics, urban-rural conflict, and all the other non-legal factors which have throughout our history entered into political districting are to some extent not to be ruled out in the undefined vista now opened up by review in the federal courts of state reapportionments. To some extent —aye, there's the rub. In effect, today's decision empowers the courts of the country to devise what should constitute the proper composition of the legislatures of the fifty States. If state courts should for one reason or another find themselves unable to discharge this task, the duty of doing so is put on the federal courts or on this Court, if State views do not satisfy this Court's notion of what is proper districting.

We were soothingly told at the bar of this Court that we need not worry about the kind of remedy a court could effectively fashion once the abstract constitutional right to have courts pass on a state-wide system of electoral districting is recognized as a matter of judicial rhetoric, because legislatures would heed the Court's admonition. This is not only a euphoric hope. It implies a sorry confession of judicial impotence in place of a frank acknowledgment that there is not under our Constitution a judicial remedy for every political mischief, for every undesirable exercise of legislative power. The Framers carefully and with deliberate forethought refused so to enthrone the judiciary. In this situation, as in others of like nature, appeal for relief does not belong here. Appeal must be to an informed, civically militant electorate. In a democratic society like ours, relief must come through an aroused popular conscience that sears the conscience of the people's representatives. In any event there is nothing judicially more unseemly nor more self-defeating than for this Court, to make *in terrorem* pronouncements, to indulge in merely empty rhetoric, sounding a word of promise to the ear, sure to be disappointing to the hope.[28]

In piecing together a liberal or radical argument for judicial self-restraint, I want to draw upon these thoughts of Justice

28. 369 U.S. 186, 266–270, 82 S.Ct. 691, 737–739 (1962).

Frankfurter, fully mindful that I may or may not be construing them with exactly his intent. In any case, it is impossible to say with certainty just what the true intent was of a man now long dead, and, secondly, what does matter most is that the intellectual possibilities of the argument have been explored so as to make it the strongest argument possible. The revisionism of what follows—if that is what it is—is also motivated by a feeling that, in the warm afterglow of the Warren Court's activist liberalism, Justice Frankfurter has too often been left to take a bum rap by most of us in the academy. He is received as he is frequently portrayed: a detached, icy, and remote figure whose philosophy of judicial self-restraint was born of a painful professorial rectitude and a perverse desire to rain on every parade. This harsh judgment is as undeserved as it is unflattering; for on very rare occasion when he would give us a glimpse of the person within the role—as in the first paragraph of his dissent in the flag salute case—this man who stepped forward to stoutly defend the innocence of Sacco and Vanzetti amid the hysteria of a post-World War I witch hunt,[29] this staunch sympathizer of social reform, could write, not so much with the force of an opinion as a fact, that the libertarian sentiments espoused by the Court represented for him "the thought and action of a lifetime." [30]

Two lines of thought dominate these remarks of Justice Frankfurter. The first focuses on what he sees as the incompleteness of the transformation process in reformulating as a justiciable issue in *Baker* what heretofore had been perceived as a "political question"; the second constitutes a general admonition about judicial activism. For our purposes, the second of these concerns is the more important, but in view of the preceding discussion of polycentric problems, the first is relevant too. Let me begin with the less important.

As Professor Fuller suggested, the apportionment of legislative districts is a polycentric problem. The reason is obvious:

29. Frankfurter, The Case of Sacco and Vanzetti (1927).

30. Most of that first paragraph is quoted in Chapter 3, note 23.

how the boundaries of any one district are drawn has direct implications for the contours of every other district. When malapportionment was initially attacked as a violation of that clause in the Constitution guaranteeing to each state a republican form of government,[31] the Court, out of institutional necessity, I would argue, avoided the issue. Framed in this light, the constitutional challenge is not judicially resolvable. Because, in short,

31. Art. IV, § 4. The first such case was Colegrove v. Green, 328 U.S. 549, 66 S.Ct. 1198 (1946). Disposition of the malapportionment issue in subsequent "political question" cases is canvassed in Justice Frankfurter's dissent in Baker v. Carr, 369 U.S. 186, 277–280, 82 S. Ct. 691, 743–744 (1962). His discussion of the Guarantee Clause follows, 369 U.S. at 289–297, 82 S.Ct. at 749–753. Says Frankfurter of *Baker*, it "involves all of the elements that have made the Guarantee Clause cases non-justiciable. It is, in effect, a Guarantee Clause claim masquerading under a different label." 369 U.S. at 297, 82 S. Ct. at 754. And further:

What, then, is this question of legislative apportionment? Appellants invoke the right to vote and to have their votes counted. But they are permitted to vote and their votes are counted. They go to the polls, they cast their ballots, they send their representatives to the state councils. Their complaint is simply that the representatives are not sufficiently numerous or powerful—in short, that Tennessee has adopted a basis of representation with which they are dissatisfied. Talk of "debasement" or "dilution" is circular talk. One cannot speak of "debasement" or "dilution" of the value of a vote

until there is first defined a standard of reference as to what a vote should be worth. What is actually asked of the Court in this case is to choose among competing bases of representation—ultimately, really, among competing theories of political philosophy—in order to establish an appropriate frame of government for the State of Tennessee and thereby for all the States of the Union.

369 U.S. at 299–300, 82 S.Ct. at 755.

Recent Burger Court decisions allowing more justifications for a *de minimis* percentage deviation from absolute equality present the prospect of backing into the very problem of which Justice Frankfurter speaks. See Mahan v. Howell, 410 U.S. 315, 93 S.Ct. 979 (1973); Gaffney v. Cummings, 412 U.S. 735, 93 S.Ct. 2321 (1973); White v. Regester, 412 U.S. 755, 93 S.Ct. 2332 (1973); White v. Weiser, 412 U.S. 783, 93 S.Ct. 2348 (1973). At what point will the present Court create so many exceptions to the one man-one vote rule and percentage deviations of what arbitrary magnitude that the Justices, in effect, return full circle to the position of being asked to decide how much representation certain interests are entitled to?

there is no one accepted definition of what constitutes representative government, adversary argument will be meaningless; the parties will talk right past one another when they state their claims. A meeting of minds about the exact nature of the issue in dispute does not exist; there is no single point at which argument can be joined. For the Court to attempt resolution of this issue in these terms would be foolhardy because the Justices would have to decide exactly what degree of representation every group within a given state is entitled to. That is the kind of task for which decision by adjudication is remarkably ill-suited. Finally, in view of what Fuller says about the way in which polycentric problems are customarily solved, it is worth noting that legislative apportionments have been handled traditionally by negotiation among the legislators themselves, that is, by simultaneous bargaining.

Litigation under the Equal Protection Clause, however, supplies a standard which was absent from the Guarantee Clause cases. The principle which is implicit is, of course, equality, or as the Court explicitly stated it two years later, one man-one vote.[32] The Court's reluctance to make this clear in *Baker* v. *Carr* is a matter of considerable concern to Justice Frankfurter. And when Justice Douglas, in a concurring opinion, writes, "Universal equality is not the test; there is room for weighting," [33] this proves too much for Frankfurter. Either the Court has not successfully transformed a "political question" into a justiciable one by providing a standard which will make adjudication possible in this kind of controversy or the Court is engaged in subterfuge—waiting for the initial uproar over its intervention into "the political thicket" to blow over before announcing what is surely a controversial standard.[34] When Jus-

---

32. Reynolds v. Sims, 377 U.S. 533, 84 S.Ct. 1362 (1964). For a description of the manner of proof, adopted in subsequent reapportionment cases, see Chapter 4, note 68.

33. 369 U.S. 186, 244–245, 82 S.Ct. 691, 724 (1962).

34. See Shapiro, Law and Politics in the Supreme Court 251–252, and Ch. 5 generally (1964); and, for a comprehensive treatment of reapportionment, see Dixon, Jr., Democratic Representation: Reapportionment in Law and Politics (1968).

tice Frankfurter writes that the majority have not announced that population is the only relevant variable in legislative apportionment—that "[r]oom continues to be allowed for weighting" other variables such as "geography, economics, urban-rural conflict, and all the other non-legal factors which have throughout our history entered into political districting"—he is surely correct in concluding that this then puts the Court precisely in the position it rejected in the Guarantee Clause cases, that is, of deciding what mix of interests qualifies as representative government. And, if the heat is so great that "the Court naturally shrinks from asserting that in districting at least substantial equality is a constitutional requirement enforceable by courts," then the Court should stay out of the kitchen.

It is also worth noting, as Professor Shapiro has pointed out, that the cost of embracing the neutral principle of one man-one vote has meant flying in the face of all we know about the reality of pluralism and the group theory of politics.[35] The abstrac-

35. See Shapiro, Law and Politics in the Supreme Court 216–250. Compare, for example, the conception of the political system evident in the following excerpt from Chief Justice Warren's opinion for the Court in Reynolds v. Sims, 377 U. S. 533, 562, 565, 84 S.Ct. 1362, 1382, 1383 (1964), with that from Justice Stewart's dissenting opinion in Lucas v. Forty-Fourth General Assembly of Colorado, 377 U.S. 713, 748–749, 84 S.Ct. 1459, 1480 (1964).

Chief Justice Warren:

Legislators represent people, not trees or acres. Legislators are elected by voters, not farms or cities or economic interests. As long as ours is a representative form of government, and our legislatures are those instruments of government elected directly by and directly representative of the people, the right to elect legislators in a free and unimpaired fashion is a bedrock of our political system.

* * *

Logically, in a society ostensibly grounded on representative government, it would seem reasonable that a majority of the people of a State could elect a majority of that State's legislators. To conclude differently, and to sanction minority control of state legislative bodies, would appear to deny majority rights in a way that far surpasses any possible denial of minority rights that might otherwise be thought to result. Since legislatures are responsible for enacting laws by which all citizens are to be governed, they should be bodies which are collectively responsive to the popular will. And the concept of equal protection has been traditionally viewed as requiring the uniform treatment of persons

tion of a justiciable issue has wedded us to the nostalgic view of the American political system as a kind of New England town meeting writ large. Also, it is conjectural whether the one man-one vote principle *per se* has particularly advantaged the weaker minorities (as compared with suburbia, for example) or whether they would not have fared better pressing for some slice of the legislative pie recognizable as their own. Furthermore, one man-one vote is no guarantee against the gerrymander. It is entirely possible that one man-one vote will make it easier to keep down the representation of certain minorities under the cover of equally but cleverly-drawn legislative districts, thus throwing an Hurculean burden on the shoulders of the underrep-

standing in the same relation to the governmental action questioned or challenged. With respect to the allocation of legislative representation, all voters, as citizens of a State, stand in the same relation regardless of where they live.

* * *

Justice Stewart:

My own understanding of the various theories of representative government is that no one theory has ever commanded unanimous assent among political scientists, historians, or others who have considered the problem. But even if it were thought that the rule announced today by the Court is, as a matter of political theory, the most desirable general rule which can be devised as a basis for the make-up of the representative assembly of a typical State, I could not join in the fabrication of a constitutional mandate which imports and forever freezes one theory of political thought into our Constitution, and forever denies to every State any opportunity for enlightened and progressive innovation in the design of its democratic institutions,

so as to accommodate within a system of representative government the interests and aspirations of diverse groups of people, without subjecting any group or class to absolute domination by a geographically concentrated or highly organized majority.

Representative government is a process of accommodating group interests through democratic institutional arrangements. Its function is to channel the numerous opinions, interests, and abilities of the people of a State into the making of the State's public policy. Appropriate legislative apportionment, therefore, should ideally be designed to insure effective representation in the State's legislature, in cooperation with other organs of political power, of the various groups and interests making up the electorate. In practice, of course, this ideal is approximated in the particular apportionment system of any State by a realistic accommodation of the diverse and often conflicting political forces operating within the State.

resented to demonstrate the requisite but difficult to prove discriminatory intent lurking behind an apportionment scheme in order to successfully challenge it in court.[36]

Ultimately, of course, the question is whether the Court should intervene at all. And this gets us to the more important question of just what the Court's role ought to be. Requoting Justice Frankfurter:

> In this situation, as in others of like nature, appeal for relief does not belong here. Appeal must be to an informed, civically militant electorate. In a democratic society like ours, relief must come through an aroused popular conscience that sears the conscience of the people's representatives. In any event there is nothing judicially more unseemly nor more self-defeating than for this Court to make *in terrorem* pronouncements, to indulge in merely empty rhetoric, sounding a word of promise to the ear, sure to be disappointing to the hope.

But what could this mean? Justice Clark apparently thought this advice was largely inappropriate given the facts of political life in Tennessee which inspired *Baker* v. *Carr*:

> But the majority of the people of Tennessee have no "practical opportunities for exerting their political weight at the polls" to correct the existing "invidious discrimination." Tennessee has no initiative and referendum. I have searched diligently for other "practical opportunities" present under the law. I find none other than through the federal courts. The majority of the voters have been caught up in a legislative strait jacket. Tennessee has an "informed, civically militant electorate" and "an aroused popular conscience," but it does not sear "the conscience of the people's representatives." This is because the legislative policy has riveted the present

36. The difficulty of establishing discriminatory intent is well-illustrated in several of the racial discrimination cases; see especially Palmer v. Thompson, 403 U.S. 217, 91 S.Ct. 1940 (1971). For discussion of the Court's approach and an indication of some of the relevant variables in imputing discriminatory intent, see Washington v. Davis, 426 U.S. 229, 96 S.Ct. 2040 (1976); Village of Arlington Heights v. Metropolitan Housing Development Corp., 429 U.S. 252, 97 S.Ct. 555 (1977).

seats in the Assembly to their respective constituencies, and by the votes of their incumbents a reapportionment of any kind is prevented.[37]

These observations of Justice Clark's to the contrary notwithstanding, Justice Frankfurter's view contains, I think, the nucleus of a progressive case for the practice of judicial self-restraint, a case for judicial nonintervention based upon a desire to promote social change, not minimize it.

We are accustomed to accept "the safety valve theory of judicial review"—the notion that one of the reasons the American system hangs together as well as it does is because when other governmental institutions grow unresponsive, timely intervention by the Court produces enough change so as to defuse the grievance and allow the system to continue functioning. In fact, however, this is very costly, at least from the standpoint of pacing social change. There are several dysfunctional aspects to the practice of judicial review. The first of these is simply the inherent conservatism of the judicial process, already discussed, whose disposition of social issues deflates and retards change. Another reason for thinking twice about the judicial absorption of social discontent as a plus is that it tends to be addictive. De Tocqueville was not alone in wondering aloud whether we would not be better off if we kicked the habit of legalistic thinking. Insofar as chronic reliance is placed upon the courts for the rectification of social ills, institutions of popular control atrophy and fall prey to those forces with ever-narrower designs on the uses of power. And finally, judicial pronouncements convey the illusion that the problem has been taken care of, when, in fact, nothing may really have been done at all, probably because the Court's judgment has been quietly disregarded. All of these are good reasons why those bent on social reform may want to think again before succumbing to the seductive allure of litigation.

37. 369 U.S. 186, 258–259, 82 S.Ct. 691, 732–733 (1962) (concurring opinion).

I think what Justice Frankfurter is saying is simply that the discontent which the safety valve theory releases ought to be allowed to build up—that judicial intervention deflates a healthy sense of social grievance and robs it of its effective force. And when he talks about conduct that "sears the conscience of the people's representatives," he is talking about alternatives of protest more serious than writing your congressman. What I think Justice Frankfurter may have in mind are the techniques of old-fashioned American pressure politics: street-marching, picketing and strikes, stand-ins and sit-ins, and public confrontations. What he is suggesting—and this is far from meaningless rhetoric—is that those disaffected by government must mount an aggressive campaign that will make it impossible for those in power to ignore away the problem. Change must come from those officials immediately concerned. The courts can promise, but, being relatively weak institutions, they cannot guarantee delivery on the promise. This is surely a credible, and, indeed, an attractive argument for the practice of judicial self-restraint by judges and potential litigants alike.

Unfortunately, this is not an argument without several flaws. The first of these deficiencies—that judicial activism may be essential because of its function in keeping open the means of organization and expression—resulted in the original case for preferred freedoms. Without the maintenance of freedoms of speech, press, and peaceable assembly, the prospect for "sear-[ing] the conscience of the people's representatives" is dim indeed.

Second, the exhortation to popular political action may be built upon a faulty empirical premise regarding the spontaneous mobilization of large groups out of a regard for a commonly-perceived self-interest. As Mancur Olson, Jr., has argued, "large or latent groups have no tendency voluntarily to act to further their common interests." [38] It is irrational, Olson contends, for

38. The Logic of Collective Action
165 (1968); but *cf.* Wilson, Political Organizations (1973).

any individual to contribute his time and money to such an enterprise if he can obtain the benefits of the group effort without personal sacrifice. Unless the group is sufficiently small so that it is worth his while to carry the burden also for others who stand to profit, he will not actively participate. Thus

> If the members of a large group rationally seek to maximize their personal welfare, they will *not* act to advance their common or group objectives unless there is coercion to force them to do so, or unless some separate incentive, distinct from the achievement of the common or group interest, is offered to the members of the group individually on the condition that they help bear the costs or burdens involved in the achievement of the group objectives. Nor will such large groups form organizations to further their common goals in the absence of the coercion or the separate incentives just mentioned. These points hold true even when there is unanimous agreement in a group about the common good and the methods of achieving it.[39]

The assumption which judicial self-restraint makes about the spontaneity of interest group activity may be more a product of wishful thinking about the group theory of politics than an accurate observation of what really happens.

Finally, the argument for judicial self-restraint unduly emphasizes the weakness of the Court. Professor Shapiro is quite right to suggest that this is, in part, the product of a self-fulfilling prophecy: we say courts are weak institutions and our endless repetition of this helps to make it so.[40] Our preoccupation with the weakness of the judiciary to an extent mistakes subtlety for weakness and also appears to be premised on an unreasonable expectation about the capacity of single institutions of American government to deliver on promises all by themselves.

The first of these short-comings fails to adequately recognize the power of the Court as the manipulator of important symbols in a legalistic culture. Frankfurter's observation about our con-

39. *Ibid.*, 2.

40. Freedom of Speech: The Supreme Court and Judicial Review 39 (1966).

fusion of legality with moral rightness, in his dissent in the flag salute case, is precisely to the point. This is not merely an interesting sociological fact, it is an important political fact as well; for it is the wedding of the two that gives the Court a weighty "moral sanction." While the employment of such a moral sanction burns up a certain amount of the Court's political capital, Professor Shapiro is right to ask what good is power if it is not used.[41] Lest the importance of the Court's legitimating power be underestimated, a brief reminder by Justice Jackson, dissenting from the Court's affirmance of the forced removal of Japanese-Americans from the Pacific coast during World War II, should suffice:

> Much is said of the danger to liberty from the Army program for deporting and detaining these citizens of Japanese extraction. But a judicial construction of the due process clause that will sustain this order is a far more subtle blow to liberty than the promulgation of the order itself. A military order, however unconstitutional, is not apt to last longer than the military emergency. Even during that period a succeeding commander may revoke it all. But once a judicial opinion rationalizes such an order to show that it conforms to the Constitution, or rather rationalizes the Constitution to show that the Constitution sanctions such an order, the Court for all time has validated the principle of racial discrimination in criminal procedure and of transplanting American citizens. The principle then lies about like a loaded weapon ready for the hand of any authority that can bring forward a plausible claim of an urgent need. Every repetition imbeds that principle more deeply in our law and thinking and expands it to new purposes. All who observe the work of courts are familiar with what Judge Cardozo described as "the tendency of a principle to expand itself to the limit of its logic." A military commander may overstep the bounds of constitutionality, and it is an incident. But if we review and approve, that passing incident becomes the doctrine of the Constitution.

41. *The Supreme Court and Constitutional Adjudication: Of Politics and Neutral Principles*, 31 Geo.   Wash.L.Rev. 587, 604 (1963); Law and Politics in the Supreme Court 30.

There it has a generative power of its own, and all that it creates will be in its own image. * * * [42]

In this light, it is more than a little questionable—unless one chooses to see the matter in only a superficial way—whether Hamilton's "least dangerous branch" appellation accurately fits the Court.

And to saddle the Court with the responsibility of vindicating every promise is to unwittingly impose the discredited all-Gaul theory of American government on it. Why should judicial power, any more than presidential power, be defined as "the power to command"? Overemphasis on delivery power is perhaps best illustrated by Justice Frankfurter's comment from the bench during the first round of oral argument in *Brown* v. *Board of Education.* Said Frankfurter, "Nothing could be worse from my point of view than for this Court to make an abstract declaration that segregation is bad and then have it evaded by tricks." [43] This seems an odd statement, indeed; for the Court's

---

42. Korematsu v. United States, 323 U.S. 214, 245–246, 65 S.Ct. 193, 207 (1944). Justice Jackson's concluding remark, that "Nothing better illustrates this danger than does the Court's opinion in this case," proved prophetic indeed. As Title II of the Internal Security Act of 1950, Congress enacted legislation which empowered the President, in a self-proclaimed "internal security emergency," "to apprehend and by order detain, pursuant to the provisions of this title, each person as to whom there is reasonable ground to believe that such person probably will engage in, or probably will conspire with others to engage in, acts of espionage or of sabotage." Emergency Detention Act of 1950, § 103(a), 64 Stat. 1019, 1021. Eighteen years later, a report of the House Un-American Ac-

tivities Committee recommended the use of detention camps for certain categories of persons arrested in urban riots, a proposal which understandably enraged blacks especially. See 1971 Cong.Quart. Wkly.Rep. 1952. Specifically, the Committee report observed that the detention centers might usefully be employed for "the temporary imprisonment of warring [urban] guerillas." House Rep. 1351, 90th Cong., 2d Sess., p. 59. The Emergency Detention Act was repealed by Congress in 1971. The repealer also contained language declaring that "[n]o citizen shall be imprisoned or otherwise detained by the United States except pursuant to an Act of Congress." 85 Stat. 347.

43. 21 U.S.L.W. 3164 (1952).

opinion, which evidenced almost a fear of stating a clear principle[44]—something for which the Court took a great deal of heat from the legal profession itself[45] and a failing which may well have contributed to the difficulty, even among well-meaning people, of understanding exactly what would constitute compliance—was "evaded by tricks" anyway. Insofar as promises go unfulfilled, it is because, as Justice Jackson wrote: "While the Constitution diffuses power the better to preserve liberty, it also contemplates that practice will integrate the dispersed powers into a workable government. It enjoins upon its branches separateness but interdependence, autonomy but reciprocity." [46]

44. As Richard Kluger has shown, Chief Justice Warren was determined to avoid an accusatory tone in the *Brown* opinion out of concern both for promoting unanimity among the Justices and to facilitate compliance with the Court's ruling. See Simple Justice, Chs. 25, 26 (1976) [hereafter referred to as Kluger]. Probably the best explanation, therefore, why the opinion seems deficient from the standpoint of being an entirely principled decision is simply that, had the Court taken the tack of Harlan, Sr.'s dissent in *Plessy* v. *Ferguson* or that advocated by Professor Charles Black, see note 45, *infra*,—both principled approaches, to be sure—an accusatory tone would have been inevitable. This is so because disposition of the case entirely in terms of principle would have meant comparing the purpose of segregation with the purpose behind the Fourteenth Amendment; the result would have constituted a harsh moral judgment. By focusing on the harmful effects of segregation, Chief Justice Warren avoids this inflammatory and thus dysfunctional tone and substitutes in its place detached and dispassionate discussion. This was not, of course, a choice without certain costs, as also would have been the case had the alternative strategy been adopted.

45. See, especially, Wechsler, *Toward Neutral Principles of Constitutional Law*, 73 Harv.L.Rev. 1 (1959), reprinted in Principles, Politics, and Fundamental Law 3–48 (1961); Black, *The Lawfulness of the Segregation Decisions*, 69 Yale L.J. 421 (1960); *cf.* Pollak, *Racial Discrimination and Judicial Integrity: A Reply to Professor Wechsler*, 108 U.Pa.L.Rev. 1 (1959).

46. Youngstown Sheet & Tube Co. v. Sawyer, 343 U.S. 579, 635, 72 S.Ct. 863, 870 (1952) (concurring opinion).

Judicial Activism and the Legitimating Role of the Court

When the advocates of judicial self-restraint argue that there is no substitute for popular political participation if there is to be effective social change, there can be little argument, even if we only occasionally live up to that expectation. Only such broad-based effort is capable of exerting sufficient pressure on those many access points of American government so as to make the system work. It is hardly open to question, I suppose, that only after the forces of popular discontent began to mobilize, beginning with the Montgomery bus boycott, could the real impetus to black civil rights be felt.[47] Desegregation was surely not achieved simply because the Court declared that racial discrimination should end "with all deliberate speed."

But this does not mean that the Court's participation was irrelevant. Far from it. If it is true that change is the child of hope and not despair,[48] then a persuasive reason for judicial activism exists precisely because of the Court's capacity for "sounding a word of promise to the ear * * *." In contrast to the way Professor Charles Black has described the legitimating role of the Court in the Constitutional Revolution of 1937 as the culmination of a process of political recognition,[49] I would argue that judicial activism makes legitimation of a claim the beginning and not the end of the political process. The Court's decree is a promise only; delivery on that promise has to be rested by popular political participation. In the struggle that follows, the Court's decision has two uses: as a rallying point for the aggrieved, and as a strategic moral recognition that the claim should be honored. To insist that the Court go further than this is both impractical and dysfunctional.

47. See Kluger, 749–750.

48. See Brinton, The Anatomy of Revolution 250 (Rev. ed. 1965).

49. The People and the Court 56–65 (1960). This contrast is important and logically suggests that legiti- mation which results from acts of judicial self-restraint, as in the Constitutional Revolution of 1937, marks the end of the process of po- litical recognition while legitima- tion conveyed through judicial ac- tivism comes near the beginning of the process.

As with most things, the choice between judicial activism and judicial self-restraint is not either-or, but more or less. In matters of constitutional interpretation which come before it, the Court must walk a tightrope that attaches its legitimating and representational roles. Its legitimating role stems from a unique capacity to render principled decisions and constitutes its claim to be taken seriously by others. Its representational role gives it a reason for being. Without principle, there is no reason for others to honor its promises; without a constituency, preoccupation with the enhancement of its political power becomes mere vanity.

*

Epilogue:
Is the Court a Continuing Constitutional Convention?

Professor Corwin quoted Woodrow Wilson as saying that the Supreme Court constituted "a kind of Constitutional Convention in continuous session."[1] At first glance, this appears to be one of those misleading metaphors or suspicious similes about social institutions which extorts a grain of truth at prohibitive cost to genuine understanding.[2] The fact is, however, that the Court is always a continuing constitutional convention in somebody's eyes, whether in Justice Black's attacks on the revisionist tendencies of the interest balancers as they apply concepts such as fairness and reasonableness, or in Justice Frankfurter's admonitions to preferred freedoms advocates not to rewrite the Constitution out of eagerness to help the underrepresented, or in the views of others assailing the literalness of Justice Black's approach by which he would have made of the Court a continuation of the original constitutional convention.[3] In itself, though, this phrase tells us little of the Court's possible role in the political system. It remains for the various modes of constitutional interpretation to breathe life into Wilson's characterization.

1. Chase and Ducat, Corwin's The Constitution and What It Means Today 5 (13th ed. 1973).

2. Landau, *On the Use of Metaphor in Political Analysis*, in Political Theory and Political Science 78–102 (1972).

3. Wilson's description would even more aptly seem to fit judicial application of Professor Rawls' concept of "justice as fairness" which stresses the timeless importance of "the original position," that is, government at its founding. See A Theory of Justice (1971).

*

INDEX

References are to Pages

294 INDEX